AF361268

THE HISTORY OF AL-ṬABARĪ

AN ANNOTATED TRANSLATION

VOLUME XIX

The Caliphate of Yazīd b. Muʿāwiyah

A.D. 680−683 / A.H. 60−64

The History of al-Ṭabarī

Editorial Board

Ihsan Abbas, University of Jordan, Amman

C. E. Bosworth, The University of Manchester

Franz Rosenthal, Yale University

Everett K. Rowson, Harvard University

Ehsan Yar-Shater, Columbia University (*General Editor*)

Estelle Whelan, *Editorial Coordinator*

SUNY

SERIES IN NEAR EASTERN STUDIES

Said Amir Arjomand, Editor

The preparation of this volume was made possible in part by a grant from the National Endowment for the Humanities, an independent federal agency.

Bibliotheca Persica
Edited by Ehsan Yar-Shater

The History of al-Ṭabarī
(Ta'rīkh al-rusul wa'l mulūk)

VOLUME XIX

The Caliphate of Yazīd b. Muʿāwiyah

translated and annotated
by

I. K. A. Howard

University of Edinburgh

State University of New York Press

Published by
State University of New York Press, Albany
© 1990 State University of New York
All rights reserved
Printed in the United States of America

No part of this book may be used or reproduced
in any manner whatsoever without written permission
except in the case of brief quotations embodied in
critical articles and reviews.

For information, address State University of New York
Press, State University Plaza, Albany, N.Y., 12246

Library of Congress Cataloging-in-Publication Data
Ṭabarī, 838?–923.
  [Taʾrīkh al-rusul wa-al-mulūk. English. Selections]
  The caliphate of Yazīd b. Muʿāwiyah/translated and annotated
by I. K. A. Howard.
    p.   cm.—(The history of al-Ṭabarī = Taʾrikh al-rusul waʾl
mulūk; v. 19) (SUNY series in Near Eastern studies) (Bibliotheca
Persica)
  Translation of extracts from: Taʾrīkh al-rusul wa-al-mulūk.
  Bibliography: p.
  Includes index.
  ISBN 0–7914–0040–9. ISBN 0–7914–0041–7 (pbk.)
  1. Islamic Empire—History—661–750. 2. Yazīd I, Caliph,
ca. 642–683. I. Howard, I. K. A. II. Title. III. Series.
IV. Series: Ṭabarī, 838?–923. Taʾrīkh al-rusul wa-al-mulūk.
English; v. 19. V. Series: Bibliotheca Persica (Albany, N.Y.)
DS38.2.T313 1985 vol. 19
[DS38.5]
909′.1 s—dc19   88–39753
[909′.097671′01]   CIP

10 9 8 7 6 5 4 3 2 1

Preface

THE HISTORY OF PROPHETS AND KINGS (*Ta'rīkh al-rusul wa'l-mulūk*) by Abū Ja'far Muḥammad b. Jarīr al-Ṭabarī (839–923), here rendered as the *History of al-Ṭabarī*, is by common consent the most important universal history produced in the world of Islam. It has been translated here in its entirety for the first time for the benefit of non-Arabists, with historical and philological notes for those interested in the particulars of the text.

Al-Ṭabarī's monumental work explores the history of the ancient nations, with special emphasis on biblical peoples and prophets, the legendary and factual history of ancient Iran, and, in great detail, the rise of Islam, the life of the Prophet Muḥammad, and the history of the Islamic world down to the year 915. The first volume of this translation will contain a biography of al-Ṭabarī and a discussion of the method, scope, and value of his work. It will also provide information on some of the technical considerations that have guided the work of the translators.

The *History* has been divided here into 38 volumes, each of which covers about two hundred pages of the original Arabic text in the Leiden edition. An attempt has been made to draw the dividing lines between the individual volumes in such a way that each is to some degree independent and can be read as such. The page numbers of the original in the Leiden edition appear on the margins of the translated volumes.

Al-Ṭabarī very often quotes his sources verbatim and traces the chain of transmission (*isnād*) to an original source. The chains of transmitters are, for the sake of brevity, rendered by only a dash

(—) between the individual links in the chain. Thus, "According to Ibn Ḥumayd—Salamah—Ibn Isḥāq" means that al-Ṭabarī received the report from Ibn Ḥumayd, who said that he was told by Salamah, who said that he was told by Ibn Isḥāq and so on. The numerous subtle and important differences in the original Arabic wording have been disregarded.

The table of contents at the beginning of each volume gives a brief survey of the topics dealt with in that particular volume. It also includes the headings and subheadings as they appear in al-Ṭabarī's text, as well as those occasionally introduced by the translator.

Well-known place names, such as, for instance, Mecca, Baghdad, Jerusalem, Damascus, and the Yemen, are given in their English spellings. Less common place names, which are the vast majority, are transliterated. Biblical figures appear in the accepted English spelling. Iranian names are usually transcribed according to their Arabic forms, and the presumed Iranian forms are often discussed in the footnotes.

Technical terms have been translated wherever possible, but some, such as dirham and imām, have been retained in Arabic forms. Others that cannot be translated with sufficient precision have been retained and italicized as well as footnoted.

The annotation aims chiefly at clarifying difficult passages, identifying individuals and place names, and discussing textual difficulties. Much leeway has been left to the translators to include in the footnotes whatever they consider necessary and helpful.

The bibliographies list all the sources mentioned in the annotation.

The index in each volume contains all the names of persons and places referred to in the text, as well as those mentioned in the notes as far as they refer to the medieval period. It does not include the names of modern scholars. A general index, it is hoped, will appear after all the volumes have been published.

For further details concerning the series and acknowledgments, see Preface to Volume I.

Ehsan Yar-Shater

Contents

Translator's Foreword

This section of Ṭabarī's history, which is devoted to the caliphate of Yazīd b. Muʿāwiyah, is in fact almost entirely concerned with the reactions of two men to his recognition as Caliph. Apart from this, Ṭabarī merely records the names of governors and *qāḍī*s and gives a brief description of a campaign in Khurāsān. These two men, al-Ḥusayn b. ʿAlī b. Abī Ṭālib and ʿAbdallāh b. al-Zubayr b. al-ʿAwwām, represent two of the most influential Islamic families. They are the sons of two great Islamic leaders and they oppose Yazīd's succession. Thus, the central question involved in the caliphate of Yazīd is the constitutional question of succession.

In order to understand Ṭabarī's handling of this problem, it is useful to examine what sources he used and how he used them. Two earlier historians, Dīnawarī (d. 282/895–6) and Yaʿqūbī (d. 292/905), have given accounts of these events. Like Ṭabarī, they concentrate on the opposition to Yazīd's caliphate from al-Ḥusayn and Ibn al-Zubayr, but their accounts are summaries and interpretations of previous historical writings without clear references to their sources; whereas Ṭabarī's account is much more detailed and through the use of *isnād*s (chains of authority) gives us a much clearer picture of the sources he used. A third historian, Balādhurī (d. 279/892), has, in his *Ansāb al-ashrāf*, provided us with a detailed picture, which enables us to check Ṭabarī's account. Sometimes Balādhurī gives summaries introduced by *qālū* ("they reported") and sometimes he gives even more detailed accounts than Ṭabarī with their *isnād*s. He also provides versions, not given by Ṭabarī, that help balance the account. A fourth earlier historian, Khalīfah b. Khayyāṭ (d. 246/860), briefly deals with al-Ḥusayn and gives more space to Ibn al-Zubayr but very limited information.

Of the later historians, Masʿūdī provides accounts which, although lacking *isnāds*, can be seen to come from the same sources as those used by Ṭabarī. The Shīʿite al-Mufīd (d. 413/1022) gives a slightly abbreviated version of Ṭabarī's account of al-Ḥusayn, which is almost certainly taken from Ṭabarī. Similarly Ibn al-Athīr uses Ṭabarī's for his version. These three accounts add very little to our knowledge about the historical writings on the event, but they do help to check and understand Ṭabarī's text. The same is the case with regard to Abū al-Faraj al-Iṣfahānī's *Maqātil al-Ṭālibiyyīn* (d. 356/967) which, by and large, provides confirmation of the basic sources used by Ṭabarī for the accounts of the deaths of al-Ḥusayn and his followers, but through a different transmission.

With regard to al-Ḥusayn, a third type of historical writing emerges in the account of Ibn Aʿtham al-Kūfī (d. 314/926). This is hagiographical literature with the feats and exploits of al-Ḥusayn exaggerated to the point of almost miraculous actions. Similar hagiographical writing is found in the clearly forged work that was attributed to Abū Mikhnaf. This tradition is continued in *Maqtal al-Ḥusayn* by al-Khwārazmī. Here he generally uses Ibn Aʿtham's account and provides interpretations, explanations, and supplements.

In his account of al-Ḥusayn, Ṭabarī has relied heavily on Hishām b. Muḥammad al-Kalbī (d. 204/819–20). The latter has provided us with the most detailed version of Abū Mikhnaf (d. 157/774). By and large this seems to follow Abū Mikhnaf word for word and in the main is confirmed as authentic by the corroborating evidence of reports in other historians, particularly Balādhurī, which have come from Abū Mikhnaf through a different transmission. Ibn al-Kalbī has supplemented this with extracts from ʿAwānah b. al-Ḥakam (d. 147/764). He also gives a few reports from the Shīʿite Jābir b. Yazīd al-Juʿfī (d. 128/746) and al-Qāsim, the son of the Shīʿite al-Aṣbagh b. Nubātah (d. 1st/7th century).

The second source used by Ṭabarī is the account purporting to be that of the fifth Shīʿite Imām Abū Jaʿfar Muḥammad al-

Bāqir (114/732) b. ʿAlī b. al-Ḥusayn by the Shīʿite ʿAmmār b. Muʿāwiyah al-Duhnī (d. 133/750–1). This account is also the one used by Masʿūdī with only minor differences. Clearly this is presented as the authentic view of Muḥammad al-Bāqir on the subject and therefore the view that ought to be accepted by the Shīʿah. In its outline, and it is brief, it is, with only slight variations, the same as Ibn al-Kalbī's version.

To these two accounts Ṭabarī adds a very brief summary from Abū al-Hudhayl Ḥusayn b. ʿAbd al-Raḥmān and a few supplementary details from ʿUmar b. Shabbah. The impression conveyed is that we have been presented with a definitive account of the event where all the evidence has been collated and presented. This impression is not altogether correct and it is appropriate in introducing Ṭabarī's version to examine it a little more closely. In order to do this, it is convenient to divide the account into the following sections:

1. The attempt to confirm Yazīd's caliphate by making important figures among the Muslims give him the oath of allegiance.
2. The letters from Kūfah to al-Ḥusayn, the appointment of Ibn Ziyād as governor of Kūfah, and the abortive mission of Muslim b. ʿAqīl.
3. Al Ḥusayn's journey to Karbalāʾ, his negotiations with ʿUmar b. Saʿd, and his death.
4. The desecration of the head of al-Ḥusayn, and the treatment of the survivors from his family.

All the sources are agreed that at his succession Yazīd was anxious to obtain the oath of allegiance from al-Ḥusayn, Ibn al-Zubayr, and many also include Ibn ʿUmar. Dīnawarī adds ʿAbd al-Raḥman b. Abī Bakr but this is clearly wrong as the latter was already dead. It is evident to all that these are leading Muslims, the sons of famous fathers, and therefore we are left with the impression in Ṭabarī's account that it was only natural that Yazīd should want them to pledge allegiance to him. There may, however, have been a little more to it than that. According to both Balādhurī and Ibn Aʿtham, Muʿāwiyah had agreed, in the treaty he made with al-Ḥasan b. ʿAlī on the latter's abdication, that there should be a consultative council (*shūrā*) to decide the succession after him. However, Ṭabarī fails to mention this. The *shūrā* was the institution introduced by ʿUmar for his succession; the six leading Muslims chose one of their number as the Caliph. Therefore al-Ḥusayn, Ibn al-Zubayr and Ibn ʿUmar could naturally have expected to have been among the group who decided on the next Caliph, and almost certainly that group would not have chosen Yazīd. What Yazīd was doing—and his father seems to have tried to do the same toward the end of his life—was trying to preempt the *shūrā* by obtaining these men's oaths of allegiance.

In presenting al-Ḥusayn's and Ibn al-Zubayr's reaction, either Ṭabarī or Ibn al-Kalbī has amalgamated two reports from Abū Mikhnaf. In the second half of the first report, the part omitted by Ṭabarī or Ibn al-Kalbī, both men have made excuses to avoid seeing al-Walīd, the governor of Medina, when he asked them to come. Guessing the reason why he has asked them, they make their escape to Mecca. The second report from Abū Mikhnaf, which in Ṭabarī's version has been tacked on to the beginning of the first report, deals with the conversation between al-Ḥusayn and al-Walīd. Ṭabarī completely ignores reports included by both Balādhurī and Khalīfah b. Khayyāt from the Baṣran historian Juwayriyyah b. Asmāʾ (d. 173/789) in which both Ibn al-Zubayr and al-Ḥusayn meet al-Walīd together and Ibn al-Zubayr is the main spokesman. The selective picture that emerges from Ṭabarī's version favors al-Ḥusayn at the expense of Ibn al-Zubayr.

All the sources are agreed upon the Kūfans' sending to al-Ḥusayn to come to them as their leader. All, too, are agreed on the mission of Muslim b. ʿAqīl to find out the situation in Kūfah. Yazīd's remedy for that situation is the appointment of ʿUbaydallāh. For this Ibn al-Kalbī's account, or Ṭabarī's version of it, leaves the main source, Abū Mikhnaf, and adopts the account of ʿAwānah b. al-Ḥakam. In this account, Yazīd's appointment of ʿUbaydallāh is as the result of advice from his Christian adviser Sarjūn, who presents it as Muʿāwiyah's advice. Clearly the appointment of ʿUbaydallāh is being laid at the door of the Christian Sarjūn and blame for what ensues is in some way removed from Yazīd. Surprisingly, the apparent Shīʿite account from Muḥammad al-Bāqir supports this report of the appointment of ʿUbaydallāh. However, since it gives this in greater detail than many of the events that one would expect someone sympathetic to al-Ḥusayn to dwell

on, that account begins to look suspect in terms of its apparent
origin. It is ʿAwānah, too, who reports the three choices given by
Yazīd of dealing with Muslim b. ʿAqīl: (a) the first to imprison
him; (b) the second to kill him; (c) and the third to banish him.
The fact that ʿUbaydallāh chooses to kill him again in some way
diminishes the responsibility of Yazīd for that action.

The Baṣran historian Wahb b. Jarīr (d. 207/822) has Muslim,
before he is killed, declare at the behest of ʿUbaydallāh that he
is a leader of rebels, in this way detracting from any heroism
Muslim may have shown. This historical report is completely
ignored by Ṭabarī.

Abū Mikhnaf's account, as reported by Ṭabarī, of al-Ḥusayn's
journey to Kūfah provides us with the most detailed account with
important speeches and letters by al-Ḥusayn. The significance of
these is that al-Ḥusayn in them makes the kind of claims about
himself and the Imāmate that are clearly of a Shīʿite character.
This indicates that there was a Shīʿite version of the events prior
to Abū Mikhnaf that Abū Mikhnaf has incorporated into his own
account along with other reports.

In the historical presentation of the account, the next major
issue is the responsibility for al-Ḥusayn's death. According to
Abū Mikhnaf, the consensus of historians at this time was that
al-Ḥusayn had offered ʿUmar b. Saʿd, ʿUbaydallāh's commander
of his forces against al-Ḥusayn at Karbalāʾ, three options: (a) he
would go back; (b) he would go to a frontier post; or (c) he would
go to Yazīd and put his hand in his and see what his view was. If
these were really offered, then ʿUbaydallāh's task was over. All
he had to do was send al-Ḥusayn to Yazīd. However, ʿUbaydallāh
insisted that al-Ḥusayn must submit to him; this was too much
for al-Ḥusayn. He, his followers, and his family accepted death.
The blame for al-Ḥusayn's death according to this is clearly the
responsibility of ʿUbaydallāh, and not Yazīd. The purpose of this
version originally may have been merely intended to transfer the
blame for al-Ḥusayn's death from Yazīd to ʿUbaydallāh. However,
it also had implications for those who believed in the Imāmate of
al-Ḥusayn, for he was, in fact, agreeing to accept Yazīd as Caliph;
he was willing to renounce his whole mission, which was the
rejection of Yazīd's caliphate. Abū Mikhnaf admits that there is a
tradition that maintains that all al-Ḥusayn offered was to go back

to Medina or go anywhere else in God's broad land. Despite this view, which would agree with the Shī'ite version, we have the Shī'ite Imām Muḥammad al-Bāqir endorsing again the attitude that does not agree with the views of the Shī'ah.

The treatment of al-Ḥusayn's head after his death is another example of the division of opinion concerning who is more blameworthy, Yazīd or 'Ubaydallāh. Abū Mikhnaf himself has reports for both Yazīd and 'Ubaydallāh, poking at the teeth in al-Ḥusayn's head. In 'Awānah's version, when the surviving prisoners are sent to Yazīd, he treats them well and declares that if he had been there he would never have killed al-Ḥusayn. From the extracts we have from 'Awānah's account, it seems that he is transferring all the blame he can from Yazīd to 'Ubaydallāh. Abū Mikhnaf provides us with a variety of versions, very few of which seem to have been edited in the same way in which the account about the oath of allegiance was edited. However, Ṭabarī has contrived to make the account of Muḥammad al-Bāqir the arbiter over such conflicts and in it the action is Yazīd's.

Despite these comments on Ṭabarī's version of the death of al-Ḥusayn, we owe to him the fact that we have the most detailed version of the narrative available to us in his report of Ibn al-Kalbī's recension of Abū Mikhnaf's work. The space given to this event, which in terms of political history was a failed revolution, emphasizes the importance of the event for Muslims in general, and the Shī'ah in particular. The death or martyrdom of al-Ḥusayn was for a long time a problem for the consciences of devout Muslims. He was, after all, the grandson of the Prophet. For the Shī'ah its significance is much deeper. Al-Ḥusayn serves in their eyes as a redemptive hero, who by his actions set an example to Muslims that should always be remembered.

After the death of al-Ḥusayn, Ṭabarī deals with the opposition to Yazīd by Ibn al-Zubayr. In fact, he introduces an account of the beginnings of that opposition that is clearly out of place. During his description of the events of the year 60/680, he gives an account of the attack by Ibn al-Zubayr's brother, 'Amr b. al-Zubayr, on Ibn al-Zubayr in Mecca. If this had been the case, it would have taken place either before al-Ḥusayn had departed or immediately afterward. That it is out of place is corroborated by

Balādhurī, who also has the incident, and puts it correctly after al-Ḥusayn's death. The account of this given by Ṭabarī is based entirely on Wāqidī. The general tenor of Ṭabarī's account of this incident is borne out by Balādhurī, who gives a much wider range of sources, including Wāqidī.

The accounts given of Yazīd's attempts to persuade Ibn al-Zubayr and the people of Medina and Mecca to accept his authority are again confirmed by much fuller accounts from Balādhurī. The same is the case for the battle of Ḥarrah and the bombardment of the Kaʿbah. There is the same tendency in the sources to try to mitigate the responsibility of Yazīd for these crimes against Islam by thrusting the blame on his generals, in this case, Muslim b. ʿUqbah and Ḥusayn b. Numayr al-Sakūnī.

One constitutional problem does emerge from Ṭabarī's treatment of his sources. This is the problem concerning the condition on which Ibn al-Zubayr was receiving the oath of allegiance. In Balādhurī it is quite clear that Ibn al-Zubayr at this juncture is receiving the oath of allegiance on the condition that there will be a *shūrā*. Ṭabarī never mentions this. On one occasion in a report that is identical with one given by Balādhurī, he deliberately omits the words "on the condition of a *shūrā*" from the statement that Ibn al-Zubayr was receiving the oath of allegiance from the people. In fact *shūrā* is only mentioned once and then, perhaps, by accident when he reports that the people of Mecca held the view that a *shūrā* was appropriate.

An answer to why this omission took place has yet to be given.

In the Arabic texts the names Ḥusayn and Ḥuṣayn have been given sometimes with the article *al-* and sometimes without it. In general for al-Ḥusayn, it is more usual that the *al-* occurs. In some accounts the *al-* is clearly missing for derogatory reasons, but in others this is not so. I have in fact followed the Arabic, and where there is al-Ḥusayn I have written it and, where not, I have omitted it. In citations from the Qurʾān, where two different numbers are given for a verse, the first is that of the official Egyptian edition and the second that of Flügel's text.

I would like to thank my former colleagues Dr. ʿAbd al-Raḥīm ʿAlī and Dr. Farid al-Shayyal for help in checking the translation. I owe thanks, too, to Dr. Carole Hillenbrand for help and advice. I must also thank Mrs. May O'Donnell and Miss Irene Crawford for their help in typing a difficult manuscript. However, any imperfections in the translation are my responsibility.

I. K. A. Howard

The
Events of the Year

60 (cont'd)
(April 22–September 30, 680)

In this year (60/680) the oath of allegiance was given to Yazīd b. Muʿāwiyah after the death of his father on 15 Rajab (April 22, 680) in the reports of some, but in the reports of others on the 20 of the month (April 27, 680), as we have mentioned earlier in the account of the death of his father, Muʿāwiyah.[1] Yazīd confirmed ʿUbaydallāh b. Ziyād[2] as governor of al-Baṣrah[3] and al-Nuʿmān b. Bashīr[4] as governor of al-Kūfah.[5]

---

1. The death of Muʿāwiyah, the previous Umayyad Caliph, is dealt with in Ṭabarī, II, 198.

2. ʿUbaydallāh b. Ziyād is one of the sons of Muʿāwiyah's earlier governor in Iraq, Ziyād b. Abīhi, literally 'Ziyād, the son of his father'. Muʿāwiyah had won the father over to his side by recognizing him to be his brother as a result of a liaison between Muʿāwiyah's father, Abū Sufyān, and Ziyād's prostitute mother, Sumayyah. ʿUbaydallāh had also attained prominence and authority. See *EI*[1], s.v. ʿUbaid Allāh b. Ziyād.

3. Al-Baṣrah is a garrison town of the Arabs, which is located in the south of Iraq. Just to the south is the site of modern Baṣrah. See *EI*[2], s.v. Al-Baṣra.

4. Al-Nuʿmān's father, Bashīr b. Saʿd, had been one of the leaders of the Anṣār. After serving the Umayyads, al-Nuʿmān later joined Ibn al-Zubayr and was killed in his service. See *EI*[1], s.v. al-Nuʿmān b. Bashīr.

5. Al-Kūfah is a garrison town of the Arabs in Iraq on the Euphrates river. See *EI*[2], s.v. Al-Kūfa.

According to Hishām b. Muḥammad (al-Kalbī)[6]—Abū Mikhnaf:[7] Yazīd succeeded at the beginning of the month of Rajab in the year 60 (April 8, 680). Al-Walīd b. ʿUtbah b. Abī Sufyān[8] was governor of Medina, al-Nuʿmān b. Bashīr al-Anṣārī of al-Kūfah, ʿUbaydallāh b. Ziyād of al-Baṣrah, and ʿAmr b. Saʿīd b. al-ʿĀṣ[9] of Mecca. Yazīd's only concern, when he assumed power, was to receive the oath of allegiance from the individuals who had refused to agree with Muʿāwiyah's demand for this oath of allegiance to Yazīd. Muʿāwiyah had summoned the people to give an oath of allegiance to him that Yazīd would be his heir.[10] Yazīd's concern was to bring their attitude to an end. Therefore he wrote to al-Walīd: "In the Name of God, the Merciful, the Compassionate, from Yazīd, Commander of the Faithful, to Walīd b. ʿUtbah. . . . Muʿāwiyah was one of the servants of God, whom God had blessed, appointed to authority, and given power and ability. He lived for a measured time and died at an appointed time. May God have mercy on him, for he lived as a praiseworthy man and died as a pious, God-fearing man. Peace be with you." He wrote to him on another parchment as small as a rat's ear: "Seize Ḥusayn, ʿAbdallāh b. ʿUmar, and ʿAbdallāh b. al-Zubayr[11]

---

6. Hishām b. Muḥammad was also known as Ibn al-Kalbī. He was an important compiler of historical traditions, who died in 204 (819) or 206 (821). See *EI²*, s.v. Al-Kalbī. His recensions of the events in Yazīd's caliphate form the basis of Ṭabarī's account.

7. Abu Mikhnaf's name was Lūṭ b. Yaḥyā. He was an important source for the early Iraqī historical tradition. He died in 157 (775). See Sezgin, *Abū Miḥnaf*.

8. Al-Walīd b. ʿUtbah b. Abī Sufyān was a newphew of Muʿāwiyah, who had a reputation for drinking. See Balādhurī, *Ansāb*, IV/1, 135. Throughout his career he is involved in the inter-Umayyad dispute over the benefits of power. His quarrel with Marwān indicates this. See p. 3, below.

9. ʿAmr b. Saʿīd b. al-ʿĀṣ was a prominent Umayyad, who later revolted against the Caliph ʿAbd al-Malik b. Marwān, claiming that Marwān had promised him the succession. Eventually ʿAbd al-Malik had him killed. See *EI²*, s.v. ʿAmr b. Saʿīd.

10. Muʿāwiyah's attempt to bring about the succession of Yazīd is reported in Ṭabarī's account of his caliphate. See Ṭabarī, II, 173–77.

11. Al-Ḥusayn, ʿAbdallāh b. ʿUmar and ʿAbdallāh b. al-Zubayr were three leading Qurashites, who all felt they had some claim to the caliphate. Al-Ḥusayn b. ʿAlī had claims to the caliphate by virtue of the fact that both his father and brother, al-Ḥasan, had occupied that position. ʿAbdallāh b. ʿUmar had a similar claim through his father, ʿUmar b. al-Khaṭṭāb. In the case of ʿAbdallāh b. al-Zubayr, his father had been a member of the group nominated by ʿUmar to form the consultative council (*shūrā*), which was to choose his successor from among themselves.

to give the oath of allegiance. Act so fiercely that they have no chance to do anything before giving the oath of allegiance. Peace be with you." [217]

When the news of Mu'āwiyah's death came to al-Walīd, it shocked and greatly disturbed him. He sent a dispatch to Marwān b. al-Ḥakam,[12] summoning him to come to him. Earlier, when al-Walīd had come to Medina, Marwān had only visited him there reluctantly. When al-Walīd perceived his attitude, he abused him in front of those who attended his gatherings. Marwān learned of this and kept away from him, cutting off all contact with al-Walīd. Marwān had continued to stay away from him until news of the death of Mu'āwiyah came to al-Walīd. Since the death of Mu'āwiyah and the order to take the oath of allegiance from this group weighed heavily on al-Walīd, he sought help for that from Marwān and summoned him. After al-Walīd read Marwān Yazīd's letter, he said, "'We belong to God and to Him we shall return.'[13] May God have mercy on him." Then al-Walīd asked Marwān's advice about the affair, saying, "How do you consider we should act?" Marwān answered, "I consider that you should send immediately to this group and summon them to give the oath of allegiance and enter into obedience. If they do so, you should accept that from them and leave them alone. If they refuse, you should take hold of them and execute them before they learn of the death of Mu'āwiyah. Indeed, if they learned of that, each one of them would rise up from a different direction, proclaim opposition and secession, and summon men to himself. I am afraid things are not that clear. However, in the case of Ibn 'Umar, I do not think that he would consider fighting. For he would only be willing to be entrusted with authority over the people if this matter were given to him spontaneously."

Therefore he sent 'Abdallāh b. 'Amr b. 'Uthmān[14]—he was a young boy then—to the two of them, al-Ḥusayn b. 'Alī and

---

12. Marwān b. al-Ḥakam was a prominent Umayyad, whose father, al-Ḥakam b. al-'Āṣ b. Umayyah, had been expelled from Medina by the Prophet. Marwān became 'Uthmān's adviser when he was Caliph and he also became Caliph in 64 (684). See *EI*[1], s.v. Marwān b. al-Ḥakam.

13. Qur'ān, 2:156 (151).

14. 'Abdallāh b. Amr b. 'Uthmān was a grandson of the Caliph 'Uthmān b. 'Affān, who seems to have had an insignificant role in affairs. See Balādhurī *Ansāb*, IV/1, 602.

'Abdallāh b. al-Zubayr. 'Abdallāh b. 'Amr b. 'Uthmān found the two sitting in the mosque. However, he came to them at a time when al-Walīd did not hold assemblies for the people; the two would not go to him at such a time. He said, "Both of you answer the summons of the governor." They replied, "Go now, we will come."

One of them approached the other.[15] 'Abdallāh b. al-Zubayr asked al-Ḥusayn, "Why do you think he has sent for us at this time when he does not hold assemblies?" The latter answered, "I have been wondering. In my view their despot has perished, and he has sent for us to get the oath of allegiance from us before news spreads among the people. I do not think it can be anything else." [218] Ibn al-Zubayr asked, "What do you intend to do?" Al-Ḥusayn said, "I will gather my servants immediately and go to him. When I reach the door, I will make them wait there, and I will go in to see him." Ibn al-Zubayr commented, "I fear for you if you go in." He replied, "I would not go to him unless I were able to resist him."

Al-Ḥusayn got up and gathered his mawālī[16] and his household around him. Then he began to walk until he came to the door of al-Walīd's house.[17] He told his followers. "I am going in. If I call you, or you hear his voice raised, all rush together to me. Otherwise, do not leave until I come out to you."

He went in and greeted al-Walīd as governor. Marwān was sitting with him. Ḥusayn said, as if he did not harbor any suspicions about Mu'āwiyah's death, "Fostering relations is better than

---

15. Balādhurī has given an almost identical account but does not include this dialogue. See *Ansāb*, IV/1, 300.

16. *Mawālī* (singular *mawlā*) denotes either patrons or clients. It was by this institution that a freed slave maintained his relationship with a tribe. The same institution was used for all newcomers to Islamic society. Although it could also mean kinsmen, here it means clients and slaves, as kinsmen are mentioned separately. See Crone, *Slaves*, 49–57, 197–200.

17. Balādhurī has two separate reports. One, which has so far been identical, apart from the dialogue, with Ṭabarī's version from Hishām b. Muḥammad al-Kalbī, deals with Ibn al-Zubayr and Ibn 'Umar with no mention of al-Ḥusayn's visit to al-Walīd. See *Ansāb*, IV/1, 299–302. He has a separate report about that visit, which is identical to Ibn al-Kalbī's version given here. See ibid., p. 302–3. Ibn al-Kalbī probably amalgamated the two reports, for the amalgamation had taken place by the time of Dīnawarī, whose version is similar to Ṭabarī. See Dīnawarī, *Akhbār*, 240–42.

severing them. May God reconcile you both." They said nothing in reply. He came forward and sat down. Then al-Walīd read him the letter, gave him the news of Muʿāwiyah's death, and demanded the oath of allegiance from him. Al-Ḥusayn said, "'We belong to God and to Him we shall return.'[18] May God have mercy on Muʿāwiyah and increase your reward. As for the oath of allegiance which you have asked me to give, a person like me should not give his oath of allegiance in secret. I do not see that you would be satisfied with less than my public oath made before all the people." Al-Walīd agreed, and al-Ḥusayn suggested, "When you come out before the people and summon them to give the oath of allegiance, you should summon us with the people. Then it will be one affair." Al-Walīd, who preferred the easy way, said to him, "Go then in the name of God and come to us with the people."

Marwān interrupted, swearing, "By God! If he leaves you now without giving the oath of allegiance, you will never have the same opportunity without much bloodshed between you and him. Hold the man; do not let him leave you until he gives the oath of allegiance or you cut off his neck." At that al-Ḥusayn jumped up and said, "O son of a blue-eyed woman![19] Would you or he kill me? By God! You are a liar and a sinner." With that he went out and passed his followers; they followed him until he reached his house.

Marwān told al-Walīd, "You disobeyed me. No, by God! He [219] will never give you the same hold over him again." Al-Walīd replied, O, Marwān, let someone other than you blame me. Indeed, you chose for me something which would have involved the destruction of my religion. By God! I would not want to have all the worldly wealth and dominion which the sun rises and sets over for having killed al-Ḥusayn. Glory be to God! Should I kill al-Ḥusayn because he said, 'I will not give the oath of allegiance?' By God! I think that on the Day of Resurrection a man who is held

---

18. Qurʾān, 2:156 (151).

19. A reference to Marwān's maternal grandmother, Māriyyah bt. Mawhab of Kindah. Her father had been a slave, probably a Christian from Armenia; and the Armenians were hated by the Arabs. Hence, the grandmother was referred to as "blue-eyed" as an insult; the insult was used against the grandson. See Balādhurī, *Ansāb*, V, 129.

responsible for the blood of al-Ḥusayn will weigh little in the scales of God." Marwān said, "If this is your opinion, then you have acted correctly." He said this to him without commending him for his view.[20]

As for Ibn al-Zubayr, he had said that he would come at that time, but then he went to his own house and hid. Al-Walīd sent for him and discovered that he was gathering his followers as a means of protecting himself. He harassed him with a great number of messengers and men, one after another. Ḥusayn, for his part, replied to them, "Stop this so that you can consider and we can consider and so that you can reflect and we can reflect."[21] On the other hand, Ibn al-Zubayr said to them, "Do not hurry me; I am coming to you. Give me time." They harassed them both all evening and during the early part of the night; however, they were more considerate to Ḥusayn. Al-Walīd sent mawālī of his to Ibn al-Zubayr, who abused him, shouting at him, "Son of Kāhiliyyah,[22] by God! You should come to the governor or he will kill you." All that day and for the early part of the night, Ibn al-Zubayr remained there answering, "I will come now." When they urged him, he replied, "By God! I am being made suspicious by the great number of requests to come and the succession of messengers. Do not hurry me until I send the governor someone who will bring me his views and his orders." He sent his brother, Jaʿfar b. al-Zubayr,[23] to al-Walīd. He said to him, "May God have mercy on you, leave ʿAbdallāh alone. You have terrified him and terrorized him with the great number of your messengers. He will come to you tomorrow, God willing. Order your messengers to leave us." Al-Walīd sent to them, and they went away.

---

20. This last sentence is omitted by Balādhurī. The narrative of Ibn al-Kalbī now returns to the first report of Balādhurī. See *Ansāb*, IV/1, 300f.

21. As a result of his careless editing of two versions, Ibn al-Kalbī has produced a contradiction in what was meant by him to be a continuous narrative.

22. This is disparaging reference to Ibn al-Zubayr. The mother of his grandfather Khuwaylid was Zuhrah bt. ʿUmar b. Ḥanthar of the clan of Kāhil of the tribe of Asad. See Balādhurī, *Ansāb*, V, 198. This reference is using his non-Qurashī female ancestor as a means of insulting him.

23. Jaʿfar b. al-Zubayr is Ibn al-Zubayr's brother from a different mother, Zaynab bt. Marthad b. ʿAmr. Despite later taking part in his brother's revolution, Jaʿfar lived to an old age and died in the caliphate of Sulaymān b. ʿAbd al-Malik, between 96 (715) and 99 (717). See Ibn Saʿd, *Ṭabaqāt*, V, 136–37.

Under cover of night, Ibn al-Zubayr left. He and his brother, Ja'far, without anyone else, took the road to al-Fur'.[24] He avoided   [220] the main road out of fear of pursuit and headed for Mecca. In the morning, al-Walīd sent for him and found that he had left. Marwān declared, "By God! If he has mistaken the road to Mecca.... So send men after him." He sent a horseman from the mawālī of Umayyah with eighty other horsemen.[25] They pursued him, but they were not able to catch up with him and so they returned. For the whole of that day until evening, they were distracted from Ḥusayn by the pursuit of Ibn al-Zubayr. Then in the evening he sent men to Ḥusayn. He answered them, "Come in the morning. Then you will consider and we shall consider."

They left him that night without harassing him. Ḥusayn left under cover of night. It was Sunday night with two days left in the month of Rajab in the year A.H. 60 (May 4, 680).

Ibn al-Zubayr had departed the night before Ḥusayn; Ibn al-Zubayr had gone on Saturday night and he had taken the road through al-Fur'. While Ibn al-Zubayr was traveling with his brother Ja'far, Ja'far recited the words of Ṣabrah al-Ḥanzalī:[26]

All the sons of one mother will find out one night
     that only one of their offspring has remained

"Glory be to God!" exclaimed 'Abdallāh. "What did you mean by what I just heard, brother?" Ja'far replied, "By God! Brother, I did not mean anything that you would dislike." 'Abdallāh said, "By God! It is even more hateful to me that this thing should be uttered by you unintentionally."

The narrator commented that it was just as if he were drawing a bad omen from the poem.

As for al-Ḥusayn, he left accompanied by his sons, his brothers, and his brother's sons. These people were most of his household,

---

24. Al-Fur' is a village between Medina and Mecca. See Yāqūt, *Mu'jam*, III, 878.

25. "If," in the previous sentence, is added from Balādhurī, who also identified the horseman as Ḥabīb b. Kurrah, and reported that there were only thirty horsemen. See *Ansāb*, IV/1, 300; also Dīnawarī, *Akhbār*, 242, where the name is Ḥabīb b. Kadīn.

26. Balādhurī attributes this verse to another poet, Mutammim b. Nuwayrah al-Ḥanzalī. See *Ansāb*, IV/1, 300.

except for Muḥammad b. al-Ḥanafiyyah.[27] The latter had said to him, "My brother, you are the most lovable of people and the dearest to me. I could not give my stored advice to any creature more entitled to it than you. Keep away from Yazīd b. Muʿāwiyah [221] with your followers, and avoid the provinces as long as you can. Then send your messengers to the people and summon them to you. If they give you the oath of allegiance, I praise God for that. If the people agree upon someone other than you, God will neither make your religion nor your reason deficient on that account; He will not remove your manliness and outstanding merit either. Yet I am afraid that you will enter one of these provinces and you will come to a group of people. They will differ among themselves: one group will be with you and another against you. They will fight, and you will be a target for the first of their spears. Then the best of all this community in person, in father, and in mother would be the one whose blood was most wastefully squandered and whose family most humiliated." Al-Ḥusayn asked him where he should go, and he answered, "Stay at Mecca. If that place is secure for you, it will serve its purpose. However, if it is unsuitable for you, you can resort to the deserts and the mountain peaks; You can move from place to place until you see what becomes of the affairs of the people and then you will know their views. You will be most correct in judgment and firmest in action as long as you can directly face matters. Affairs will never be more abstruse for you than when you turn your back on them." Al-Ḥusayn replied, "Brother, you have given good advice and shown your concern. I hope that your judgment is correct and appropriate."

According to Abū Mikhnaf—ʿAbd al-Malik b. Nawfal b. Musāḥiq[28]—Abū Saʿīd al-Maqburī:[29] I watched al-Ḥusayn en-

---

27. Muḥammad b. al-Ḥanafiyyah is a son of ʿAlī b. Abī Ṭālib by a Ḥanifite woman called Khawlah. After the death of al-Ḥusayn, he was described as the imām and mahdī by al-Mukhtār b. Abī ʿUbayd. He neither declined the title nor accepted it, but he did give the oath of allegiance to ʿAbd al-Malik. See *EI*[1], s.v. Muḥammad b. al-Hanifiyya.

28. ʿAbd al-Malik b. Nawfal b. Musāḥiq was a well-known traditionist and an authority of Abū Mikhnaf, who lived during the first half of the second (eighth) century. See Sezgin *Abū Miḥnaf*, 193—94.

29. Abū Saʿīd al-Maqburī was Kaysān, a mawlā of Kinānah. He died in 100 (718—19) or in the caliphate of al-Walīd b. ʿAbd al-Malik, 86—96 (705—15). See Ibn Saʿd, *Ṭabaqāt*, V, 61—62.

tering the mosque of Medina. As he walked, he was leaning on two men. First he leaned on one man and then on the other. He was reciting the verses of Ibn Mufarrigh:[30]

May I not terrify the camels when I lead a raid at the morning dawn!
    May I not be called Yazīd
If ever I accept humiliation for dignity
    while death is watching whether I flinch.

I said to myself, "By God, he is only reciting those two verses [222] because of something he is intending to do." It was only two days later when I was told that he had left for Mecca.

Then al-Walīd sent for 'Abdallāh b. 'Umar; he demanded that 'Abdallāh give the oath of allegiance to Yazīd. He answered, "When the people give the oath of allegiance, so will I." A man said, "What stops you from giving the oath of allegiance? You only want the people to argue among themselves, to fight, and destroy each other. Then, when that exhausts them, they will say: 'Have 'Abdallāh b. 'Umar in authority over you, for no one else remains. So give the oath of allegiance to him.'" 'Abdallāh retorted, "I want them neither to fight each other nor to argue among themselves and destroy each other. However, when the people give their oath of allegiance, and no one is left except me, I will give my oath of allegiance." They left him, for they were not afraid of him.

Ibn al-Zubayr set out and came to Mecca while 'Amr b. Sa'īd was governor there. When he entered he said, "I am seeking refuge." However, he did not attend their prayer, nor did he participate in the procession [from 'Arafah] with them.[31] He kept apart with his followers, making procession and praying with them alone.

When al-Ḥusayn set off for Mecca he recited: "Then he left it out of fear while he kept on the lookout. He said: 'My Lord, save me from the unjust people.'"[32] As he entered Mecca, he recited:

---

30. Ibn Mufarrigh's verses are given by Iṣfahānī, *Aghanī*, XVII, 51 and 68; and Balādhurī, *Ansāb*, IV/1, 303.

31. The procession (*ifādah*) from 'Arafah took place on Dhū al-Ḥijjah as part of the rituals of the pilgrimage (*hajj*). See *EI*², s.v. *Hadjdj*. It obviously refers to something that happened later.

32. Qur'ān, 28:21.

"And when he set out toward Midian, he said: 'Perhaps my Lord will guide me in the right path.'"[33]

In the month of Ramaḍān of this year (60/June, 680) Yazīd dismissed al-Walīd b. ʿUtbah from Medina. He appointed ʿAmr b. Saʿīd al-Ashdaq to be in charge. ʿAmr b. Saʿīd b. al-ʿĀṣ came to Medina in Ramaḍān.

Al-Wāqidī[34] claimed that Ibn ʿUmar was not in Medina when the news of the death of Muʿāwiyah and the demand that the oath of allegiance be given to Yazīd came to al-Walīd. When Ibn al-Zubayr and al-Ḥusayn were summoned to give the oath of allegiance to Yazīd, they refused; they left for Mecca on the same night. They met Ibn ʿAbbās[35] and Ibn ʿUmar coming from Mecca. The latter two both asked them what the situation was like in Medina. They answered, "The death of Muʿāwiyah, and the demand for the oath of allegiance is to be made to Yazīd." Ibn ʿUmar warned them to be pious toward God and not to divide the unity of the Muslims; he went to Medina and stayed there for some days. He waited until the oath of allegiance came from the provinces. Then he went to al-Walīd b. ʿUtbah and gave him his oath of allegiance. Ibn ʿAbbās also gave him his oath of allegiance.

In this year, ʿAmr b. Saʿīd sent ʿAmr b. al-Zubayr[36] to combat his brother ʿAbdallāh b. Zubayr.[37]

The Attack of ʿAmr b. al-Zubayr

Muḥammad b. ʿUmar al-Wāqidī has mentioned that ʿAmr b. Saʿīd b. al-ʿĀṣ al-Ashdaq came to Medina in Ramaḍān 60 (June, 680). When the people of Medina visited him, they found him to be a dignified and eloquent man.

---

33. Qur'ān, 28:22.

34. Al-Wāqidī was a leading historical and religious authority, who died in 207 (822–23). See *EI*[1], s.v. al-Wāqidī.

35. Ibn ʿAbbās, a son of al-ʿAbbās and cousin of the Prophet, is the man from whom the ʿAbbāsids are descended. He was an important Companion of the Prophet; he was regarded as an expert on the Qur'ān and the traditions. He supported ʿAlī during his Caliphate but withdrew toward the end of it. See *EI*[2], s.v. ʿAbdallāh b. ʿAbbās.

36. ʿAmr b. al-Zubayr's mother was from the Umayyads; he spent most of his time with them. As he had received much money and power from them, he had a hostile attitude toward his own family. See Balādhurī, *Ansāb*, IV/1, 310.

37. Ṭabarī's dating of this event is highly suspect. See the Introduction.

According to Muḥammad b. ʿUmar al-Wāqidī—Hisham b. Saʿd[38]—Shaybah b. Niṣāḥ:[39] The messengers went back and forth between Yazīd b. Muʿāwiyah and Ibn al-Zubayr about giving the oath of allegiance. Yazīd swore that he would not accept it from him until he was brought in chains.

Al-Ḥārith b. Khālid al-Makhzūmī was in charge of leading the prayer but Ibn al-Zubayr stopped him.[40] When he stopped him, Yazīd wrote to ʿAmr b. Saʿīd to send an army against Ibn al-Zubayr. At the time that ʿAmr b. Saʿīd had come to Medina, he had put ʿAmr b. Zubayr in command of his police[41] because he was aware of the animosity between him and ʿAbdallāh b. al-Zubayr. ʿAmr b. al-Zubayr had sent for a group of the people of Medina and had them flogged violently.

According to Muḥammad b. ʿUmar al-Wāqidī—Shuraḥbīl b. Abī ʿAwn[42]—his father:[43] ʿAmr b. al-Zubayr looked for all those who favored Ibn al-Zubayr and had them flogged. Among those who were flogged were al-Mundhir b. al-Zubayr,[44] his son Muḥammad b. al-Mundhir,[45] ʿAbd al-Raḥmān b. al-Aswad b. ʿAbd

[224]

---

38. Hishām b. Saʿd was a well-known traditionist and authority of Wāqidī's. He died in 158 (775) or 160 (776–77). See Ibn Ḥajar, *Tahdhīb*, XI, 39–41.

39. Niṣāḥ has been left without any diacritical marks on the first letter. However, Shaybah b. Niṣāḥ is an authority of Hishām b. Saʿd. See Wāqidī, *Maghāzī*, index. Shaybah was regarded as having Shīʿite inclinations. He died in the caliphate of Marwān b. Muḥammad, 127–32 (744–50). See Ibn Ḥajar, *Tahdhīb*, IV, 377–78.

40. According to Balādhurī, there is an incorrect report that al-Ḥārith b. Khālid al-Makhzūmī was governor of Mecca and ʿAmr b. Saʿīd was governor of Medina when Muʿāwiyah died. See Balādhurī, *Ansāb*, IV/1, 299. However, Wāqidī reports that he was governor of Mecca when Yazīd died. See ibid., p. 354. Al-Ḥārith was probably the deputy for the governor in charge of the prayer, and it was later than the last months of 60 (May–September, 680) that Ibn al-Zubayr would have been able to take such an action.

41. The Arabic for police is *shurṭah*. Its function seems to be to keep order in the towns. See *EI*[1], s.v. Shurṭa.

42. Shuraḥbīl b. Abī ʿAwn was an authority of Wāqidī; he probably lived in the middle of the second (eighth) century. He usually reported from his father. See Ṭabarī, index.

43. Abū ʿAwn was only reported from by his son Shuraḥbīl. See Ṭabarī, index.

44. Al-Mundhir was a brother of Ibn al-Zubayr who was killed in the course of supporting his brother. See p. 223, below.

45. The only further information on this nephew, Muḥammad b. al-Mundhir, of Ibn al-Zubayr is that his mother was ʿĀtikah bt. Saʿīd b. Zayd. See Ibn Saʿd, *Ṭabaqāt*, V, 135.

Yaghūth,[46] ʿUthmān b. ʿAbdallāh b. Ḥakīm b. Ḥizām,[47] Khubayb b. ʿAbdallāh b. al-Zubayr,[48] and Muḥammad b. ʿAmmār b. Yāsir.[49] He had them flogged from forty to fifty or sixty lashes. ʿAbd al-Raḥmān b. ʿUthmān[50] and ʿAbd al-Raḥmān b. ʿAmr b. Sahl[51] fled with some other men to Mecca.

ʿAmr b. Saʿīd asked ʿAmr b. al-Zubayr, "What man should we send against your brother?" He answered, "You will never find anyone to send against him who hates him more than I do." He took out a few dozen men on the dīwān,[52] and many of the mawālī of the people of Medina also went out. Unays b. ʿAmr al-Aslamī[53] set out with him with seven hundred men. He sent the latter ahead in his vanguard while he camped at al-Jurf.[54] Marwān b. al-Ḥakam came to ʿAmr b. Saʿīd and warned him, "Do not attack Mecca. Fear God and do not violate the sanctity of the House of God. Leave Ibn al-Zubayr alone. He has grown into an obstinate old man of over sixty years of age. By God! If you do not kill him, he will surely die." ʿAmr b. al-Zubayr interjected, "By God! Let us fight against him, and let us attack him in the heart of Kaʿbah, and let those who hate it, hate it." Marwān replied, "By God! That grieves me."

---

46. ʿAbd al-Raḥmān b. al-Aswad b. ʿAbd Yaghūth was from Quraysh and had settled in Medina. See Ibn Saʿd, *Ṭabaqāt*, V, 2.

47. ʿUthmān b. ʿAbdallāh b. Ḥakīm b. Ḥizām's father was killed in the Battle of the Camel while he was supporting Ibn al-Zubayr and his father against ʿAlī. See Ṭabarī, II, 3207. He was married to al-Zubayr's sister. See Balādhurī, *Ansāb*, IV/1, 361.

48. Khubayb b. ʿAbdallāh b. al-Zubayr was given a pardon after his father's defeat by al-Ḥajjāj b. Yūsuf. See Ṭabarī, II, 845.

49. It is surprising to find Muḥammad, the son of ʿAlī's great supporter ʿAmmār b. Yāsir, associating with the supporters of Ibn al-Zubayr. On him see Ibn Saʿd, *Ṭabaqāt*, V, 181.

50. The only apparent report about ʿAbd al-Raḥmān b. ʿUthmān concerns this episode.

51. The only apparent report about ʿAbd al-Raḥmān b. ʿAmr b. Sahl concerns this episode.

52. The dīwān is an institution for registering the names of those who are to take part in campaigns in order that they can be paid. As the fighters normally came from the Arabs, the recruitment of mawālī would seem to be a temporary measure for this campaign. See *EI²*, s.v. Dīwān.

53. The only apparent report about Unays b. ʿAmr al-Aslamī concerns this incident.

54. Al-Jurf is a place near Mecca. See Yāqūt, *Muʿjam*, II, 63.

Unays b. 'Amr al-Aslamī advanced as far as Dhū Ṭuwā[55] while 'Amr b. al-Zubayr went on until he stopped at al-Abṭaḥ.[56] He sent to his brother, "Fulfill the oath of the Caliph by putting a chain of silver around your neck, which will not be seen, so that the people will not fight each other. Therefore, be pious toward God, for you are in a sacred town." Ibn al-Zubayr answered, "Your meeting place is the mosque."

Ibn al-Zubayr sent 'Abdallāh b. Ṣafwān al-Jumaḥī[57] against Unays b. 'Amr in the direction of Dhū Ṭuwā, while some of the people who lived around Mecca joined 'Abdallāh b. Ṣafwān. They fought against Unays b. 'Amr and inflicted a dreadful defeat on him. The bulk of 'Amr b. al-Zubayr's followers scattered, and he went into the house of Ibn 'Alqamah.[58] 'Ubaydah b. al-Zubayr[59] came to him and gave him protection. He went to 'Abdallāh b. al-Zubayr and said, "I have given him protection." Ibn al-Zubayr retorted, "Are you giving protection at the expense of the people? This is not appropriate."   [225]

According to Muḥammad b. 'Umar al-Wāqidī, he transmitted this account to Muḥammad b. 'Ubayd b. 'Umayr,[60] and the latter reported that 'Amr b. Dīnār[61] informed him that Yazīd b. Mu'āwiyah wrote to 'Amr b. Sa'īd to put 'Amr b. al-Zubayr in command of an army and to send him with Unays b. 'Amr against Ibn al-Zubayr. 'Amr b. al-Zubayr went on until he stopped at his house at al-Ṣafā[62] while Unays b. 'Amr stopped at Dhū Ṭuwā.

---

55. In the valley of Mecca at the gateway into Mecca. See Ibn Manẓūr, *Lisān*, s.v. *ṭwy*.

56. Al-Abṭaḥ is a stony valley near Mecca and Minā. See Yāqūt, *Mu'jam*, I, 92.

57. 'Abdallāh b. Ṣafwān al-Jumaḥī was from Quraysh; he supported Ṭalḥah and al-Zubayr against 'Alī. Later he became a loyal supporter of Ibn al-Zubayr. When al-Ḥajjāj defeated him, his head was cut off. See Ṭabarī, I, 1910, and II, 852.

58. Text has been emended to Ibn 'Alqamah, as in *Addenda et Emendanda*, DCL. Ibn 'Alqamah's house was very close to the Ka'bah in Mecca. See Ṭabarī, I, 1130.

59. 'Ubaydah b. al-Zubayr was a brother of Ibn al-Zubayr. The brothers seemed to be in conflict with one another. At one time, 'Ubaydah was appointed governor of Mecca but then he was dismissed. See Balādhurī, *Ansāb*, IV/1, 353.

60. Muḥammad b. 'Ubayd b. 'Umayr seems to be mentioned only in connection with this report.

61. 'Amr b. Dīnār was an important traditionist and jurist; he died in 126 (743–44). See Ibn Sa'd, *Ṭabaqāt*, V, 353–54.

62. Al-Ṣafā was a hill in Mecca associated with the pilgrimage rites. The pilgrims ran to and from it and another hill called al-Marwah. See Yāqūt, *Mu'jam*, III, 397.

ʿAmr b. al-Zubayr usually led the prayer for the people; ʿAbdallāh b. al-Zubayr usually prayed behind him. When he left he knotted his fingers together [in frustration]. There did not remain one of the Quraysh who failed to come to ʿAmr b. al-Zubayr. However, ʿAbdallāh b. Ṣafwān kept away. ʿAmr b. al-Zubayr said, "What disturbs me is that I do not see ʿAbdallāh b. Ṣafwān. By God! If I went against him, he would know that the clan of Jumaḥ and the others who have taken refuge with him are few." His words were reported to ʿAbdallāh b. Ṣafwān; they roused him. He said to ʿAbdallāh b. al-Zubayr, "I see that you are acting as if you want to spare your brother." The latter replied, "Abū Ṣafwān (i.e., ʿAbdallāh b. Ṣafwān), do I want to spare him? By God! If I could get even the help of small ants against him, I would use them." ʿAbdallāh b. Ṣafwān said to him, "I will take care of Unays for you, and you take care of your brother for me." Ibn al-Zubayr agreed.

ʿAbdallāh b. Ṣafwān went against Unays b. ʿAmr, who was at Dhū Ṭuwā. He met him with a numerous crowd of Meccans and other supporters. Unays b. ʿAmr and those with him were defeated. They killed those who fled and the wounded. Muṣʿab b. ʿAbd al-Raḥmān[63] advanced against ʿAmr while his followers scattered from him. Eventually he escaped to ʿUbaydah b. al-Zubayr.[64] ʿUbaydah b. al-Zubayr told ʿAmr that he would give him protection. He went to ʿAbdallāh b. al-Zubayr and told him that, as he had given protection to ʿAmr, ʿAbdallāh should grant him protection for his sake. However, ʿAbdallāh refused to give him protection. He had him flogged for all those who had been flogged by him in Medina; he imprisoned him in the prison at ʿĀrim.[65]

Al-Wāqidī reported that they had given many reports to him about the account of ʿAmr b. al-Zubayr and that he had recorded

[226]

---

63. Muṣʿab b. ʿAbd al-Raḥmān was the son of the famous Companion of the Prophet, ʿAbd al-Raḥmān b. ʿAwf. He was killed in the siege of Mecca. See p. 223, below.

64. The Arabic text says: "He escaped to ʿAmr b. al-Zubayr." ʿAmr has been emended to ʿUbaydah.

65. ʿĀrim means "wicked" or "violent." It was the name given to Zayd, a servant of Muṣʿab b. ʿAbd al-Raḥmān. A prison of four square cubits was built for him; he was jailed there until he died. See Balādhurī, Ansāb, IV/1, 315; and p. 16, below.

them all. According to Khālid b. Ilyās[66]—Abū Bakr b. 'Abdallāh b. Abī Jahm:[67] When 'Amr b. Sa'īd came to Medina as governor, he came in the month of Dhū al-Qa'dah in the year 60 (July/ August 680). He put 'Amr b. al-Zubayr in command of his police and said, "The Commander of the Faithful has sworn that he will not accept the oath of allegiance from Ibn al-Zubayr unless he is brought in a chain. Let the oath of the Commander of the Faithful be fulfilled. I will make a light chain of silver or gold; he can wear a cloak over it so that it will not be noticed, that is, unless its sound is heard." Then he recited:

Take it. True, it is not a course of action for the strong.
　　Even a humiliated man would hesitate to accept it.
Yet, 'Āmir, the people have offered you such a course of action.
　　And no one among the neighbors is going to blame you.[68]

According to Muḥammad (b. 'Umar al-Wāqidī)—Riyāḥ b. Muslim[69]—his father:[70] 'Amr b. Sa'īd raised an army to go against 'Abdallāh b. al-Zubayr. Abū Shurayḥ[71] said, "Do not attack Mecca, for I heard the Messenger of God say: 'God has only permitted fighting in Mecca for one hour of one day. Then the city returned to its inviolable status.'" 'Amr refused to listen to what he said and retorted, "We know more about its inviolable status than you, Shaykh."

'Amr b. Sa'īd sent an army with 'Amr b. al-Zubayr. With the latter went Unays b. 'Amr al-Aslamī and Zayd, the servant of Muḥammad b. 'Abdallāh b. al-Ḥārith b. Hishām.[72] They num-

---

66. Khālid b. Ilyās was a well-known traditionist who lived in the second (eighth) century. Some critics accuse him of forging tradition. See Ibn Ḥajar, *Tahdhīb*, III, 80–81.

67. Abū Bakr b. 'Abdallāh was a well-known traditionist who seems to have been alive at the beginning of the second (eighth) century. See Ibn Ḥajar, *Tahdhīb*, XII, 26.

68. The first line of this poem is quoted by Balādhurī. See *Ansāb*, IV/1, 305, 311. A fuller version is given by Iṣfahānī, *Aghānī*, XVI, 311. Both verses with slight variations are later used by Marwān. See pp. 191–92, below.

69. Apart from two accounts both concerned with Ibn al-Zubayr and both quoted by Wāqidī, Riyāḥ b. Muslim seems to be otherwise unknown.

70. Riyāḥ's father Muslim seems to be unknown.

71. Abū Shurayḥ's name was Khuwaylid b. Ṣakhr. He was converted to Islam before the conquest of Mecca and died in 68 (687–88). See Ibn Sa'd, *Ṭabaqāt*, IV/2, 32.

72. There are no reports of either Zayd or his master in any other context.

bered about two thousand. The people of Mecca fought against them. Unays b. ʿAmr and al-Muhājir, the mawlā of al-Qalammas, were killed amid many people.[73] The army of ʿAmr b. al-Zubayr was defeated. He went to ʿUbaydah b. al-Zubayr, who told his brother that he was under his protection and that he would give him the guarantee of neighborly protection. He went with him to ʿAbdallāh b. al-Zubayr, who said, "What is this blood that is on your face, you wicked man?" ʿAmr recited:

[227]

Our wounds do not bleed on our heels [through retreating],
    but they drip blood on our feet [through going forward].[74]

Ibn al-Zubayr had him imprisoned; he betrayed ʿUbaydah's protection, asking him, "Did I tell you to give protection to this grave sinner who sought to violate those things made inviolable by God?" Then all those whom ʿAmr had flogged took vengeance on him except for al-Mundhir and his son. They both refused to take vengeance on him. ʿAmr died under the lashes.

The narrator commented that the prison of ʿĀrim was only called this because of a slave called Zayd ʿĀrim. The prison was named after him. Ibn al-Zubayr imprisoned his brother ʿAmr in this place.

According to al-Wāqidī—ʿAbdallāh b. Abī Yaḥyā[75]—his father: There were two thousand with Unays b. ʿAmr.

In this year (60/680) the people of al-Kūfah sent messengers to Ḥusayn, while he was in Mecca, calling on him to come to them. He sent his cousin Muslim b. ʿAqīl b. Abī Ṭālib to them.

The Kūfans' Invitation to Ḥusayn and the Mission of Muslim b. ʿAqīl

According to Zakariyyāʾ b. Yaḥyā al-Ḍarīr[76]—Abū al-Walīd Aḥmad b. Janāb al-Maṣṣīṣī[77]—Khālid b. Yazīd b. Asad b. ʿAbdallāh al-

---

73. There are no reports of either Muhājir or al-Qalammas in any other context.

74. Also quoted by Balādhurī. See *Ansāb*, IV/1, 314.

75. ʿAbdallāh b. Abī Yaḥyā is an occasional authority of Wāqidī; otherwise he and his father Abū Yaḥyā cannot be identified.

76. Yaḥyā al-Ḍarīr is a little known traditionist, who was blind (*ḍarīr*). See Dhahabī, *Mīzān al-Iʿtidāl*, II, 75.

77. Abū Walīd Aḥmad b. Janāb al-Maṣṣīṣī was a well-known and respected traditionist from Baghdad; he died in 220 (835). See Ibn Ḥajar, *Tahdhīb*, I, 22.

Qasrī[78]—'Ammār al-Duhnī[79] reported that he asked Abū Ja'far[80] to tell him about the killing of al-Ḥusayn so that he might think that he was present at al-Ḥusayn's death. Abū Ja'far reported that Mu'āwiyah had died while al-Walīd b. 'Utbah b. Abī Sufyān was [228] governor of Medina. He sent to al-Ḥusayn b. 'Alī asking for his oath of allegiance. Al-Ḥusayn asked him to grant him a delay and to show favor to him. He granted him a delay, and al-Ḥusayn left for Mecca. The Kūfans and their messengers came to him, saying, "We have kept ourselves exclusively for you. We do not attend the Friday prayer with the governor, so come to us." Al-Nu'mān b. Bashīr al-Anṣārī was governor of al-Kūfah.

Al-Ḥusayn sent for Muslim b. 'Aqīl b. Abī Ṭālib, his cousin, and told him, "Go to al-Kūfah and investigate what they have written to me. If it is true, we will go to them." Muslim departed to Medina. He took two guides, who went with him into the desert. They were overcome by thirst, and one of the two guides died. Muslim wrote to al-Ḥusayn asking him to relieve him, but al-Ḥusayn wrote back to him telling him to go on to al-Kūfah. He continued his journey until he arrived. He stayed with one of the inhabitants called Ibn 'Awsajah.[81] When news of his arrival was circulated among the Kūfans, they streamed to him to give the oath of allegiance. Twelve thousand of them gave the oath of allegiance to him.

One of the men who favored Yazīd b. Mu'āwiyah stood up before al-Nu'mān b. Bashīr and told him, "You are either a weak man or you are acting like a weak man. The town has been corrupted." Al-Nu'mān answered, "I would prefer to be a weak man in obedience to God than a strong man in disobedience of God. I would not tear off a cover that God has spread."

---

78. Khālid b. Yazīd b. Asad b. 'Abdallāh al-Qasrī was a little-known traditionist who seems to have lived in the second half of the second (eighth) century.

79. 'Ammār al-Duhnī's full name was 'Ammār b. Mu'āwiyah al-Duhnī. He was a traditionist, who was accused of Shī'ite tendencies by Ibn Ḥajar; he was claimed as a Shī'ite by Shī'ite writers. He died in 133 (750–51). See Ibn Ḥajar, *Tahdhīb*, VIII, 7–8, and al-Ṭūsī, *Fihrist*, 235.

80. Abū Ja'far's name is Muḥammad b. 'Alī b. al-Ḥusayn. He was the fifth Imām of the Shī'ah. He died in 114 (732). See Mufīd, *Irshād* (trans. Howard), 393–407.

81. Ibn 'Awsajah was a leading Kūfan Shī'ite, who died with al-Ḥusayn. See pp. 137–38, below. Abū Mikhnaf's account has Muslim staying with al-Mukhtār. See p. 28, below.

The words of al-Nuʿmān were reported to Yazīd. He summoned a mawlā of his called Sarjūn,[82] who used to advise him, and gave him the news. Sarjūn asked whether he would accept the advice of Muʿāwiyah if he were alive. When he agreed, Sarjūn said, "Then accept it from me. The only man for al-Kūfah is ʿUbaydallāh b. Ziyād. Give him authority over the city." Yazīd had been very angry with ʿUbaydallāh b. Ziyād; he had been intending to dismiss him from al-Baṣrah. Yet now he wrote to him expressing satisfaction with him; he gave him authority over al-Kūfah together with al-Baṣrah. He also wrote to him to hunt for Muslim b. ʿAqīl and to kill him if he found him.

[229]   ʿUbaydallāh approached with some of the nobles of the people of al-Baṣrah. He entered al-Kūfah veiled; every group of people whom he passed and greeted said, "Greetings, son of the daughter of the Apostle of God," for they thought that he was al-Ḥusayn b. ʿAlī. When ʿUbaydallāh reached the palace, he summoned a mawlā of his, gave him three thousand dirhams, and told him, "Go and ask about his man to whom the Kūfans are giving their oath of allegiance. Let it be known that you are a man from the people of Ḥimṣ[83] who has come for this purpose and that you give him this money in order to strengthen his position." The mawlā kept on being generous and helpful until he was led to a shaykh among the Kūfans, who was in charge of receiving the oath of allegiance. He met him and told him his story. The shaykh said to him, "Your meeting both pleases and grieves me. What pleases me is the way God has guided you, but what grieves me is the fact that our plans are not yet properly established." The shaykh introduced him to Muslim, who took the money from him and received his oath of allegiance. Then he returned to ʿUbaydallāh and gave him the information.

On ʿUbaydallāh's arrival, Muslim had moved from the house in which he had been staying to the house of Hāniʾ b. ʿUrwah al-Murādī.[84] Muslim b. ʿAqīl had written to al-Ḥusayn b. ʿAlī, in-

---

82. Sarjūn was Muʿāwiyah's secretary and adviser; he was probably a Christian; see Ṭabarī, II, 205.

83. Ḥimṣ is a town in Syria to the north of Damascus; it is located halfway between Damascus and Aleppo. See Yāqūt, *Muʿjam*, II, 334.

84. Hāniʾ b. ʿUrwah al-Murādī was one of the tribal leaders of Madhḥij, a Yemenī tribe.

forming him of the oath of allegiance made by twelve thousand of the Kūfans and advising him to come. Then ʿUbaydallāh asked the Kūfan nobles, "Why is it that Hāniʾ b. ʿUrwah has not come to visit me among the others?" Muḥammad b. al-Ashʿath[85] went out to get him with a group of his tribe. Hāniʾ was at the door of his house. They said to him, "The governor has mentioned you and considers you tardy. So go to him." They remained with him, and he rode with them to ʿUbaydallāh. With the latter was Shurayḥ, the qāḍī.[86] When ʿUbaydallāh saw him, he said to Shurayḥ, "His own legs have brought you one who will be destroyed."[87] After greeting Hāniʾ, he asked him where Muslim was. When he answered that he did not know, ʿUbaydallāh ordered his mawlā, the man with the dirhams, to come out to him. When Hāniʾ saw him, he was deeply troubled by him and pleaded, "May God benefit the governor. By God! I did not invite him to my house. He came and threw himself on me." ʿUbaydallāh demanded that [Muslim] be brought to him, but he replied, "By God! If he were under my two feet, I would not lift them from him to give him to you." ʿUbaydallāh ordered that Hāniʾ be brought closer. He was brought nearer, and ʿUbaydallāh struck him on the forehead and cut it open. Hāniʾ reached toward the sword of one of the police to pull it out, but he was pushed away from it. ʿUbaydallāh declared that God had made it permissible to take his blood and ordered him to be imprisoned in a part of the palace.

[230]

A different account from Abū Jaʿfar's says that the one who brought Hāniʾ b. ʿUrwah to ʿUbaydallāh b. Ziyād was ʿAmr b. al-Ḥajjāj al-Zubaydī.[88]

According to ʿAmr b. ʿAlī[89]—Abū Qutaybah[90]—Yūnus b. Abī

---

85. Muḥammad b. al-Ashʿath was the tribal leader of Kindah, a Yemenī tribe. His father had been rehabilitated after fighting in the war of Riddah. On the tribal groupings and attitudes in Kūfah, see M. Hinds, "Kūfan Political Alignments and Their Background in the Mid-Seventh Century A.D." *International Journal of Middle East Studies*, 1971.

86. Shurayḥ b. al-Ḥārith al-Kindī was appointed qāḍī over al-Kūfah by ʿUmar in 19 (640) and remained in his post until 80 (699–700).

87. An Arabic proverb. See Ibn Manẓūr, *Lisān*, s.v. ḥyn.

88. ʿAmr b. al-Ḥajjāj al-Zubaydī was a leader of a clan of the Yemenī tribe of Madhḥij.

89. ʿAmr b. ʿAli was a well-known traditionist, who died in 249 (863). See Ibn Hajar, *Tahdhīb*, VIII, 80–81.

90. Abū Qutaybah was Salm b. Qutaybah; he was a well-known traditionist,

Isḥāq[91]—al-ʿAyzār b. Ḥurayth[92]—ʿUmārah b. ʿUqbah b. Abī Muʿayṭ:[93] ʿUmārah b. ʿUqbah was sitting in the assembly of Ibn Ziyād talking. He said, "Today I have driven out some zebras; I have struck and lamed one of them." ʿAmr b. al-Ḥajjāj al-Zubaydī retorted, "A zebra that you lamed would be a stupid one." ʿUmārah said, "Shall I tell you of something stupider than all this? A man whose father was an unbeliever was brought to the Apostle of God. He ordered him to be executed. The man pleaded, 'Muḥammad, who will there be for the children?' He answered, 'Hell-fire.' You are one of the children and you will be in Hell-fire." Ibn Ziyād laughed.

Continuation of ʿAmmār al-Duhnī's Account from Abū Jaʿfar

While Hāni' was in this position, news of it got out to Madhḥij. There was an uproar at the gate of the palace. ʿUbaydallāh heard it and asked what it was. They told him that it was Madhḥij. He ordered Shurayḥ to go out to them and inform them that he had only detained Hāni' for questioning. However, he sent one of his mawālī as a spy to listen to what Hāni' would say. As he went past Hāni' b. ʿUrwah, Hāni' said to him, "Fear God, Shurayḥ, for he will kill me." However, Shurayḥ went out, stood at the gate of the palace, and said, "There is no need for concern about him. [231] The governor is only detaining him to question him." They told each other that that was true and that there was no need for concern for their colleague; they dispersed.

The news of Hāni' reached Muslim. He had the battle cry called out, and four thousand of the Kūfans gathered to him. He sent forward his vanguard and drew up his right and left wings. He himself advanced with the center toward ʿUbaydallāh. In the

---

who lived in al-Baṣrah and died in either 200 (815–16) or 201 (816–17). See Ibn Ḥajar, *Tahdhīb*, IV, 133.

91. Yūnus b. Abī Isḥāq was a well-known Kūfan traditionist; he died in either 152 (769) or 159 (775–76). See Ibn Ḥajar, *Tahdhīb*, XI, 433–34.

92. Al-ʿAyzār was a Kūfan traditionist; he died while Khālid al-Qasrī was governor of Iraq, 105–20 (723–38). See Ibn Ḥajar, *Tahdhīb*, VIII, 203–4.

93. ʿUmārah b. ʿUqbah b. Abī Muʿayṭ was a member of the Umayyad family who seems to have settled in al-Kūfah.

meantime, 'Ubaydallāh had sent to the nobles of the Kūfans and gathered them with him in the palace. When Muslim reached him and came to the gate of the palace, they were able to look down on their clansmen. They began to speak to them; they tried to make them go away. The followers of Muslim began to slip away, so that by late afternoon he only had five hundred. As darkness spread, even the five hundred had gone.

When Muslim saw that he had been left alone, he began to wander through the streets. He came to a door and stopped. A woman came out to him; he asked her to give him a drink. She gave him a drink and then returned inside her house. She delayed for as long as God decreed and then came back out to find him still at the door. She said, "Servant of God, your staying here is suspicious. Go away." He replied, "I am Muslim b. 'Aqīl. Will you shelter me?" She told him to enter.

Her son was a mawlā of Muḥammad b. al-Ashʿath. When the boy recognized him, he went to Muḥammad and told him. Muḥammad went to 'Ubaydallāh and told him. 'Ubaydallāh sent 'Amr b. Ḥurayth,[94] the commander of his police, to get him. With him went 'Abd al-Raḥmān b. Muḥammad b. al-Ashʿath.[95] Muslim was not aware of what was happening until the house was surrounded. When he realized, he went out against them with his sword and fought them. 'Abd al-Raḥmān gave him a guarantee of safe-conduct and thus got him into his power. He brought him to 'Ubaydallāh. The latter ordered that he should be taken up to the top of the palace and executed. Then his body was thrown down to the people. He then ordered Hāni' to be dragged to al-Kunāsah,[96] and there he was crucified. Their poet said of that:

If you do not know what death is, then look

    at Hāni' and Ibn 'Aqīl in the marketplace.

[232]

---

94. 'Amr b. Ḥurayth was a leading Qurashite living in al-Kūfah; he was given many official posts by the Umayyads. See Wellhausen, *Religio-Political*, trans. Ostle and Walzer, 97, 121. According to Abū Mikhnaf, Ḥusayn b. Tamīm was in command of 'Ubaydallāh's police in al-Kūfah. See p. 53, below.

95. 'Abd al-Raḥmān was later known as Ibn al-Ashʿath. He led the abortive revolution that was put down by al-Ḥajjāj b. Yūsuf; he was killed in 85 (705). See Shaban, *Islamic History*, I, 110–11; and *EI*², s.v. Ibn al-Ashʿath.

96. Al-Kunāsah (rubbish dump) was a camel market in al-Kūfah.

The command of the governor struck them down
    and they became legends for those who strive along every
    road.
Is Asmāʾ riding in peace a mount which moves at walking pace
    while Madhḥij is seeking vengeance against him?[97]

Abū Mikhnaf's Account

As for Abū Mikhnaf, he gives a fuller and more complete account
of the story of Muslim b. ʿAqīl's visit to al-Kūfah and his death
than the report of ʿAmmār al-Duhnī from Abū Jaʿfar, which we
have just mentioned.

According to Hishām b. Muḥammad (al-Kalbī)—Abū Mikhnaf—
ʿAbd al-Raḥmān b. Jundab[98]—ʿUqbah b. Simʿān,[99] mawlā of al-
Rabāb bt. Imruʾ al-Qays of Kalb, the wife of Ḥusayn—al-Rabāb
was with Sukaynah[100] bt. Ḥusayn, and ʿUqbah had become a
mawlā of her father's; she was a young girl at that time: We set
out from Mecca and we stayed on the main road. A member of
al-Ḥusayn's household said to him, "If you avoided the high
road, like Ibn al-Zubayr, the pursuit would not be able to catch up
with you." He replied, "No, by God! I will not leave it until God
judges what is pleasing to Him." On the way we met ʿAbdallāh b.
Muṭīʿ,[101] who asked al-Ḥusayn, "I wish I could offer my life for
yours. Where are you going?" He answered. "For the present, I am
going to Mecca. After that, I will leave the choice to God." ʿAbdallāh b. Muṭīʿ advised him, "May God choose well for you but,
when you reach Mecca, beware of approaching al-Kūfah. It is an
unlucky place; there your father was killed and your brother deserted and struck unawares by a blow that almost took his life.

---

97. In Abū Mikhnaf's account, more verses are given that are attributed to al-
Farazdaq. See p. 63, below. Similar verses are also given by Balādhurī who attri-
butes them to ʿAbdallāh b. Zabīr al-Asadī. See Balādhurī, *Ansāb*, II/1, 83. For
Asmāʾ, see p. 37 n. 169, below.

98. ʿAbd al-Raḥmān b. Jundab was an authority of Abū Mikhnaf; he was not
used by other historical traditionists. See Sezgin, *Abū Miḥnaf*, 193.

99. ʿUqbah b. Simʿān was an important eyewitness. He remained with al-
Ḥusayn until he died but managed to save his own life. See pp. 109, 162, below.

100. Sukaynah went on to lead a rather indulgent life. See Wellhausen, *Arab
Kingdom*, trans. M. G. Weir, 161.

101. ʿAbdallāh b. Muṭīʿ was a Qurashite who lived in Medina; he was a loyal
supporter of Ibn al-Zubayr. See Ibn Saʿd, *Ṭabaqāt*, V, 106–10.

Stay at the Ḥaram, for you are the lord of the Arabs, and the inhabitants of the Ḥijāz will not treat anyone as your equal. By God! The people will come from every side to support you. Do not leave the Ḥaram, may my uncles on both sides of my family sacrifice their lives for you, for by God, if you die, then we will be enslaved after you." [233]

Al-Ḥusayn went on and stayed in Mecca. Its inhabitants began to visit him frequently, as did those who had come to make the ʿumrah[102] and [other] people from far and wide. Ibn al-Zubayr had settled himself there, near the Kaʿbah, where he used to stand in prayer and perform the circumambulation of the Kaʿbah throughout the day. He would come to visit Ḥusayn with the others who came to visit him. He would come to him for two successive days. Sometimes he would come to him once every two days; he would advise Ḥusayn according to his view. Yet Ḥusayn was the most unwelcome of God's creatures in the eyes of Ibn al-Zubayr because he realized that the people of the Ḥijāz would not give the oath of allegiance to him and follow him as long as Ḥusayn was in the town. In their eyes and hearts, al-Ḥusayn was greater and more capable of commanding the people's obedience than he.

When the Kūfans learnt of the death of Muʿāwiyah, the Iraqīs spread rumors about Yazīd. They said that Ḥusayn and Ibn al-Zubayr had sought a secure place and both of them had gone to Mecca. The Kūfans wrote to Ḥusayn. At that time al-Nuʿmān b. Bashīr was their governor.

According to Abū Mikhnaf—al-Ḥajjāj b. ʿAlī[103]—Muḥammad b. Bishr al-Hamdānī:[104] The Shīʿah in al-Kūfah gathered in the house of Sulaymān b. Ṣurad al-Khuzāʿī.[105] There we discussed

---

102. The ʿumrah is a lesser pilgrimage made when visiting Mecca. Its rituals are confined to Mecca. It was originally the pre-Islamic pilgrimage to Mecca in the month of Rajab; see *EI*[1], s.v. ʿUmra.

103. Al-Ḥajjāj b. ʿAlī was an authority of Abū Mikhnaf; otherwise he is unknown. See Sezgin, *Abū Miḥnaf*, 204.

104. Muḥammad b. Bishr al-Hamdānī was a Shīʿite of al-Kūfah. Apart from his reports, nothing is known of him; see Sezgin, *Abū Miḥnaf*, 202 and 205.

105. It was claimed that Sulaymān b. Ṣurad al-Khuzāʿī was a Companion of the Prophet. He had been a supporter of ʿAlī and his family and had become the leader of the Shīʿah in al-Kūfah. After the failure of al-Ḥusayn, he led the penitents (*tawwābūn*), who wanted to avenge al-Ḥusayn. They were decisively defeated. See Jafri, *Origins and Early Development*, 82, 159, 177, 182, 222–32.

the death of Muʿāwiyah, and praised and glorified God for that. Sulaymān b. Ṣurad announced to us, "Muʿāwiyah is dead. Al-Ḥusayn has withheld giving his oath of allegiance to the Umayyads and has gone to Mecca. You are his Shīʿah and the Shīʿah of his father. If you know that you will be his helpers and fighters against his enemy, then write to him and tell him. But if you fear failure and weakness, do not tempt the man to risk his own life."

They declared, "No, indeed we will fight his enemy, and our lives will be given for him." He said, "Then write to him." They wrote to him: "In the name of God, the Merciful, the Compassionate, to al-Ḥusayn b. ʿAlī, from Sulaymān b. Ṣurad, al-Musayyab b. Najabah,[106] Rifāʿah b. Shaddād,[107] Ḥabīb b. Muẓāhir,[108] and his Shīʿah of the believers and Muslims among the Kūfans. Peace be

[234] with you. We commend the praise of God, other than Whom there is no deity, to you. Praise be to God Who has broken your enemy, the obstinate tyrant who had leapt upon his community, stripped it of its authority, plundered its *fayʾ*,[109] and seized control of it without its consent. Then he killed the choice members of it and preserved the wicked members of this place. He made God's wealth something that circulates only among the community's tyrants and the wealthy. He was destroyed as Thamūd was destroyed.[110] There is no imām over us. Therefore come, so God may unite us in the truth through you. Al-Nuʿmān b. Bashīr is in

---

106. Al-Musayyab b. Najabah was a leading Shīʿite in al-Kūfah, who had been a supporter of ʿAlī; he lost his tribal authority when Muʿāwiyah came to power. He took part in the movement of penitents after the death of al-Ḥusayn. See Jafri, *Origins and Early Development*, 118, 177, 222–23, 232.

107. Rifāʿah b. Shaddād was a long-standing Shīʿite in al-Kūfah, who had taken part in Ḥujr b. ʿAdī's revolt against Muʿāwiyah in 51 (671). After al-Ḥusayn's failure, he took part in the movement of penitents, which he survived. He joined al-Mukhtār. See Jafri, *Origins and Early Development*, 177, 223–24, 232.

108. Ḥabīb b. Muẓāhir was a leading Shīʿite in al-Kūfah. Of the four who wrote this letter, he is the only one who managed to get to al-Ḥusayn and die with him. See Jafri, *Origins and Early Development*, 177, 182, 189, 206.

109. *Fayʾ* literally means "booty" but it has implications beyond that. It refers to the conquered lands that had not been divided among the Muslim conquerors and whose income these Kūfans felt should go to them, not to Syria. See Shaban, *Islamic History*, I, 46–51.

110. The Thamūd were a people who rejected the prophet Ṣāliḥ. They hamstrung a she-camel that was sent as a sign. For their sins, they were destroyed by an earthquake. The theme is frequently repeated in the Qurʾān. For one example, see Qurʾān, 7:73–79 (71–77).

the governor's palace; we do not gather with him for the Friday prayer. Nor do we accompany him out of the mosque for the Festival prayer.[111] If we hear that you will agree to come to us, we will drive him away until we pursue him to Syria, if God wills. The peace and mercy of God be with you."

We despatched the letter with 'Abdallāh b. Sabu' al-Hamdānī[112] and 'Abdallāh b. Wālī.[113] We ordered them to go quickly. The two men hurried off and came to al-Ḥusayn at Mecca on 10 Ramaḍān (June 14, 680). Two days later we sent Qays b. Mushir al-Ṣaydāwī,[114] 'Abd al-Raḥmān b. 'Abdallāh b. Kadan al-Arḥabī[115] and 'Umārah b. 'Ubayd al-Salūlī[116] to him. With them they took about fifty-three letters, each letter being from one man or a group of two or four. We delayed a further two days and then sent Hāni' b. Hāni' al-Sabī'ī[117] and Sa'īd b. 'Abdallāh al-Ḥanafī.[118] With them we had written: "In the name of God, the Merciful, the Compassionate, to al-Ḥusayn b. 'Alī, from the believers and Muslims of his Shī'ah. Make haste. The people are waiting for you. They think of no one but you. Therefore, speed, speed! Peace be with you."

Shabath b. Rib'ī,[119] Ḥajjār b. Abjar,[120] Yazīd b. al-Ḥārith b.   [235]

---

111. On the Festival of Sacrifice ('īd al-aḍḥā) and the Festival for the End of the Fast ('īd al-fiṭr), a special prayer was said in the morning outside the mosque. See EI[1], s.v. Muṣallā.

112. Balādhurī gives his name as 'Abdallāh b. Sabī'. See Ansāb, II/2, 158. The latter was mentioned as fighting with al-Mukhtār. See Ṭabarī, II, 653.

113. 'Abdallāh b. Wālī was a supporter of 'Alī, who died fighting for the penitents from al-Kūfah with Sulaymān b. Ṣurad. See Ṭabarī, I, 3422–28, and II, 569.

114. Qays b. Mushir al-Ṣaydāwī was regularly used as a messenger by the Shī'ah in al-Kūfah and al-Ḥusayn; he was captured on one of his journeys and then killed. See p. 84, below.

115. Balādhurī records the name as Kadir and Dhī Kadir instead of Kadan. See Ansāb, II/2, 158, 159. However, he also records Kadan with his correct name as being killed fighting for al-Ḥusayn. See Ansāb, II/2, 196.

116. Balādhurī records the name 'Abd instead of 'Ubayd. See Ansāb, II/2, 158, 159. He was a leading member of the Kūfan Shī'ah.

117. This journey and Hāni' al-Sabī'ī's journey back are the only times he is mentioned.

118. Sa'īd b. 'Abdallāh al-Ḥanafī is one of the leaders of the Kūfan Shī'ah.

119. Shabath b. Rib'ī, at first a staunch supporter of 'Alī, then became a Khārijite but quickly returned to 'Alī and fought against them. After writing this letter, he changed sides again. See Wellhausen, Religio-Political, 119.

120. Ḥajjār b. Abjar was an important tribal leader in al-Kūfah; he changed sides after writing the letter. See pp. 49, 125, below.

Yazīd b. Ruwaym,[121] ʿAzrah b. Qays,[122] ʿAmr b. al-Ḥajjāj al-Zubaydī and Muḥammad b. ʿUmayr al-Tamīmī[123] had also written: "The Janāb has grown green; the fruit has ripened; the waters have overflowed. Therefore, if you want to, come to an army that has been gathered for you. Peace be with you."

When all the messengers gathered together with him, he read the letters and asked the messengers about the people's situation. He wrote back with Hāni' b. Hāni' al-Sabīʿī and Saʿīd b. ʿAbdallāh al-Ḥanafī, who were the last two messengers: "In the name of God, the Merciful, the Compassionate, from al-Ḥusayn b. ʿAlī to the leaders of the believers and the Muslims. Hāni' and Saʿīd have brought me your letters; they are the last two of your messengers who have come to me. I have understood everything that you have described and mentioned. The statement of most of you is: 'There is no imām over us. Come, God may unite us in guidance and truth through you.' I am sending you my brother, Muslim b. ʿAqīl, who is my cousin and the trustworthy representative from my family. I have instructed him to write to me about your circumstances, situation, and views. If he writes to me that the opinion of your leaders and of the men of wisdom and merit among you is united in the same way as the messengers who have come to me have described, and as I have read in your letters, I will come to you speedily, God willing, for, by my life, what is the imām except one who acts according to the Book, one who upholds justice, one who professes the truth, and one who dedicates himself to [the essence of] God? Peace be with you."

According to Abū Mikhnaf—Abū al-Mukhāriq al-Rāsibī:[124] Some members of the Shīʿah in al-Baṣrah had been meeting for some days in the house of a woman from the tribe of ʿAbd al-Qays, who was called Māriyyah bt. Saʿd or Munqidh. She had

---

121. Yazīd b. al-Ḥārith b. Yazīd Ruwaym was a Yemenī leader in al-Kūfah; he changed sides after writing the letter. See p. 125, below.

122. ʿAzrah b. Qays was a Yemenī leader in al-Kūfah; he also changed sides after writing the letter. See pp. 105–13, 120–21, 139, 164, below.

123. Muḥammad b. ʿUmayr was a leader of Tamīm in al-Kūfah. After writing the letter, he seems to have kept a very low profile.

124. Abū al-Mukhāriq al-Rāsibī was an authority of Abū Mikhnaf, who was a Kūfan traditionist at the beginning of the second (eighth) century. See Sezgin, *Abū Miḥnaf*, 189.

sympathy toward the Shī'ah, and her house had become a place where they held discussions.[125]

The coming of al-Ḥusayn had been reported to Ibn Ziyād, and he wrote to his administrator ('āmil) in al-Baṣrah to send out scouts and take control of the road. However, Yazīd b. Nubayṭ[126]—he was from the tribe of 'Abd al-Qays—decided to go to support al-Ḥusayn. He had ten sons and he asked them, "Which of you will come with me?" Two of his sons, 'Abdallāh and 'Ubaydallāh, volunteered to go with him. Then he told his companions in the house of that woman (i.e., Māriyyah), "I have decided to go. Now I am leaving." They said to him, "We fear for you because of the followers of Ibn Ziyād." He replied, "By God! If the feet of my she-camel are set on the plain desert, I do not care whoever seeks to overtake me." [236]

Yazīd set out, hurrying along the road, until he reached Ḥusayn. He joined al-Ḥusayn's encampment at al-Abṭaḥ. Al-Ḥusayn received news of Yazīd's arrival and began to look for him. When the man came to al-Ḥusayn's encampment and was told that he had gone to his house, the man went after him. When al-Ḥusayn did not find him, he sat in his encampment waiting for him. The Baṣran came back and found him sitting. Then he recited: "In the favor and mercy of God, in that let them rejoice."[127] He greeted al-Ḥusayn, sat with him, told him about the reason why he had come, and prayed for good with him. Then he set out with him, and fought alongside him. Yazīd and his two sons were killed with him.

Then[128] al-Ḥusayn summoned Muslim b. 'Aqīl and despatched him with Qays b. Mushir al-Ṣaydāwī, 'Umārah b. 'Ubayd al-Salūlī, and 'Abd al-Raḥmān b. 'Abdallāh b. Kadan al-Arḥabī. He enjoined him to be pious before God, to be discreet, and to be courteous. Al-Ḥusayn instructed Muslim that, if he saw that the people were united and committed, then he should inform him speedily. Muslim departed and came to Medina. There he prayed

---

125. Apart from this incident, Māriyyah was not mentioned again.
126. Apart from this account, Yazīd was not mentioned again.
127. Qur'ān, 10:59 (58).
128. The narrative now returns to the account reported to Abū Mikhnaf from al-Ḥajjāj b. 'Alī.

in the Mosque of the Apostle of God and said farewell to the dearest members of his family. Then he hired two guides from the tribe of Qays. These two set out with him, but they missed the way and went astray. They were struck by severe thirst. The two guides, on the point of dying of thirst, told him, "Follow this path to reach water."

[237]

Muslim b. ʿAqīl wrote a letter to Ḥusayn and sent it with Qays b. Mushir—this was at al-Maḍīq in the valley of al-Khubayt:[129] "... I set out from Medina with two guides and they missed the way and got lost. All of us were overcome by thirst; the two guides soon died. But we kept going until we came to a watering-hole. We were only saved at the last moment of our lives. That wateringhole is in a place called al-Maḍīq in the valley of al-Khubayt. I have taken this as a bad omen for my mission. If you consider it so, you could relieve me and send another in my place. Peace be with you."

Al-Ḥusayn wrote back: "... I am afraid that your urging me in the letter to relieve you of the task that I sent you on is only prompted by cowardice. Therefore go on with the task that I gave you. Peace be with you." When Muslim read the letter, he said, "It is not for myself that I am afraid." So he continued until he came to a wateringhole belonging to the tribe of Ṭayyi'. He stopped with them. As he rode off there was a man hunting. He saw him shoot a fawn as it came into his sight, and kill it. Muslim said, "Thus will our enemies be killed, God willing."

Muslim went on until he entered al-Kūfah. There he stayed in the house of al-Mukhtār b. Abī ʿUbayd,[130] which is called today the house of Muslim b. al-Musayyab.[131] The Shīʿah began to come regularly to him. Whenever a group of them gathered together with him, he would read the letter of al-Ḥusayn, and they would begin to weep.

---

129. Al-Maḍīq is a village between Mecca and Medina. See Yāqūt, *Muʿjam*, IV, 560. Al-Khubayt is a valley in that area. See ibid., II, 398.

130. Al-Mukhtār b. Abī ʿUbayd was a political opportunist of Shīʿite persuasion, who became a revolutionary Shīʿite leader; he won control of al-Kūfah for two years, 65–67 (684–86). See Wellhausen, *Religio-Political*, 125–45; and *EI*[1], s.v. al-Mukhtār b. Abī ʿUbaid.

131. Muslim b. al-Musayyab was governor of Shīrāz for the Umayyads; he was killed in 129 (746–47) during the Shīʿite revolution of ʿAbdallāh b. Muʿāwiyah. See Ṭabarī, II, 1977.

'Ābis b. Abī Shabīb al-Shākirī[132] stood up. After praising and glorifying God, he said, "I cannot speak to you for the people because I do not know what is in their hearts, nor would I deceive you about them. By God! I can, however, tell you about what I have decided for myself. By God! I will answer you when you call me. I will fight your enemies alongside you. I will strike with my sword in defense of you until I meet God, seeking nothing but God's reward." Next Ḥabīb b. Muẓāhir al-Faqʿasī got up and spoke, "May God have mercy on you! You have explained what is in your heart by your concise words." Then he said, "By God other than Whom there is no deity! I am of the same view as he is." Al-Ḥanafī[133] said the same.

[238]

According to al-Ḥajjāj b. 'Alī, he asked Muḥammad b. Bishr whether he had said anything. He answered, "Even though I wanted God to strengthen my colleagues with victory, I did not like killing and I was unwilling to lie."

The Shīʿah began to visit Muslim b. 'Aqīl so frequently that his place of residence became well known, and al-Nuʿmān b. Bashīr learnt of the location.

According to Abū Mikhnaf—Numayr b. Waʿlah[134]—Abū al-Waddāk:[135] Al-Nuʿmān ascended the pulpit and after praising God said, "Servants of God, fear God and do not rush into rebellion and discord, for in that men will be destroyed, blood will be shed, and property will be plundered." He was a tolerant, pious man who preferred the gentle approach. He went on, "I do not fight anyone who does not fight me. Nor do I come against anyone who does not come against me. Nor do I revile you. I do not oppose you. Nor will I apprehend anyone merely on grounds of suspicion, accusation, or hearsay. However, if you disclose your real intentions, violate your oath of allegiance, and oppose your imām, by God other than Whom there is no deity, I will strike you with my sword as long as its hilt remains in my hand, even though I do

---

132. 'Ābis b. Abī Shabīb al-Shākirī was a leader of the Kūfan Shīʿah, who managed to get to al-Ḥusayn; he was killed with him. See pp. 147–48, below.

133. Al-Ḥanafī is Saʿīd b. 'Abdallāh al-Ḥanafī.

134. Numayr b. Waʿlah was a reporter of historical traditions, who reported from al-Shaʿbī, as well as being an authority for Abū Mikhnaf. See Sezgin, *Abū Miḥnaf*, 215.

135. Abū al-Waddāk is Jabr b. Nawf al-Hamdānī, a well-known traditionist. See Sezgin, *Abū Miḥnaf*, 215.

not have any of you to help me. Yet I hope that those among you who know the truth are more numerous than those whom falsehood will destroy."

ʿAbdallāh b. Muslim b. Saʿīd al-Ḥaḍramī,[136] an ally of the Banū Umayyah, stood before him and said, "O, governor, what you see can only be adequately dealt with by violence. Your view about what should be done between you and your enemy is that of the weak." Al-Nuʿmān answered, "I would prefer to be one of the weak while remaining in obedience to God than to be one of the mighty while being in rebellion against God." Then he descended from the pulpit.

ʿAbdallāh b. Muslim went out and wrote the following letter to Yazīd b. Muʿāwiyah: ". . . Muslim b. ʿAqīl has come to al-Kūfah, and the Shīʿah have given the oath of allegiance to him on behalf of al-Ḥusayn b. ʿAlī b. Abī Ṭālib. If you have any need of al-Kūfah, then send a strong man there, who will carry out your orders and act in the same way as you would against your enemy. Al-Nuʿmān b. Bashīr is a weak man, or he is acting like a weak man." He was the first to write to him. Then ʿUmārah b. ʿUqbah wrote to him in a similar vein, as did ʿUmar b. Saʿd b. Abī Waqqāṣ.[137]

According to Hishām (b. Muḥammad al-Kalbī)—ʿAwānah:[138] When the letters reached Yazīd—and there were only two days between their letters—he summoned Sarjūn, a mawlā of Muʿāwiyah and asked him, "What is your view of the fact that Ḥusayn has directed his attention toward al-Kūfah, and Muslim b. ʿAqīl is in al-Kūfah receiving the oath of allegiance on his behalf? I have also learnt that al-Nuʿmān is weak; I have had other bad reports of him." Then he read him their letters [and asked], "Whom do you think that I should appoint as governor of al-Kūfah?" Now Yazīd was angry with ʿUbaydallāh b. Ziyād, so Sarjūn answered him, "Do you think, if Muʿāwiyah were recalled to life for you, that

[239]

---

136. Apart from this incident, ʿAbdallāh b. Muslim Saʿīd al-Ḥadramī is not mentioned.

137. ʿUmar was the son of the famous Companion of the Prophet Saʿd b. Abī Waqqāṣ and later led the Kūfan army against al-Ḥusayn. See pp. 103, 115, below.

138. Ibn al-Kalbī breaks his narrative from Abū Mikhnaf and introduces connecting material from ʿAwānah b. al-Ḥakam al-Kalbī. The latter is an important historical traditionist. He died in 147 (764) or 153 (770). See *EI*², s.v. ʿAwāna b. al-Ḥakam.

you would take his advice?" He answered, "Yes." Sarjūn produced
a letter of appointment for ʿUbaydallāh b. Ziyād as governor of al-
Kūfah and said, "This is the advice of Muʿāwiyah written before
he died." So he took his advice, joined the two cities under the
authority of ʿUbaydallāh, and sent him his letter of appointment.

After this Yazīd summoned Muslim b. ʿAmr al-Bāhilī[139]—who
was there with him—and he sent him to al-Baṣrah to ʿUbaydallāh with his letter of appointment, and he wrote to him as well:
"... My followers among the people of al-Kūfah have written
to me to inform me that Ibn ʿAqīl is in al-Kūfah gathering units
in order to spread rebellion among the Muslims. Therefore, when   [240]
you read this letter of mine, go to al-Kūfah and search for Ibn
ʿAqīl, as if you were looking for a bead, until you find him. Then
bind him in chains, kill him, or expel him. Peace be with you."

Muslim b. ʿAmr went to ʿUbaydallāh at al-Baṣrah. ʿUbaydallāh ordered that preparations should begin immediately and
that the departure for al-Kūfah would take place on the next day.

Earlier Ḥusayn had written a letter to the Baṣrans.

According to Hishām (b. Muḥammad al-Kalbī)—Abū Mikhnaf—
al-Ṣaqʿab b. Zuhayr[140]—Abū ʿUthmān al-Nahdī:[141] Ḥusayn
wrote a letter to the Baṣrans with a mawlā of his [family's] called
Sulaymān.[142] It was written in one copy but [addressed to] the
heads of the five divisions in al-Baṣrah[143] and to the nobles:
it was written to Mālik b. Mismaʿ al-Bakrī,[144] al-Aḥnaf b.

---

139. Muslim b. ʿAmr al-Bāhilī was from Syria. After being sent to ʿUbaydallāh
in al-Baṣrah, he stayed. Then he became a supporter of Ibn al-Zubayr. He died
during the revolt of Ibn al-Zubayr. See Crone, *Slaves*, 136–37.

140. Al-Ṣaqʿab b. Zuhayr was a well-known traditionist, who lived during the
first half of the second (eighth) century. See Sezgin, *Abū Mikhnaf*, 220.

141. Abu ʿUthmān al-Nahdī was ʿAbd al-Raḥmān b. Mill. He was born before
Islam and lived until after 75 (694). See Sezgin, *Abū Miḥnaf*, 220.

142. Sulaymān is only mentioned in connection with this incident; he was
killed.

143. When Ziyād was appointed governor of al-Baṣrah in 44 (664), he divided
the people into five divisions for the purpose of administration and distribution of
pay. The division was not made entirely on a tribal basis. See Shaban, *Islamic
History*, I, 86.

144. It is strange that Mālik b. Mismaʿ al-Bakrī should have been written to by
al-Ḥusayn. He was a leader in al-Baṣrah of Bakr b. Wāʾil and had fought against
ʿAlī at the Battle of the Camel. He then joined Muʿāwiyah. He fought against
Mukhtār later for Ibn al-Zubayr but then returned to the Umayyads. See Crone,
Slaves, 116–17.

Qays,[145] al-Mundhir b. al-Jārūd,[146] Masʿūd b. ʿAmr,[147] Qays b. al-Haytham,[148] and ʿUmar b. ʿUbaydallāh b. Maʿmar.[149] A single copy of it was given to all the [Baṣran] nobles [which was as follows]: "God gave preference to Muḥammad before all His creatures. He graced him with prophethood and chose him for His message. After he had warned His servants and informed them of what he had been sent with, God took him to Himself. We are his family, those who possess his authority (awliyāʾ), those who have been made his trustees (awṣiyāʾ), and his inheritors; we are those who have more right to his position among the people than anyone else. Our people selfishly claimed our exclusive right to that. Yet we consented [to what they did] since we hated disunion and desired the well-being [of the community]. However, we know that we have greater claim to that right, which was our entitlement, than those who have seized it. They have done well, set many things right, and sought truth. May God have mercy on them and forgive us and them. I have sent my messenger to you with this letter. I summon you to the Book of God, the Sunnah of His Prophet. Indeed the Sunnah has [almost] been killed while innovation has been given life. If you hear my words and obey my commands, I will guide you along the path of righteousness. Peace and the mercy of God be with you."

[241]   Each one of the nobles who read the letter kept it secret, except al-Mundhir b. al-Jārūd. He claimed he was afraid that the messenger was a plotter sent by ʿUbaydallāh. He brought the messenger to ʿUbaydallāh on the evening before the morning when he was intending to depart to al-Kūfah. ʿUbaydallāh read the letter and

---

145. Al-Aḥnaf b. Qays was a very powerful leader of the Banū Saʿd of Tamīm in al-Baṣrah; he had had a good relationship with Muʿāwiyah but was reluctant to accept Yazīd. See Wellhausen, *Arab Kingdom*, 138, 142.

146. Al-Mundhir b. al-Jārūd had been a governor for ʿAlī but was at this time leaning toward the Umayyads. One of his daughters married ʿUbaydallāh. See Crone, *Slaves*, 15.

147. Masʿūd b. ʿAmr was the tribal leader of Rabīʿah in al-Baṣrah, who was killed in the feuding that took place in al-Baṣrah after the death of Yazīd. See Wellhausen, *Arab Kingdom*, 209.

148. Qays b. al-Haytham was a leader of the Banū Sulaym in al-Baṣrah; he also played an important role in Khurāsān. See Wellhausen, *Arab Kingdom*, 414–15.

149. ʿUmar b. ʿUbaydallāh b. Maʿmar was an important leader of Tamīm in al-Baṣrah.

ordered the messenger to be beheaded. Then ʿUbaydallāh ascended the pulpit at al-Baṣrah. After praising and glorifying God, he said, "By God! There is no difficulty that I cannot overcome,[150] Nor does the rattling of the dry skin [of a camel] affect me.[151] Indeed I am a scourge of those who are my enemies and a deadly poison to those who fight against me. Whoever competes with [the tribe of] al-Qārah in shooting arrows does her justice.[152] People of al-Baṣrah, the Commander of the Faithful has appointed me governor of al-Kūfah, and I am going there in the morning. I have appointed over you ʿUthmān b. Ziyād b. Abī Sufyān.[153] Beware of opposition and spreading rumors, for, by Him other than Whom there is no deity, if I hear a word of opposition from any man among you, I will kill him and his ʿarīf[154] and his patron (walī). I will hold those who are near responsible for those who are distant so that you all may hear me and there will not be any opponent or rebel among you. I am the son of Ziyād, whom I [most] resemble among [all] who tread on stones. I do not betray any resemblance to an uncle or to a cousin."

He left al-Baṣrah after he had made his brother ʿUthmān his deputy, and he set off for al-Kūfah. He took with him Muslim b. ʿAmr al-Bāhilī and Sharīk b. al-Aʿwar al-Ḥārithī,[155] together with his entourage and his household. When he reached al-Kūfah, he was wearing a black turban and he was veiled. News of Ḥusayn's departure had reached the people; they were expecting his arrival. When ʿUbaydallāh came, they thought that he was al-Ḥusayn. ʿUbaydallāh could not pass a group of people without their greeting him. They said, "Welcome, son of the Apostle of God,

---

150. An Arabic proverb. Its literal meaning is: "There is no difficult camel which cannot be ridden by me." See Ibn Manẓūr, *Lisān*, s.v. *qrn*.

151. An Arabic proverb. When the camel is frightened, it makes a rattling sound by rubbing its dry skin. The proverb means that he will not be deceived or frightened. See Ibn Manẓūr, *Lisān*, s.v. *qʿqʿ*.

152. An Arabic proverb. Qārah was a tribe famous for its archers. The proverb means: "Don't shoot arrows at people who can shoot better than you." See Ibn Manẓūr, *Lisān*, s.v. *qwr*.

153. ʿUthmān b. Ziyād b. Abī Sufyān was a brother of ʿUbaydallāh.

154. An ʿirāfah was a small group of tribesmen collected together for the purpose of distribution of revenue. The head of each of these was an ʿarīf appointed by the government. See Shaban, *Islamic History*, I, 87–88.

155. Sharīk b. al-Aʿwar al-Ḥārithī was a man of influence in al-Baṣrah; he had supported ʿAlī in the battles of the Camel and Ṣiffīn.

your arrival is a happy event." He saw in their joy at seeing al-Ḥusayn something to trouble him. Muslim b. ʿAmr said, when they overdid it, "Retire, for this is the governor, ʿUbaydallāh b. Ziyād." As he came in view, he checked his mount,[156] and he only had some ten men with him. When he entered the palace and the people realized that he was ʿUbaydallāh b. Ziyād, they felt great sorrow and grief. What he had heard from the people made ʿUbaydallāh very angry, and he said, "Will I only see these people as I have seen them?"

[242]

According to Hishām (b. Muḥammad al-Kalbī)—Abū Mikhnaf—al-Muʿallā b. Kulayb[157]—Abū Waddāk: After he had settled in the palace, the call was made among the people: "The prayer is a general prayer that all should gather for (al-ṣalāt jāmiʿatan)."[158] The people gathered and he went out to them. After praising and glorifying God, he said, "The Commander of the Faithful (Yazīd), may God make him prosperous, has appointed me to be in charge of your town and your frontier post. He has ordered me to give justice to the oppressed among you, to be generous to those of you who are deprived, and to treat the obedient among you with kindness, but to be violent against those of you who are suspicious and disobedient. I will follow his instructions concerning you and will carry out his authorization among you. I will be like a kind father to the good and obedient among you, but I will use my whip and sword against those who abandon my commands and oppose my appointment. Let each man save himself. Truthfulness should avert evil from you without threat of punishment (waʿīd)."[159]

Then he went down; he put the ʿarīfs and the people to a severe test and said, "Write to me about the strangers, those among you who are sought by the Commander of the Faithful, those among

---

156. The Arabic is ẓahr. The term was used for the outskirts of al-Kūfah. In this context, it must mean "his mount."

157. Al-Muʿallā b. Kulayb was an unknown authority of Abū Mikhnaf. See Sezgin, *Abū Miḥnaf,* 210.

158. *Al-ṣalāt al-jāmiʿah* was the regular form of call to prayer used whenever the governor wanted to address the people. It has been suggested that it was the first form of the call to prayer. See E. Mittwoch, "Zur Enstehungsgeschichte des islamischen Gebets und Kultus," 25.

159. An Arabic proverb. See Ibn Manẓūr, *Lisān,* s.v. *nbw.*

you from Ḥarūriyyah,[160] and the troublemakers whose concern is discord and turmoil. Whosoever of you makes these lists for us will be safe from harm. But those of you who do not write anyone will have to guarantee that there is no opponent in his ʿirāfah who will oppose us, and no wrongdoer who will try to wrong us. Anyone who does not do so will be denied protection, and his blood and his property will be permitted to us. Any ʿarīf in whose ʿirāfah is found anyone who is wanted by the Commander of the Faithful, whom he has not reported to us, will be crucified at the door of his house, and I will cancel that ʿirāfah from [the dīwān of] payment, or he will be sent to a position in ʿUmān [or] al-Zarrah."[161]

As for ʿĪsā b. Yazīd al-Kinānī,[162] according to ʿUmar b. Shab-   [243] bah[163]—Hārūn b. Muslim[164]—ʿAlī b. Ṣāliḥ[165]—[ʿĪsā b. Yazīd al-Kinānī]: When Yazīd's letter to ʿUbaydallāh b. Ziyād came, he chose five hundred of the Baṣrans, among whom were ʿAbdallāh b. al-Ḥārith b. Nawfal[166] and Sharīk b. al-Aʿwar; the latter was a member of the Shīʿah of ʿAlī. Sharīk was the first of the people to fall behind. He is said to have feigned falling behind as a result of overcrowdedness, as did the people with him. Then ʿAbdallāh b. al-Ḥārith fell behind, and the people with him. They hoped that ʿUbaydallāh would turn aside to them and that al-Ḥusayn would get to al-Kūfah before him. However, he did not take any notice of those who had fallen behind but went on until he reached al-

---

160. Ḥarūriyyah refers to the Khārijites by the name of the place where the first group broke away from ʿAlī. See Wellhausen, *Religio-Political*, 2.

161. "Or" has been inserted because there does not appear to have been any place called "ʿUmān al-Zarrah." However, there is ʿUmān on the Persian gulf. See Yāqūt, *Muʿjam*, III, 716. Nearby on the island of Baḥrayn there was a large village called "al-Zarrah." See ibid., II, 907.

162. ʿĪsā b. Yazīd al-Kinānī was a historical traditionist, who died c.134 (750). See Petersen, *ʿAlī and Muʿāwiyah*, 60.

163. ʿUmar b. Shabbah was an important historian, who died in 262 (875–76). He was accused of pro-Shīʿite tendencies. See Petersen, *Alī and Muʿāwiyah*, 150–51.

164. Hārūn b. Muslim was a little-known traditionist; he was an authority of ʿUmar b. Shabbah.

165. ʿAlī b. Ṣāliḥ was a little-known traditionist.

166. ʿAbdallāh b. al-Ḥārith b. Nawfal was a Hāshimite, who later, in 65 (684), was nominated by the Baṣrans to the caliphate but he gave way to Ibn al-Zubayr's governor. See Wellhausen, *Arab Kingdom*, 404–10.

Qādisiyyah. [There] his mawlā, Mihrān,[167] fell behind. ʿUbayd-allāh said to him, "Mihrān, are you in this predicament too? If you keep going until you see the palace, you will have a hundred thousand [dirhams]." However, Mihrān's answer was, "No, by God! I cannot."

ʿUbaydallāh stopped and took out clothes made of Yemenī cloth and put on a Yemenī band. He mounted his mule and traveled on by himself. As he passed the guard post, the guards, whenever they saw him, had no doubt that he was al-Ḥusayn. "Welcome, son of the Apostle of God," they said. But he did not speak to them. The people began to come out to him from their houses. Al-Nuʿmān b. Bashīr heard them and locked the door on him and his entourage. ʿUbaydallāh came toward him, and al-Nuʿmān did not doubt that he was al-Ḥusayn, for around him was a crowd of people making a great noise. He called out, "I ask you in the name of God withdraw from me..., for I will not hand over my office (amānah) to you, and I have no wish to kill you." ʿUbayd-allāh did not answer him but he went closer while the other man was hanging over the balcony. Then he began to say to him, "Open; you may not be able to, for you have been slumbering for a long time." A man behind him heard this and withdrew to the people. He said, "O people, it is Ibn Marjānah,[168] by Him other than Whom there is no deity." They replied, "Shame on you! It is none other than al-Ḥusayn." Then al-Nuʿmān opened the door for him, and he entered. They slammed the door in the face of the people, who dispersed.

[244]

In the morning, ʿUbaydallāh sat on the pulpit. He said, "People, I am aware that the men who marched with me and showed obedience to me are enemies of al-Ḥusayn, even though they thought that al-Ḥusayn had come into the land and gained as-cendancy in the town. But, by God, I did not recognize any of you." Then he came down from the pulpit.

ʿUbaydallāh learnt that Muslim b. ʿAqīl had arrived the night before him and was staying within al-Kūfah. He summoned a mawlā of the Banū Tamīm and gave him some money. He told

---

167. Mihrān seems to have been the personal servant of ʿUbaydallāh.
168. Marjānah was ʿUbaydallāh's mother. It was a disparaging way to refer to ʿUbaydallāh.

him, "Pretend to be believing in this matter and help them with
the money. Go to Hāni' and Muslim, and stay with him." The
mawlā went to Hāni' and told him that he was a member of the
Shī'ah, and that he had some money to give.

In the meantime Sharīk b. al-A'war had become ill. He told
Hāni', "Tell Muslim to come to me, for 'Ubaydallāh will pay me
a sick visit." Sharīk said to Muslim, "Do you think that, if I gave
you the opportunity, you would strike the head of 'Ubaydallāh
with your sword?" Muslim replied, "Yes, by God!" 'Ubaydallāh
did come to pay Sharīk a sick visit in the house of Hāni'. Sharīk
had told Muslim, "When you hear me say, 'Give me a drink of
water,' come out and strike him." 'Ubaydallāh sat beside Sharīk's
bed and Mihrān stood behind him. When Sharīk called out, "Give
me a drink of water," a servant girl came out with a cup. However,
she saw Muslim and disappeared. Sharīk called out again, "Give
me a drink of water." Then he called out a third time, "Shame on
you! Do you prevent me from having water? Bring me a drink of
water, even though my life is taken away by it." Mihrān realized
the situation and winked at 'Ubaydallāh; he jumped up. Sharīk
said, "Governor, I want to make my will to you." He replied, "I
will come to visit you again," Mihrān began to hurry him away.
Mihrān told him, "By God! He wanted you to be killed." He replied, "How is that possible with my kindness to Sharīk, and in the
house of Hāni' whom my own father treated with great favor?"

When he got back he sent for Asmā' b. Khārijah[169] and Muḥammad b. al-Ash'ath.

He told them, "Bring me Hāni'." They answered, "He will not   [245]
come without a guarantee of safe-conduct." He said, "What does
he want with a guarantee of safe-conduct? Has he done anything
wrong? Go to him and, if he won't come without a guarantee of
safe-conduct, give it to him." They went and asked him to come.
He replied, "If 'Ubaydallāh gets hold of me, he will kill me." But
they kept urging him and finally brought him while 'Ubaydallāh
was delivering the Friday sermon and sat in the mosque. Hāni'
combed his two plaits of hair [while he waited]. When 'Ubaydallāh had performed the prayer, he called out to Hāni'. The latter

---

169. Asmā' b. Khārijah was a tribal leader of Fazārah of Qays. See Wellhausen,
Religio-Political, 117.

followed him, entered, and greeted him. ʿUbaydallāh said "Didn't you know, Hāniʾ, when my father came to this land, he did not spare the life of anyone of this Shīʿah except for your father and Hujr?[170] You know what happened to Hujr. Then he continued to treat you as well as a good companion. He wrote to the governor of al-Kūfah, 'All that I want from you is to take good care of Hāniʾ.'" Hāniʾ agreed. ʿUbaydallāh demanded, "Is my reward, then, that you hide a man in your house so that he may kill me?" Hāniʾ said, "I have not done such a thing." However, ʿUbaydallāh brought out the man from the tribe of Tamīm, who had been a spy on them. When Hāniʾ saw him, he realized that ʿUbaydallāh had been told [everything]. So he said, "Governor, what you have been told is true, but I will never ignore your favor to me. You and your family are guaranteed safe-conduct. Go wherever you wish." ʿUbaydallāh smoldered [with anger] at that. Mihrān was standing at his side with a cane in his hand, and he said to ʿUbaydallāh, "What a humiliation! This slave of a weaver guarantees your safe-conduct in [the province under] your authority!" ʿUbaydallāh said, "Seize him." He threw down the cane, took hold of the two plaits of Hāniʾ's hair, and pulled them across Hāniʾ's face. ʿUbaydallāh struck Hāniʾ on the face with the cane. The iron head of the cane came off and stuck into the wall. Then ʿUbaydallāh struck his face again; he broke Hāniʾ's nose and brow.

The people heard the uproar. The news reached the tribe of Madhhij. They came and began to surround the building. ʿUbaydallāh ordered Hāniʾ to be thrown into a room while Madhhij were shouting. ʿUbaydallāh ordered Mihrān to take Shurayh to Hāniʾ. [246] Mihrān went out and took Shurayh to Hāniʾ, and the police came in with him. Hāniʾ appealed to him, "Shurayh, do you see what has been done to me?" Shurayh answered, "I see that you are alive." He retorted, "Am I alive despite what you can see? Tell my tribe that, if they go away, he will kill me." Shurayh went back to ʿUbaydallāh and said, "I saw that he was alive, but I saw marks of cruel [treatment]." He replied, "Do you deny the

---

170. Hujr b. ʿAdī was a Shīʿite whom ʿUbaydallāh's father, Ziyād, had first tried to reconcile. Then when he emerged in the revolution, Ziyād put the revolution down with force and sent him to Muʿāwiyah, who executed him. See Wellhausen, *Religio-Political*, 95–101.

governor the right to punish his subjects? Go out to those men and tell them." Shurayḥ went out, but ʿUbaydallāh ordered a man to accompany him. Shurayḥ called to them, "What is this wicked behavior? The man is alive. His governor has reprimanded him with a few blows without taking his life. Go away and do not give grounds for bringing punishment on yourselves and your colleague." So they went away.

According to Hishām (b. Muḥammad al-Kalbī)—Abū Mikhnaf—al-Muʿallā b. Kulayb—Abū al-Waddāk: Sharīk b. al-Aʿwar stayed with Hāniʾ b. ʿUrwah al-Murādī. Sharīk was a member of the Shīʿah and had been present at the Battle of Ṣiffīn with ʿAmmār.[171]

When Muslim b. ʿAqīl heard of the coming of ʿUbaydallāh to al-Kūfah, of what he had said and his treatment of the ʿarīfs and the people, he left the house of al-Mukhtār, where he was well known, and went to the house of Hāniʾ b. ʿUrwah al-Murādī. He came inside his door and sent in for Hāniʾ to come out. Hāniʾ did not want him to be there when he saw him, but Muslim said to him, "I have come to you that you should give me neighborly protection and make me your guest." Hāniʾ replied, "May God have mercy on you, you have put a great burden on me. If it were not for the fact of your entry into the house and your trust, I would have preferred to ask you to leave me. Yet a guarantee of protection is required of me. It is not possible for a person like me to refuse a person like you out of ignorance. Come in." The Shīʿah began to visit him in the house of Hāniʾ b. ʿUrwah.

Ibn Ziyād summoned a mawlā of his called Maʿqil. He told him, "Take three thousand dirhams, and look for Muslim b. ʿAqīl and look for his followers. Give them these three thousand dirhams. Tell them to use it to help in the war against their enemy. Let them know that you are one of them, for if you give them the dirhams they will be sure of you, have confidence in you, and they will not keep any of their information hidden from you. Then keep visiting them." Maʿqil did that. He traveled until he came near Muslim b. ʿAwsajah al-Asadī of the Banū Saʿd b. Thaʿlabah in the Great Mosque. The latter was praying, and Maʿqil heard some people saying that this man had pledged al-

[247]

---

171. ʿAmmār b. Yāsir was a famous Companion of the Prophet and supporter of ʿAlī; he died in the Battle of Ṣiffīn. See *EI*[2], s.v. ʿAmmār b. Yāsir.

legiance to al-Ḥusayn. He sat and waited until Muslim b. ʿAwsajah had finished praying. Maʿqil said, "O servant of God, I am a Syrian, a mawlā of Dhū al-Kalāʿ,[172] whom God has blessed with love for this House (*bayt*) and love for those who love them. Here are three thousand dirhams that I want to give to one of them whom I have learnt has come to al-Kūfah in order to receive oaths of allegiance on behalf of the son of the daughter of the Apostle of God. I have been wanting to meet him, but I have neither found anyone who will direct me to him nor anyone who knows the place. I was sitting [here] earlier and I heard a group of Muslims saying that there was a man who knew about this. Therefore I have come to you so that you may take this money and introduce me to your leader. If you wish, you may receive my oath of allegiance to him before my meeting him." Muslim b. ʿAwsajah replied, "I thank God for your meeting me, and it gives me joy that you will get what you desire; God should help the House of His Prophet through you. Yet your knowledge of my involvement in this affair before it has developed troubles me; I fear this tyrant and his severity." Before he left, he took his oath of allegiance and testaments, strongly supported by oaths that he would be sincere and keep the matter concealed. Maʿqil gave him whatever assurances would satisfy him. Muslim b. ʿAwsajah told him, "Come to me at my house regularly for some days, for I will seek permission for you [to visit] your master." He began to go to visit Muslim b. ʿAwsajah frequently with the people, and the latter sought permission for him.

[248] Hāniʾ b. ʿUrwah fell ill, and ʿUbaydallāh came on a sick visit to him. ʿUmārah b. ʿUbayd al-Salūlī told Hāniʾ, "[The purpose of] our group and our planning is to kill this despot. Now God has given you power over him, so kill him." Hāniʾ replied, "I would not like him to be killed in my house." So ʿUbaydallāh left [unharmed].

Only a week later, Sharīk b. Aʿwar fell sick. He was held in great regard by Ibn Ziyād and other governors; yet he was a steadfast Shīʿite. ʿUbaydallāh sent to him that he should come to him in the evening. Sharīk said to Muslim, "This reprobate is going to

---

172. Dhū al-Kalāʿ was an important Yemenī family of Ḥimṣ. See Crone, *Slaves*, 95.

pay me a sick visit in the evening. When he is sitting down, come out against him and kill him. Then go and take his place in the palace, for no one will prevent you. If I recover from the pain during the next few days, I will go to al-Baṣrah and I will be able to take control of it on your behalf."

In the evening, ʿUbaydallāh set off to pay Sharīk a sick visit. Muslim b. ʿAqīl had taken up a strategic position in order that he could enter. Sharīk had said, "Don't let him escape you when he sits down." Hāniʾ b. ʿUrwah rose and told Muslim b. ʿAqīl, "I don't want him to be killed in my house," as if he loathed that idea. Ibn Ziyād arrived and came in and sat down. He asked Sharīk about his illness, "What is it that you seem [to have] and when did you feel ill?" After Sharīk had spent a long time in answering him and he still saw that Muslim had not come out, he became afraid that Ibn Ziyād would escape and he began to recite: "What are you waiting for to greet Salmā? Quench my thirst [with a sip of water], even though my life is in that." He repeated that twice or three times. ʿUbaydallāh remarked, without discovering his real situation, "Have you noticed that he is talking deliriously?" Hāniʾ replied, "Yes, may God make you prosperous. This behavior has been going on from early this morning, when it was still dark, until now."

Ibn Ziyād rose and departed. Then Muslim came out. Sharīk   [249] demanded, "What stopped you from killing him?" He replied, "Two things. One of them was Hāniʾ's dislike for him to be killed in his house. The other was a tradition that the people tell on the authority of the Prophet. 'Faith controls killing and a believer should not commit murder.'" Hāniʾ said, "By God! If you had killed him, you would have killed a grave sinner (*fāsiq*), a profligate [*fājir*], and an unbeliever (*kāfir*). Yet I disliked the idea of his being killed in my house."

Sharīk only lingered on for three nights after that, and then he died. Ibn Ziyād came out and led the prayer for him. Later, after he had killed Muslim and Hāniʾ, Ibn Ziyād was told, "The words that you heard Sharīk speak during his illness were only to urge Muslim and tell him to come out to kill you." Ibn Ziyād retorted, "By God! I will never pray at the funeral of an Iraqī again. By God! If Ziyād were not buried among them, I would take Sharīk out of his grave."

Maʿqil, the mawlā of Ibn Ziyād, whom the latter had insinuated into [the circles of] Ibn ʿAqīl and his followers by money, had regularly visited Muslim b. ʿAwsajah for some days, so that Muslim b. ʿAwsajah would introduce him to Ibn ʿAqīl. After the death of Sharīk b. al-Aʿwar, Muslim b. ʿAwsajah brought Maʿqil to introduce him to Ibn ʿAqīl. Then Maʿqil got to know all the information about Ibn ʿAqīl. Muslim b. ʿAqīl received his oath of allegiance and told Abū Thumāmah al-Ṣāʾidī[173] to take the money that he had brought. The latter was the one who collected money from them in order to help each other; he used to buy their arms. He was an expert in weapons, one of the horsemen (fāris) of the Arabs and one of the notables of the Shīʿah. Maʿqil began to visit them regularly. He was the first to enter and the last to leave in order to hear all their news and to learn their secrets. Then he reported the secrets in the ear of Ibn Ziyād.

Hāniʾ b. ʿUrwah was in the habit of going every morning and evening to ʿUbaydallāh. When Muslim came to stay with him, he stopped going and pretended to be sick. He began not to go out. Ibn Ziyād asked those who did attend, "Why is it I don't see [250] Hāniʾ?" They replied, "He is sick." Ibn Ziyād said, "If I had been informed of his illness, I would have paid him a sick visit."

According to Abū Mikhnaf—al-Mujālid b. Saʿīd:[174] ʿUbaydallāh summoned Muḥammad b. al-Ashʿath and Asmāʾ b. Khārijah.

According to Abū Mikhnaf—al-Ḥasan b. ʿUqbah al-Murādī:[175] ʿUbaydallāh sent ʿAmr b. al-Ḥajjāj al-Zubaydī with them.

According to Abū Mikhnaf—Numayr b. Waʿlah—Abū al-Waddāk: Rawʿah, sister of ʿAmr b. al-Ḥajjāj, was married to Hāniʾ b. ʿUrwah; she was the mother of Yaḥyā b. Hāniʾ.[176]

ʿUbaydallāh asked them, "What prevents Hāniʾ b. ʿUrwah from coming to visit us?" They answered, "We don't know, may

---

173. Abū Thumāmah al-Ṣāʾidī helped run the Shīʿah organization in al-Kūfah. He was able to join al-Ḥusayn; he died with him. See pp. 142–44, below.

174. Al-Mujālid b. Saʿīd was a well-known historical authority in al-Kūfah, who died in 144 (762). See Sezgin, *Abū Miḥnaf*, 210–11.

175. His name may be al-Ḥusayn b. ʿUqbah, for that name is also given as an authority of Abū Mikhnaf. He is unknown under either name. See Sezgin, *Abū Miḥnaf*, 207.

176. Yaḥyā b. Hāniʾ also reported some accounts used by Abū Mikhnaf. See Sezgin, *Abū Miḥnaf*, 224.

God make the governor prosperous, but it seems that he is sick."
Ibn Ziyād replied, "I have heard that he has recovered and that he
sits at the door of his house. Go and tell him that he should not
abandon his duty toward us, for I do not like one of the Arab
nobles like him to behave rudely to me." When he was sitting at
his door, they went to him in the evening and stood in front of his
house. They asked him, "What is preventing you from seeing the
governor? He has mentioned you and said that, if he had been told
you were ill, he would have paid you a sick visit." He answered,
"An illness has prevented me." They said, "He has been informed
that you sit at the door of your house every evening. He finds you
tardy. Tardiness and churlish behavior are things that the authorities will not tolerate. We adjure you to ride with us."

He called for his clothes and got dressed. Then he called for
a mule and rode with them. When he got near the palace, he
began to feel some apprehension. He said to Ḥassān b. Asmā'
b. Khārijah,[177] "Nephew, by God, I fear this man. What do you
think?" Ḥassān replied, "By God! Uncle, I do not fear anything for
you. Why do you make a pretext against yourself when you are
innocent?"

They claimed that Asmā' did not know why 'Ubaydallāh had   [251]
sent for Hāni' while Muḥammad did know.

The group went into 'Ubaydallāh b. Ziyād, and [Hāni'] went in
with them. When 'Ubaydallāh looked up, he said, "His own legs
have brought you one who will be destroyed."[178]

'Ubaydallāh had just married Umm Nāfi' bt. 'Umārah b.
'Uqbah. When Hāni' had drawn near Ibn Ziyād, Shurayḥ, the
qāḍī, was sitting with him. Ibn Ziyād turned toward Hāni' and
recited:

I wish him all the good and yet he seeks my life.
    Who would side with you against your friend from the tribe
    of Murād?[179]

---

177. This appears to be the only time Ḥassān b. Asmā' is mentioned.
178. Arabic proverb. See note 87, above.
179. A verse recited by 'Alī when his future murderer, 'Abd al-Raḥmān b.
Muljam al-Murādī, gives the oath of allegiance to him. See Mufīd, *Irshād*, 7. The
verse itself is well known and is attributed to 'Amr b. Ma'dīkarib.

He was referring to his earlier kindness and gentleness to Hāniʾ. Hāniʾ asked "What is that, governor?" Ibn Ziyād replied, "Yes, Hāniʾ b. ʿUrwah, what are these matters that have been hatching in your houses against the Commander of the Faithful and the general community of the Muslims? You have brought Muslim b. ʿAqīl and taken him into your house. You have gathered arms and men for him in houses around you. You thought that was hidden from me." Hāniʾ said, "I have not done that, and Muslim is not with me." Ibn Ziyād declared, "O yes, you have!" Hāniʾ repeated his denial, and Ibn Ziyād [again] said, "Yes, you have!" After the argument between them had gone on for some time, and Hāniʾ persisted in contradicting and denying [the accusations], Ibn Ziyād summoned that spy, Maʿqil. He came and stood before him. Ibn Ziyād asked him whether he knew Hāniʾ, and he said that he did. At that Hāniʾ realized that he had been a spy against them and had brought information about them. For a moment he was bewildered; then his spirit returned to him. He said, "Listen to me and believe what I say. I swear by God that I do not lie. By God, other than Whom there is no deity! I did not summon him to my house. I did not know anything about his business until I saw him sitting at my door. He asked to stay with me. I was too ashamed to refuse him. As a result of that, the duty of giving him protection fell upon me. Therefore, I took him into my house and gave him lodging and refuge. Then his affair [developed] as you have been

[252]   informed. If you wish, I will give you strongly sworn testaments and whatever you can trust that I will not do you any harm. If you wish, I will give you a guarantee that I will put in your hand to ensure that I return to you. Then I will go to him and order him to leave my house for wherever in the land he wants to go. Then I will be rid of his right of protection." Ibn Ziyād said "No, by God! You will never leave me unless you bring him." Hāniʾ refused, saying, "No, by God! I will not bring him to you. How could I bring you my guest so that you can kill him!" Ibn Ziyād [again] insisted, "By God! Bring him to me." Hāniʾ repeated, "By God! I will not bring him."

After the argument between them had gone on for some time, Muslim b. ʿAmr al-Bāhilī rose. There was no other Syrian or Baṣran in al-Kūfah except him. He said, "May God make the governor prosperous! Leave me with him so that I can speak to

him." He had seen Hāni''s obstinacy and refusal to comply with
Ibn Ziyād's order. He told Hāni' to come over to him so that he
could speak to him; he arose and took him aside from Ibn Ziyād.
They were where Ibn Ziyād could see them. When they raised
their voices, he could hear what they were saying. Muslim said to
him, "I adjure you before God, Hāni', not to kill yourself and
bring tribulation on your tribe and your clan. By God! I hold you
too precious to be killed." Hāni' thought his clan would move to
rescue him, but Muslim continued, "Ibn ʿAqīl is the cousin of the
Umayyads, so they will neither kill him, nor harm him. Therefore
deliver him to Ibn Ziyād. There will be no shame and blemish on
you in doing that, for you would only be handing him over to the
authorities." Hāni' replied, "By God! Indeed, there would be
shame and disgrace for me if I were to hand over one who has
come under my protection and is my guest, while I am still alive
and sound. I can hear; I see well; I have a strong arm and many
helpers. By God! If I were the only one without any helper, I would
not hand him over until I had died on his behalf." He pressed
further, but Hāni' went on saying, "By God! I will never hand him
over to you."

Ibn Ziyād heard that and ordered him to be brought to him. They
brought him, and Ibn Ziyād said to him, "By God! Bring Muslim
b. ʿAqīl to me or I will have your head cut off." Hāni' replied,
"Then there will be much flashing [of swords] around your house."
Ibn Ziyād retorted, "That is your error. Do you frighten me with
the flashing [of swords]?"

Hāni' thought his clan would defend him. Ibn Ziyād ordered   [253]
that he should be brought closer to him. He was brought nearer,
and Ibn Ziyād struck his face with his cane; he went on beating at
his nose, forehead and cheeks so that Hāni''s nose was broken and
the blood flowed from it onto his clothes, and the flesh of his
cheeks and forehead was splattered over his beard. Eventually the
cane broke. Hāni' stretched out his hand toward the hilt of the
sword of one of the police but the man pulled it away from him
and prevented him. Ibn Ziyād yelled at him, "Have you become
one of the Ḥarūrī today? So you have legally brought punishment
on yourself. Therefore, killing you is permitted to us. Take him
away and throw him into one of the rooms in the building. Lock
the doors on him and put guards on him." That was done. How-

ever, Asmāʾ b. Khārijah arose and said, "Are we messengers of treachery from now on? You told us to bring the man to you. Yet, when we brought him to you, you smashed his nose and face; you made his blood flow on his beard. Then you claimed that you would kill him." ʿUbaydallāh said, "Are you still here?" And he ordered him to be struck and shaken. Then he was left in prison. Muḥammad b. al-Ashʿath said that the tribal leaders were satisfied with the governor's attitude, whether for them or against them; and that the governor was only giving due punishment. However, when it was reported to ʿAmr b. al-Ḥajjāj that Hāniʾ had been killed, he advanced with Madhḥij and surrounded the palace. He had a great crowd with him. He called out, "I am ʿAmr b. al-Ḥajjāj, and these are the horsemen and leading men of Madhḥij, who have neither broken away from obedience nor separated from the community. But it has been reported to them that their colleague has been killed; they regard that as a great crime."

ʿUbaydallāh was told that Madhḥij were at the gate. He told the qāḍī, Shurayḥ, to go in to their colleague, look at him and then go out and inform them that he was still alive and had not been killed, for he had seen him. Shurayḥ went in and looked at him.

According to Abū Mikhnaf—al-Ṣaqʿab b. Zuhayr—ʿAbd al-Raḥmān b. Shurayḥ[180] heard Shurayḥ telling Ismāʿīl b. Ṭalḥah:[181] I went in to Hāniʾ. When Hāniʾ saw me, he said, with blood flowing down his beard, "Oh, God! Oh, Muslim! Has my clan perished? Where are the people of religion? Where are the people of the town? Have they vanished, abandoning me to their enemy and the son of their enemy?" When he heard the tumult at the door of the palace, and I was about to go out, he followed me and said, "I think those are the voices of Madhḥij and my group of the Muslims. If ten of them got in, they would be able to rescue me." I went out to them accompanied by Ḥumayd b. Bukayr al-Aḥmarī,[182] whom Ibn Ziyād had sent with me—he was a member

[254]

---

180. ʿAbd al-Raḥmān b. Shurayḥ later became one of the supporters of al-Mukhtār in his revolution. See Sezgin, *Abū Miḥnaf*, 220.

181. Ismāʿīl was the son of Ṭalḥah b. ʿUbaydallāh, who opposed ʿAlī at the Battle of the Camel.

182. Bakr in text has been emended to Bukayr as in *Addenda et Emendanda*, DLII. Ḥumayd b. Bukayr al-Aḥmarī was a member of the police, who was also present at the battle against al-Ḥusayn. See p. 164, below.

of his police who used to stand beside him. I swear by God that, if he had not been with me, I would have told Hāni''s colleagues what Hāni' had asked me. But when I went out to them, I said, "When the governor learnt about your attitude and your statements concerning your colleague, he ordered me to go and see him. I went and I saw him. Then he ordered me to inform you that he is still alive; the report that he had been killed was false." 'Amr b. al-Ḥajjāj and his colleagues praised God that he had not been killed. Then they went away.

According to Abū Mikhnaf—al-Ḥajjāj b. 'Alī—Muḥammad b. Bishr al-Hamdānī: When 'Ubaydallāh struck Hāni' and imprisoned him, he was afraid that because of it the people would create a disturbance. He went out and ascended the pulpit. With him were the nobles, his police and his entourage. After praising and glorifying God, he said, "O people, hold fast to obedience to God and to your imāms. Do not cause division and discord, for you will be destroyed, humiliated, killed, harshly treated or deprived. He who speaks the truth to you is your brother.[183] He who warns you is excused."[184] He was on the point of descending the pulpit, when the lookouts at the date sellers' gate of the mosque rushed in yelling, "Muslim b. 'Aqīl has come!" 'Ubaydallāh quickly went into the palace and locked the gates.   [255]

According to Abū Mikhnaf—Yūsuf b. Yazīd[185]—'Abdallāh b. Khāzim:[186] By God! I was Ibn 'Aqīl's messenger to the palace to see what became of Hāni'. When he was beaten and imprisoned, I mounted my horse and was the first to enter the house to bring information of him to Muslim b. 'Aqīl. There some women of Murād had gathered and they were crying out, "O calamity! O bereavement!" I went in to see Muslim with the news. He ordered me to summon his supporters. The houses around him were full of them. Of the eighteen thousand who had given him the oath of allegiance, there were four thousand men there. He

---

183. An Arabic proverb. See Ibn Manẓūr, *Lisān*, s.v. *akhw*.

184. An Arabic proverb meaning that the one who warns cannot be blamed for the punishment of those who ignore the warning. See Ibn Manẓūr, *Lisān*, s.v. *ndhr*.

185. Yūsuf b. Yazīd was a frequent authority of Abū Mikhnaf; otherwise he is unknown. See Sezgin, *Abū Miḥnaf*, 226.

186. The only apparent report about 'Abdallāh b. Khāzim seems to concern this episode.

told me to yell with his battle cry *"yā manṣūr amit"* ("ye who have been promised victory, kill!").[187] So I cried out, *"yā manṣūr amit."* Then the Kūfans gathered around him.

Muslim gave the command of the quarter Kindah and Rabīʿah to ʿUbaydallāh b. ʿAmr b. ʿUzayz al-Kindī.[188] He told him to go in front of him with the cavalry. He put Muslim b. ʿAwsajah al-Asadī in charge of the Madhḥij and Asad quarter, and since he was in command of them he ordered Muslim to dismount with the foot soldiers. Over the quarter of Tamīm and Hamdān, he appointed Abū Thumāmah al-Ṣāʾidī. He gave command of the quarter [of the people] from Medina to ʿAbbās b. Jaʿdah al-Jadalī.[189] Then he advanced toward the palace. When ʿUbaydallāh was informed of his coming, he barricaded himself in the palace and locked the gates.

According to Abū Mikhnaf—Yūnus b. Abī Isḥāq—ʿAbbās al-Jadalī: Four thousand of us went out with Ibn ʿAqīl. When we reached the palace, we were only three hundred. Muslim began to move forward with the people from Murād until he had surrounded the palace. The people answered the call and gathered; it was only a short time before the mosque and the marketplace were full of people. They continued to gather until the afternoon (*masāʾ*). ʿUbaydallāh's situation was grim. All his energy was concentrated on holding the door of the palace, for he only had [256] thirty members of his police, twenty nobles, and his family and mawālī with him in the palace. The nobles began to come to him through the door that adjoined the building of the Byzantines. Then those who were with Ibn Ziyād began to look down on the people. They looked down at them; they had to guard against the stones that the people threw at them as they cursed them. Nor were they remiss in cursing ʿUbaydallāh and his father. Ibn Ziyād summoned Kathīr b. Shihāb b. al-Ḥusayn al-Ḥārithī[190] and ordered

---

187. This was the battle cry used at Badr by the Muslims. See Wāqidī, *Maghāzī,* I, 8.

188. The only apparent report about ʿUbaydallāh b. ʿAmr b. ʿUzayz al-Kindī seems to concern this episode.

189. The only apparent report about ʿAbbās b. Jaʿdah al-Jadalī seems to concern this episode.

190. Kathīr b. Shihāb b. al-Ḥusayn al-Ḥārithī was a powerful Yemeni tribal leader, whose influence was only reported on this occasion, for he took the leading role in sending away Madhḥij. In this attempted revolt, the other important Madhḥij leader, ʿAmr b. al-Zubaydī, seems to have played no part on either side.

him to go out among those of Madhḥij who obeyed him, to go round al-Kūfah and to make the people desert Ibn ʿAqīl; he should make them afraid of war and threaten them with the authorities' punishment. Then he ordered Muḥammad b. al-Ashʿath to go out among those of Kindah and Ḥaḍramawt who obeyed him; he should raise a standard that would guarantee safe-conduct to those people who came to him. He gave similar instructions to al-Qaʿqāʿ b. Shawr al-Dhuhlī,[191] Shabath b. Ribʿī al-Tamīmī, Ḥajjār b. Abjar al-ʿIjlī' and Shamir b. Dhī al-Jawshan al-ʿĀmirī.[192] He kept the rest of the nobles of the people with him, not wishing to be without them because of the small number of people who were with him. Kathīr b. Shihāb went out and encouraged the people to desert Muslim.

According to Abū Mikhnaf—Abū Janāb al-Kalbī:[193] Kathīr met a man from Kalb called ʿAbd al-Aʿlā b. Yazīd.[194] He was carrying arms with the intention of joining Ibn ʿAqīl with his fellow youths. He seized him and took him to Ibn Ziyād. Kathīr told Ibn Ziyād about the man, but the man told Ibn Ziyād that he had been intending to come to him. Ibn Ziyād retorted, "Sure! Sure! I remember that you promised me that!" Ibn Ziyād ordered the man to be imprisoned.

Muḥammad b. al-Ashʿath went out until he reached the houses of the Banū ʿUmārah. ʿUmārah b. Salkhab al-Azdī[195] came to him; he was on his way to Ibn ʿAqīl and was carrying arms. Muḥammad b. al-Ashʿath seized him and sent him to Ibn Ziyād, who imprisoned him. Ibn ʿAqīl sent ʿAbd al-Raḥmān b. Shurayḥ al-Shibāmī against Muḥammad b. al-Ashʿath from the mosque. When Muḥammad b. al-Ashʿath saw the great number of those who had come against him, he deviated and held back. Al-Qaʿqāʿ   [257]

---

191. Al-Qaʿqāʿ b. Shawr al-Dhuhlī was one of the tribal leaders in al-Kūfah.

192. Shamir b. Dhī al-Jawshan al-ʿĀmirī was a Yemenī tribal leader in al-Kūfah; he fought for ʿAlī at Ṣiffīn but later switched sides. He was killed by al-Mukhtār in vengeance for the part he played against al-Ḥusayn. See Ṭabarī, I, 3305; II, 661–63.

193. Abū Janāb al-Kalbī's name was Yaḥyā b. Abī Ḥayyah. He was a well-known traditionist and an authority of Abū Mikhnaf; he died in 147 (764). See Sezgin, Abū Miḥnaf, 223–24.

194. ʿAbd al-Aʿlā b. Yazīd was only mentioned with regard to this incident and his execution for his part in it. See p. 62, below.

195. ʿUmārah b. Salkhab al-Azdī was only mentioned with regard to this incident and his execution for his part in it. See p. 62, below.

b. Shawr al-Dhuhlī then sent to Muḥammad b. al-Ashʿath, "I have gone around Ibn ʿAqīl from al-ʿArār.[196] Stay away from his position." He went back to Ibn Ziyād through the building of the Byzantines.

When Kathīr b. Shihāb, Muḥammad and al-Qaʿqāʿ, together with those of their tribesmen who obeyed them, had gathered with Ibn Ziyād, Kathīr spoke to him while they were giving sincere advice to Ibn Ziyād. Kathīr b. Shihāb said, "May God make the governor prosperous. You have many of the nobles of the people with you, [as well as] your police, family, and servants. Let us go out against them." ʿUbaydallāh refused, but he gave Shabath b. Ribʿī a standard and sent him out.

The people with Ibn ʿAqīl continued to increase and gather until the afternoon. Their situation was strong. ʿUbaydallāh sent for the nobles and assembled them. Then he said to them, "Look down on the people; promise additional [money] and kind treatment to those who obey. Intimidate the disobedient with [threats of] dispossession and punishment and tell them that the army from Syria is on the march toward them."

According to Abū Mikhnaf—Sulaymān b. Abī Rāshid[197]—ʿAbdallāh b. Khāzim al-Kuthayrī of the clan of Kuthayr in the tribe of Azd: The nobles looked down on us. Kathīr b. Shihāb, the foremost of the people, spoke until the sun was about to set. He said, "O people, go back to your families. Do not hurry into evil actions. Do not expose yourselves to death. These are the soldiers of the Commander of the Faithful, Yazīd, who are approaching. The governor has given God a promise that, if you persist in fighting him and do not go away by nightfall, he will deprive your children of their [right to a] state allotment of money (ʿaṭāʾ). Also [258] he will scatter your soldiers in Syrian campaigns without rations (ṭamaʿ), holding the healthy responsible for the sick and those present for those who are absent until none of the rebellious people remain who have not tasted the evil consequences of what their hands have earned." The other nobles spoke in a similar vein.

---

196. Al-ʿArār seems to have been the name of a place in al-Kūfah.

197. Sulaymān b. Abī Rāshid was a frequent authority of Abū Mikhnaf; however, he does not seem to have been used by other historians. See Sezgin, *Abū Mikhnaf*, 217.

After the people had heard what they had to say, they began to
disperse and go away.

According to Abū Mikhnaf—al-Mujālid b. Saʿīd: Women began
to come to their sons and brothers, urging them to go away as
the people would be enough without them. Every man went to
his son or his brother telling him, "Tomorrow, the Syrians will
come against you. What have you to do with war and this evil
doing? Go away." Thus, each took someone away. They continued
to disperse so that by the time evening came Muslim b. ʿAqīl
only had thirty men with him in the mosque. At the evening
prayer Muslim b. ʿAqīl prayed with only thirty men. When he
saw that it was evening, and he only had a small group with him,
he left the mosque and headed for the gates of Kindah. He reached
the gates with only ten of his men with him. When he left the
gate, there was no one with him. He looked around but could see
no one to guide him along the road, no one to show him to a
house or to give him personal support if an enemy appeared before
him.

He wandered amid the lanes of al-Kūfah, turning to right and
left without knowing where he was going until he came to the
houses of the Banū Jabalah of Kindah. He walked on until he
came to a door where there was a woman called Ṭawʿah. She had
been a slave wife[198] of al-Ashʿath b. Qays; he had freed her. She
had then married Asīd al-Ḥaḍramī[199] and she had borne him [a
son called] Bilāl. Bilāl had gone out with the people, and his
mother was standing at the door waiting for him. Ibn ʿAqīl greeted
her and she returned the greeting. He said, "Servant of God, give
me water to drink." She entered her house and brought him a
drink; he sat down. She took the vessel inside and then came out
again asking, "Servant of God, haven't you had your drink?" He
replied, "Yes." She told him to go to his people but he was silent.

[259]

---

198. The Arabic is *umm walad*. This is a term used to denote a concubine who
has given birth to a child whom the master has recognized as his own; therefore,
the child becomes free. There was a tendency for these women to be given their
freedom, at least on the death of their masters. While the translation "slave wife"
is not a complete description, it seems closest to the concubine's situation. See J.
Schacht, *Origins*, 264–65. Neither she nor her son Bilāl was mentioned after this
event.

199. Asīd b. Mālik al-Ḥaḍramī was present at the battle against al-Ḥusayn and
was said to have killed ʿAbdallāh b. Muslim b. ʿAqīl there. See p. 181, below.

She repeated it but he was still silent. A third time she said, "Fear God in [your treatment of] me! Glory be to God! Servant of God, go to your people. May God give you health. It is not right for you to sit at my door; I will not permit you to do it any longer." He got up and said, "Servant of God, I have neither house nor clan in this town. Would you show me some generosity and kindness? Perhaps I will be able to repay you later on." She asked him who he was, and he told her that he was Muslim b. ʿAqīl, and that the Kūfans had lied to him and incited him. She repeated, "Are you really Muslim?" He said, "Yes." She told him to enter her home. She took him into a room in her house but not the room that she used. She spread out a carpet for him and offered him supper, but he could not eat.

Soon her son returned. He saw her going to and fro between the rooms and exclaimed, "By God! The number of times that you have gone into and come out of that room this evening makes me suspect that you are occupied in something important." She answered, "My little son, forget about this." However, he insisted, "By God! Tell me." She told him to get on with his own business and not to ask her about anything. But he persisted until she said, "My little son, don't tell any of the people anything about what I am going to tell you." She made him take an oath. After he had sworn, she told him. Then he went to bed without saying anything. Some claim that he was a mere fugitive, while others say that he was drinking with his friends that night.

A long time passed for Ibn Ziyād. He did not hear the supporters of Ibn ʿAqīl as he had heard them before. He told his followers to look down at the people and see whether they could see any of them. They looked down and did not see anyone. Then he told them to see whether the people were in the shadows, lying in ambush for them. Ibn Ziyād's followers ascended the central parts [of the walls] of the mosque; they lowered the torches of fire in their hands, so that they could see whether there was anyone in the shadows. Sometimes the torches gave enough light and sometimes they did not give as much light as the followers would have wished. They let down the torches and sticks of cane tied with ropes that were set on fire. They were lowered until they reached the ground. They did this in [places of] the deepest darkness, as well as those parts that were closer and those that were in

[260]

between. They also did that in the darkness around the pulpit. When they saw that there was nothing in the shadows, they informed Ibn Ziyad. Then he opened the doorway into the mosque. He came out and ascended the pulpit. His followers also came out with him. He told them to sit around him for a little while before the night prayer. He ordered 'Amr b. Nāfi'[200] to call out that there would only be a guarantee of safe-conduct for any man of the police, the 'arīfs, the supporters, and the fighters who prayed the night prayer in the mosque. Not an hour passed before the mosque was full of people. After ordering his caller [to call for prayer], he began the prayer. Al-Ḥusayn b. Tamīm[201] said to him, "Either you pray with the people or someone else should pray with them while you go into the palace and pray there. This is up to you. I am afraid you will not be secure here against any of your enemies' trying to assassinate you." 'Ubaydallāh told him, "Order my guard to stand behind me just as they used to do and go round among them. I am not going inside."

After praying with the people, he stood up. He praised and glorified God, saying, ". . . Ibn 'Aqīl, stupid and ignorant man as he is, has attempted the opposition and rebellion that you have seen. There will be no security from God for a man in whose house we find him. Whoever brings him will have the reward for his blood. Fear God, you servants of God, and keep to obedience and your oath of allegiance. Do not do anything against yourselves. Ḥusayn b. Tamīm, may your mother lose you if any of the gates of the lanes of al-Kūfah are open, or this man gets away, and you do not bring him to me. I give you authority over the houses of the inhabitants of al-Kūfah. Send lookouts to the entrances of the lanes. Tomorrow morning clear the people from the houses. Search their houses thoroughly so that you can bring me this man."

Al-Ḥusayn was in charge of the police and was of the Banū Tamīm. After this, Ibn Ziyād went back into the palace. He gave 'Amr b. Ḥurayth his standard and put him in charge of the people. In the morning, he held an assembly and gave permission for   [261]

---

200. 'Amr b. Nāfi' was the secretary of 'Ubaydallāh. See p. 63, below.
201. Al-Ḥusayn b. Tamīm was in charge of 'Ubaydallāh's police in al-Kūfah; he played an active part in the defeat of al-Ḥusayn.

people to come to him. Muḥammad b. al-Ashʿath approached. Ibn Ziyād said to him, "Welcome to one of those whose loyalty is above suspicion." Ibn Ziyād sat Muḥammad b. al-Ashʿath by his side.

That same morning the son of that old woman—he was Bilāl b. Asīd; it was his mother who had given refuge to Ibn ʿAqīl—went to ʿAbd al-Raḥmān b. Muḥammad b. al-Ashʿath and told him about Muslim b. ʿAqīl being with his mother. ʿAbd al-Raḥmān went to his father, who was with Ibn Ziyād and whispered the secret to him. Ibn Ziyād asked what he had said, and Muḥammad b. al-Ashʿath answered that he had told him that Ibn ʿAqīl was in one of their houses. Ibn Ziyād poked a cane into his side and told him, "Get up and bring him to me immediately."

According to Abū Mikhnaf—Qudāmah b. Saʿīd b. Zāʾidah b. Qudāmah al-Thaqafī:[202] When Ibn al-Ashʿath arose to bring Ibn ʿAqīl to Ibn Ziyād, the latter sent to ʿAmr b. Ḥurayth, who was his deputy in leading the people in the mosque, that he should send sixty or seventy men, all from the tribal grouping of Qays, with Ibn al-Ashʿath. He was unwilling to send Ibn al-Ashʿath's own tribal grouping (qawm) because he was aware that every tribe [of the group] would be unwilling that a man like Ibn ʿAqīl should be found and arrested among them. ʿAmr b. Ḥurayth sent ʿAmr b. ʿUbaydallāh b. ʿAbbās al-Sulamī[203] and with him sixty or seventy men from Qays. They went to the house where Muslim b. ʿAqīl was staying. When the latter heard the beating of horses' hooves and the voices of men, he knew that they had come for him. He was about to strike out against them with his sword drawn, but they rushed blindly at him into the house. He fell upon them and struck them with his sword; he drove them out of the house. They repeated the attack, and Muslim counterattacked in the same way. Bukayr b. Ḥumrān al-Aḥmarī[204] exchanged blows with him. Bukayr struck him in the mouth, cutting his top lip and slicing down to the lower lip; he knocked out two of

---

202. Qudāmah b. Saʿīd was an authority of Abū Mikhnaf but only for this incident. See Sezgin, *Abū Miḥnaf*, 216.

203. ʿAmr b. ʿUbaydallāh b. ʿAbbās al-Sulamī was mentioned in connection with this incident.

204. Bukayr b. Ḥumrān al-Aḥmarī was an assistant of the officials in al-Kūfah, who helped Ziyād against Ḥujr b. ʿAdī. See Ṭabarī, II, 129–30.

Muslim's teeth. Muslim struck him a terrible blow on the head
and repeated it, cutting a nerve along his shoulder. The blow   [262]
almost reached Bukayr's stomach. When the people saw this,
they [went up and] looked down on Muslim from the upper part of
the house and began to hurl stones at him. They also lit sticks of
cane with fire and threw them at him from the top of the house.
When he saw that, he went out against them into the lane with
his sword drawn and fought them. Muḥammad b. al-Ashʿath
came toward him, saying, "Young man, you can have my guarantee
of safe-conduct. Don't kill yourself." However, he continued to
fight against the people, saying:

I swear I will only be killed as a free man,
Even though I see death as something horrible.
Every man one day will meet an evil.
Then the cold will be blended with a bitter heat
And the ray of the sun will be deflected and the sun will [forever]
    set.
I fear that I will be cheated and deluded.[205]

Muḥammad b. al-Ashʿath assured Muslim that he would not
be cheated, deluded or deceived. He told him that the Umayyads
were his cousins; they would not kill or strike him. Muslim had
been oppressed by the stones and weakened by the fighting. He
was out of breath, so he propped his back up against the wall
of the house. Muḥammad b. al-Ashʿath came closer and said,
"You can have a guarantee of safe-conduct." When Muslim
asked whether he was really granted safe-conduct, Muḥammad b.
al-Ashʿath said, "Yes." The people also said, "You are given a   [263]
guarantee of safe-conduct," except ʿAmr b. ʿUbaydallāh b. al-
ʿAbbās al-Sulamī. He said as he turned aside, "I will have no part
in this."[206] Muslim declared, "Had you not granted me safe-
conduct, I would not have put my hand in yours."

A mule was brought, and he mounted, but then they gathered
around him and pulled his sword out of his grasp. At that he was
in despair for his life, and his eyes filled with tears. He cried out,

---

205. These verses with slight variations are quoted by Ibn Aʿtham al-Kūfī. See
Ibn Aʿtham, *Futūḥ*, V, 93.
206. Literally, "I will have no she-camel or male camel in this."

"This is the beginning of betrayal." Muḥammad b. al-Ashʿath said, "I hope no harm will come to you." Muslim asked, "Is it only hope? Where then is your guarantee of safe-conduct? Indeed we belong to God and to Him we shall return."[207] And he started weeping. ʿAmr b. ʿUbaydallāh b. al-ʿAbbās goaded him saying, "One who has sought for the like of what you have sought for should not weep when there befalls him what has befallen you." Muslim replied, "I do not weep for myself, nor do I grieve for my own death, even though I have not the slightest desire for destruction. But I am weeping for my family who are coming to me. I am weeping for Ḥusayn and the family of Ḥusayn."

Then he went closer to Muḥammad b. al-Ashʿath and said, "O servant of God, by God, I see that you are unable to grant me a guarantee of safe-conduct. Yet do you have the goodness to send one of your men with my message so that it will get to Ḥusayn? For I have no doubt that he has now set out toward you, or will be setting out soon with his family. That was the reason for my outburst of grief. The message will say: 'Ibn ʿAqīl has sent me to you. He is a prisoner in the hands of the people, and he does not think that you should come to be killed. He says that you should return with your family and not let the Kūfans tempt you, for they were the followers of your father, yet he desired to leave them, even through death or murder. The Kūfans have lied to you and lied to me. A liar has no judgment.'" Ibn al-Ashʿath said, "By God! I will do that, and I will inform Ibn Ziyād that I have given you a guarantee of safe-conduct."

According to Abū Mikhnaf—Jaʿfar b. Ḥudhayfah al-Ṭāʾī[208]—
[264] Saʿīd b. Shaybān[209] also knew the report: Muḥammad b. al-Ashʿath summoned Iyās b. al-ʿAthl al-Ṭāʾī, of the Banū Mālik b. ʿAmr b. Thumāmah, who was a poet[210] and frequently visited Muḥammad. Muḥammad b. al-Ashʿath told him, "Meet Ḥusayn and give him this letter." In the letter was written what Ibn ʿAqīl had told him. Then he said to him, "Here are your provisions,

---

207. Qurʾān, 2:156 (151).
208. Jaʿfar b. Ḥudhayfah al-Ṭāʾī was a traditionist and an authority of Abū Mikhnaf. See Sezgin, *Abū Mikhnaf*, 203.
209. Saʿīd b. Shaybān is an unknown authority who only seems to report this account.
210. Neither Iyās b. al-ʿAthl nor his poetry seems to be known.

equipment and goods for your family." Iyās asked, "Where will I get a mount, for I have exhausted my own animal?" Ibn al-Ashʿath said, "Here is a mount. Ride it for this journey."

Iyās departed and met al-Ḥusayn at Zubālah[211] four nights later. He gave him the news and handed him the message. Ḥusayn said, "Everything that has been decreed will come to pass. We find satisfaction and recompense for ourselves and our corrupted community with God."

When Muslim b. ʿAqīl had moved to Hāniʾ b. ʿUrwah's house and eighteen thousand had given the oath of allegiance to him, he had sent a letter to Ḥusayn with ʿĀbis b. Abī Shabīb al-Shākirī: "The trusted early messenger does not lie to his own people. Eighteen thousand of the Kūfans have given the oath of allegiance to you. Hurry and come when my letter reaches you. All the people are with you. None of them has any regard or desire for the clan of Muʿāwiyah. Peace be with you."

Muḥammad b. al-Ashʿath went with Ibn ʿAqīl to the door of the palace. He asked permission to enter. Permission was given him. He gave a report to ʿUbaydallāh about Ibn ʿAqīl and Bukayr's blow against him. ʿUbaydallāh said, "May God destroy him." Then Muḥammad b. al-Ashʿath told him about what he had done and about his own guarantee of safe-conduct to him. ʿUbaydallāh said, "What have you to do with a guarantee of safe-conduct? As if we sent you to guarantee him safe-conduct when we only sent you to bring him!" Ibn al-Ashʿath fell silent.

Ibn ʿAqīl came to the door of the palace and he was thirsty. At the palace door there were people sitting waiting for permission to enter. Among them were ʿUmārah b. ʿUqbah b. Abī Muʿayṭ, ʿAmr b. Ḥurayth, Muslim b. ʿAmr and Kathīr b. Shihāb.

According to Abū Mikhnaf—Qudāmah b. Saʿīd:[212] When [265] Muslim b. ʿAqīl came to the palace door there was a jug of cold water that had been placed at the doorway. He asked, "Give me a drink of that water." Muslim b. ʿAmr said, "See how cold it is. By God! You will never taste a drop of it until you taste the heat

---

211. Zubālah was a well-known halt on the road from Mecca to al-Kūfah. When a traveler approached from Mecca, it was before the low ground leading toward al-Kūfah. See Yāqūt, *Muʿjam*, II, 912.

212. Saʿd has been emended to Saʿīd as in the *isnād* on p. 54, above.

of Hell-fire." Ibn ʿAqīl cried out, "Shame on you. Who are you?" Muslim b. ʿAmr al-Bāhilī retorted, "I am the one who recognized the truth when you denied it, the one who was sincere to his imām when you deceived him, and the one who was attentive and obedient to him when you rebelled against him and opposed him. I am Muslim b. ʿAmr al-Bāhilī." Ibn ʿAqīl said, "May your mother be bereft of a son! How coarse you are, how rough, how hard your heart is, how rude you are! Man of Bāhilah, you are more appropriate for the heat of Hell-fire and to remain there forever than I am." He sat down, propping himself against a wall.

According to Abū Mikhnaf—Qudāmah b. Saʿīd:[213] ʿAmr b. Ḥurayth sent a boy called Sulaymān to bring him water in the jug in order to give him a drink.

According to Abū Mikhnaf—Saʿīd b. Mudrik b. ʿUmārah:[214] ʿUmārah b. ʿUqbah sent a boy of his called Qays to bring him a jug with a napkin and a cup. He poured water into the cup and gave Muslim a drink. But, whenever he went to drink, he filled the cup with blood. When he filled the cup for the third time, he went to drink but his two teeth fell into the cup. He said, "Praise be to God! If it had been a provision granted me, I could have drunk it."

Muslim was taken into Ibn Ziyād; however, he did not greet him as governor. The guard demanded, "Don't you greet the governor?" He replied, "If he wants my death, what is the point of my greeting him with words of peace? If he did not want my death, my greetings of peace to him would be profuse." Ibn Ziyād said, "By my life! You will be killed." Muslim said, "Is it so?" He replied that, indeed, it was. Then Muslim asked if he could make his will to one of his fellow tribesmen. Ibn Ziyād agreed.

Muslim looked at those sitting with ʿUbaydallāh. Among them was ʿUmar b. Saʿd (b. Abī Waqqāṣ). He said to him, "ʿUmar, there is kinship between you and me and I have a need that you could carry out successfully. But it is secret." ʿUmar refused to let him say anything. However, ʿUbaydallāh told him not to [266]   refuse to consider the need of his cousin. So ʿUmar got up with

---

213. Saʿd has been emended to Saʿīd as on p. 54, above.
214. This appears to have been the only report from Saʿīd b. Mudrik b. ʿUmārah; he is otherwise unknown.

him and sat where Ibn Ziyād could watch him. Muslim said, "I have a debt in al-Kūfah. I borrowed seven hundred dirhams when I came to al-Kūfah. Pay it for me. Take care of my corpse. Ask Ibn Ziyād to give it to you and then bury my body. Send someone to Ḥusayn to tell him to return, for I have written to him telling him that the people are with him and now I can only think that he is coming."

ʿUmar said to Ibn Ziyād, "Do you know what he said to me, governor? He mentioned these things." Ibn Ziyād replied, "The faithful would not betray you, but the traitor might be confided in. As for your money, it is yours. We will not prevent you from doing with it what you like. As for Ḥusayn, if he does not intend harm to us, we will not intend harm to him. As for his body, we will never accept your intercession with regard to it. He is not worthy of being granted that. He fought against us and opposed us; he strove for our destruction." They also claim that he said, "As for the body when we have killed it, we do not care what is done with the corpse."

Then Ibn Ziyād said, "Ibn ʿAqīl, you came to the people while they were all united and [spoke] with one voice; you scattered them and divided their opinions so that they attacked each other." Ibn ʿAqīl replied, "I did not come for that, but the people of the town claimed that your father had killed their best men, shed their blood and appointed governors among them like the governors of Chosroe and Caesar. We came to enjoin justice and to urge rule by the Book." Ibn Ziyād exclaimed. "What have you to do with that, you great sinner? Have we not done that among them when you were drinking wine in Medina?" Muslim cried out, "I, drink wine! By God! God knows you are not speaking the truth and have spoken without any knowledge, for I am not like you have said. It is more appropriate to be described as a wine drinker then a man who laps the blood of Muslims, who takes the life that God has forbidden, who takes life when no other life [has been taken], who sheds inviolable blood, and who kills out of usurpation, enmity and evil opinion, while he enjoys himself and plays as if he had done nothing." Ibn Ziyād shouted, "You great sinner! Your own soul made you desire what God denied you, for God did not regard you as worthy of it." Muslim replied, "Who is then worthy of it, Ibn Ziyād?" Ibn Ziyād answered, "The   [267]

Commander of the Faithful, Yazīd." Muslim declared, "Praise be to God! We will accept God's judgment between you and us in every circumstance." Ibn Ziyād remarked, "You speak as if you think that you have some right in the matter." Muslim answered, "By God! It is not opinion but certainty." At this Ibn Ziyād declared, "May God kill me, if I do not kill you in such a way as no one in Islam has been killed before." Muslim retorted, "You are the person with the most right to commit crimes of innovation in Islam. You will never abandon evil murder, wicked punishment, shameful practice, and avaricious domination. None of the people is more worthy of these things than you." Ibn Sumayyah[215] began to curse him, and to curse Ḥusayn, ʿAlī, and ʿAqīl, while Muslim did not speak to him.

The authorities (ahl al-ʿilm) claim that ʿUbaydallāh ordered him to be given water in a common earthenware vessel. Then he said, "Only our unwillingness that you should become protected by drinking from it prevented us from giving you a drink from it [earlier] and then killing you. It is for that reason that we have given you a drink in this way." Then he ordered, "Take him up to the top of the palace, cut off his head and throw his body after his head." Muslim said, "Ibn al-Ashʿath, if you had not given me a guarantee of safe-conduct, I would not have surrendered. Therefore, arise with your sword on my behalf and let your pledge be fulfilled." Then he said, "Ibn Ziyād, by God, if there were any kinship between you and me, you would not kill me." Ibn Ziyād asked where the man was whose head and shoulder Ibn ʿAqīl had struck with his sword. He was summoned, and Ibn Ziyād told him to climb up and be the one who cut his head off. He ascended with him. Muslim said, "God is greater." He sought forgiveness from God and prayed for blessings to be with His angels and His Apostle, saying: "O God, judge between us and a people who have enticed us, lied against us and humiliated us." They took him to a part

---

215. Ibn Sumayyah is a reference to the prostitute mother of ʿUbaydallāh's father, Ziyād. Ziyād has been persuaded to join Muʿāwiyah by the latter, declaring that Muʿāwiyah's own father Abū Sufyān had fathered Ziyād when he had visited Sumayyah in al-Ṭāʾif. See Shaban, *Islamic History*, I, 86. It should be noted that this appellation is not given to ʿUbaydallāh as part of the dialogue but by the narrator himself, who is clearly indicating where his sympathies lay.

that overlooked where the butchers are today. His head was cut off, and his body was thrown after his head.

According to Abū Mikhnaf—al-Saqʿab b. Zuhayr—ʿAwn b. Abī Juḥayfah:[216] The Aḥmarī, Bukayr b. Ḥumrān, who killed Muslim came down, and Ibn Ziyād asked him if he had killed him? He answered that he had, and Ibn Ziyād asked him what Muslim had been saying while he was climbing to the top of the palace with him? He told him, "He was saying, 'God is greater.' He glorified God and sought His forgiveness. When I approached him to kill him, he said, 'O God, judge between us and a people who lied to us, deceived us, betrayed us and killed us!' I said to him, 'Come near me, praise be to God Who has given me vengeance over you.' Then I struck him a blow that was not sufficient for anything. He said, 'Slave, don't you see that a scratch that you can make on me is a suitable payment for your own blood?'" Ibn Ziyād remarked, "Proud, even in the face of death." Bukayr continued, "Then I struck him a second time and killed him." [268]

Muḥammad b. al-Ashʿath then approached ʿUbaydallāh b. Ziyād and spoke to him of Hāniʾ b. ʿUrwah. He said, "You know of the position of Hāniʾ b. ʿUrwah in the town and the position of his house in the clan. His tribe knows that I and my colleague brought him to you. I adjure you before God, hand him over to me, for I would not like to face the enmity of his tribe. They are the most powerful people in the town and the most numerous among the Yemenīs." Ibn Ziyād promised to do what he could but, since the affair of Muslim b. ʿAqīl had gone the way it had gone, he had changed his mind about Hāniʾ. He refused to do what he had promised. After Muslim b. ʿAqīl had been killed, he ordered Hāniʾ b. ʿUrwah to be taken to the market and his head to be cut off.

Hāniʾ was taken in bonds until he was brought to a place where sheep were sold. He began to shout, "O Madhḥij! There is no Madhḥij for me today. O Madhḥij! And how to get to Madhḥij?" When he realized that no one was going to help him, he pulled his

---

216. Erroneously given as ʿAwf in the text; see *Addenda et Emendanda*, DCLII. ʿAwn b. Abī Juḥayfah is a traditionist who may have been present at these events; however, he would have been very young, for he died in 116 (734). See Sezgin, *Abū Miḥnaf*, 190.

hand and wrenched it free of the bond, crying, "Is there no stick, knife, stone or bone with which a man can defend his life?" They jumped upon him and tied the bonds tightly. He was told to stretch out his neck, but he answered, "I am not one who generously gives away my life. I will not help you to take my life." A Turkish mawlā of ʿUbaydallāh called Rashīd[217] struck him with a sword, but it did not do anything. Hāniʾ called out, "To God is the return. O God! To Your mercy and Your paradise." Then Rashīd struck him with another blow and killed him.

[269]

ʿAbd al-Raḥmān b. al-Ḥusayn al-Murādī[218] saw Rashīd later at Khāzir while the letter was with ʿUbaydallāh b. Ziyād. The people said that he was the killer of Hāniʾ b. ʿUrwah. Ibn al-Ḥusayn declared, "May God kill me if I do not kill him, or may I be killed instead of him." He attacked him with a spear that he thrust into him. He killed him.

After Muslim b. ʿAqīl and Hāniʾ b. ʿUrwah had been killed, ʿUbaydallāh b. Ziyād summoned ʿAbd al-Aʿlā al-Kalbī whom Kathīr b. Shihāb had apprehended with the Banū Fityān. He was brought, and ʿUbaydallāh b. Ziyād asked him to tell him about what happened to him. He said, "May God make you prosperous, I went out to see what the people were doing, and Kathīr b. Shihāb apprehended me." ʿUbaydallāh said, "You must give solemnly sworn oaths that you only went out for the reasons that you claim." He refused to swear. So ʿUbaydallāh ordered him to be taken to the cemetery of al-Sabīʿ and that his head be cut off there. He was taken and executed. He [also] had ʿUmārah b. Ṣalkhab al-Azdī brought—he was one of those who had intended to help Muslim b. ʿAqīl—and ʿUbaydallāh asked him from which tribe he was. ʿUmārah b. Ṣalkhab answered that he was from Azd. ʿUbaydallāh ordered that he should be taken to his people and his head cut off.

Concerning the killing of Muslim b. ʿAqīl and Hāniʾ b. ʿUrwah, ʿAbdallāh b. al-Zabīr al-Asadī said—it is also claimed that al-Farazdaq said [these words]:[219]

---

217. Rashīd does not seem to have been mentioned in any other context.

218. ʿAbd al-Raḥmān b. al-Ḥusayn al-Murādī does not seem to have been mentioned in any other context.

219. Some of these verses were quoted earlier. See pp. 21–22, above.

If you do not know what death is, then look
    at Hāni' and Ibn 'Aqīl in the marketplace.
Look at a hero whose face the sword has covered with wounds
    and another who fell dead from a high place.
The command of the governor struck them down,   [270]
    and they became legends for those who travel on every road.
You see a corpse whose color death has changed
    and a spattering of blood that has flowed abundantly,
A young man who was even more bashful than a shy young woman
    yet was more decisive than the polished blade of a two-edged
    sword.
Is Asmā' riding in peace a mount that moves at walking pace
    while Madhḥij seeks vengeance against him?
All Murād throng around him. Each one of them,
    whether a questioner or a questioned, is apprehensively
    watchful.
If you do not avenge your two brothers,
    then be harlots, satisfied with little.

According to Abū Mikhnaf—Abū Janāb Yaḥyā b. Abī Ḥayyah
al-Kalbī: When Muslim and Hāni' were killed, 'Ubaydallāh b.
Ziyād sent their heads with Hāni' b. Abī Ḥayyah al-Wādi'ī[220]
and al-Zubayr b. al-Arwaḥ al-Tamīmī[221] to Yazīd b. Mu'āwiyah.
He ordered his secretary (kātib), 'Amr b. Nāfi', to write to Yazīd
about what had happened to Muslim and Hāni'. The secretary
wrote. He was very elaborate. He was the first to be elaborate in
writing letters. When 'Ubaydallāh saw the letter, he disliked it.
He said "What is this prolixity and this excess? Write: 'Praise
be to God, Who has exacted the dues of the Commander of the   [271]
Faithful and given him sufficient provisions against his enemy. I
inform the Commander of the Faithful, may God be generous to
him, that Muslim b. 'Aqīl took refuge in the house of Hāni' b.
'Urwah al-Murādī. I set spies on them and concealed men against
them. I tricked them until I brought them out. God gave me

---

220. Hāni' b. Abī Ḥayyah al-Wādi'ī was from the tribe of Hamdān and was
anti-Shī'ite in his attitude. He bore witness against Ḥujr b. 'Adī earlier and tried
to incriminate al-Mukhtār later. See Ṭabarī, II, 134 and 521.
221. Al-Zubayr b. al-Arwaḥ al-Tamīmī seems to have had a pro-Umayyad
attitude. Later he fought for al-Ḥajjāj against the Khārijites. See Ṭabarī, II, 890.

power over them. Thus, I brought them forward and had them executed. I have sent their heads to you with Hāni' b. Abī Ḥayyah al-Hamdānī and al-Zubayr b. Arwaḥ al-Tamīmī. They are both people who are attentive and in obedience to you, and they are sincere. Let the Commander of the Faithful ask them whatever he wants to know about the affair, for they have knowledge and truth, understanding and self-restraint. Farewell. Peace be with you."

Yazīd b. Muʿāwiyah wrote back: "You have not gone beyond how I wanted you to be. You have acted with decision. You have launched into the attack with the violence of a man who has control of his emotions. You have satisfied me, been sufficient for the task, corroborated my view of you and my opinion of you. I have summoned your two messengers, questioned them, and talked to them. I found them in their views and their merit as you had mentioned. Receive them both with kindness on my recommendation. I have been informed that al-Ḥusayn b. ʿAlī has set out for Iraq. Therefore set lookouts and watches, and be vigilant against suspicious characters. Arrest anyone on suspicion but only kill those who fight against you. Write to me about all the news that occurs. Peace and the mercy of God be with you."

According to Abū Mikhnaf—al-Ṣaʿqab b. Zuhayr—ʿAwn b. Abī Juḥayfah: Muslim b. ʿAqīl's rising in al-Kūfah was on Tuesday, 8 Dhū al-Ḥijjah, A.H. 60 (September 9, 680).[222] It is [also] said that it was on Wednesday, 7 Dhū al-Ḥijjah, A.H. 60 (September 8, 680). The Day of ʿArafah was the day after al-Ḥusayn's departure from Mecca on his way to al-Kūfah. Al-Ḥusayn had left Medina for Mecca on Sunday, with two days remaining in Rajab in the Year A.H. 60 (May 4, 680). He had entered Mecca on Friday, 3 Shaʿban (May 9). He stayed in Mecca for Shaʿban and for the months of Ramaḍān, Shawwāl and Dhū al-Qaʿdah (May, June, July, and August). Then he set out from there on Tuesday, 8 Dhū al-Ḥijjah, [that is,] the Day of Tarwiyah,[223] the day on which Muslim b. ʿAqīl had made his rising.

[272]

---

222. It was actually a Sunday.
223. The Day of Tarwiyah was a day on which the pilgrims received provisions of water before going to Minā. See EI^2, s.v. Ḥadjdj.

According to Hārūn b. Muslim[224]—ʿAlī b. Ṣāliḥ—ʿĪsā b. Yazīd: Al-Mukhtār b. Abī ʿUbayd and ʿAbdallāh b. al-Ḥārith b. Nawfal came out in rebellion with Muslim. Al-Mukhtār carried a green standard, and ʿAbdallāh carried a red standard. The latter was also wearing red clothes. Al-Mukhtār brought his standard and fixed it at ʿAmr b. Ḥurayth's door. He declared, "I only came out to strengthen ʿAmr."

Ibn al-Ashʿath, al-Qaʿqāʿ b. Shawr and Shabath b. Ribʿī had fought a fierce battle against Muslim and his followers on the evening when Muslim had come against Ibn Ziyād's palace. Shabath b. Ribʿī had said, "Wait until night falls for them. Then they will disperse." Al-Qaʿqāʿ had replied, "You have blocked the way of the people. Let room be made for them to escape."

ʿUbaydallāh ordered al-Mukhtār and ʿAbdallāh b. al-Ḥārith to be searched for. He assigned a reward for their arrest, brought them to him and had them imprisoned.

In this year al-Ḥusayn set out from Mecca to go to al-Kūfah.

Al-Ḥusayn's Departure from Mecca for al-Kūfah

According to Hishām (b. Muḥammad al-Kalbī)—Abū Mikhnaf—al-Ṣaqʿab b. Zuhayr—ʿUmar b. ʿAbd al-Raḥmān b. al-Ḥārith b. Hishām al-Makhzūmī:[225] When the letters of the Iraqīs reached al-Ḥusayn and he had made preparations to go to Iraq, I went and visited him while he was in Mecca. After I had praised and glorified God, I told him, "Cousin, I have come to you because of something important that I want to tell you as advice, that is, if you would consider receiving advice from me. If not, then you should refrain from listening to what I want to say." He said, "Speak. By God! I do not think that you have bad judgment, nor are you fond of evil in any matter or action." I said to him, "I have learnt that you are intending to go to Iraq. I am anxious about your going. You would be arriving in a country where there are Yazīd's tax

[273]

---

224. ʿUmar b. Shabbah has been omitted. He was Ṭabarī's authority for a report with this *isnād* previously. See p. 35, above.

225. Apart from reporting some of these events at which he was present, ʿUmar b. ʿAbd al-Raḥmān b. al-Ḥārith b. Hishām al-Makhzūmī was from Quraysh and a close adviser of Ibn al-Zubayr; he later acted on his behalf in matters related to al-Mukhtār. See Ṭabarī, II, 687.

collectors and leaders. They have control of the treasuries. The population are slaves to the dirham and the dīnār. I could not be sure that those who have promised you their help would not fight against you, and that those who have greater love for you [than him] would be among those who will fight against you on his behalf." He replied, "May God give you a good reward, cousin. By God! I know that you have brought good advice and you have spoken reasonably. Whatever is destined will happen whether I take your advice or ignore it. In my view, you are a most praiseworthy counselor and a sincere adviser."

I left him and went to al-Ḥārith b. Khālid b. al-ʿĀṣ b. Hishām.[226] He asked me if I had met al-Ḥusayn. I told him that I had. He questioned me about what he had said to me, and what I had said to him. I told him that I had said such-and-such to him, and he had said such-and-such to me. He said, "By the Lord of gray and white stone of al-Marwah![227] You have given him good advice. By the Lord of the Sacred House! The sound view is what you have put forward, [whether he accepts] it or leaves it." Then he recited:

Many a person from whom advice is sought lies and causes
    destruction.
    Many a person who is suspected turns out to be a good
    adviser.

According to Abū Mikhnaf—al-Ḥārith b. Kaʿb al-Wālibī[228]—ʿUqbah b. Simʿān: When Ḥusayn decided to go to al-Kūfah ʿAbdallāh b. ʿAbbās came to him and said, "Cousin, people are spreading reports that you are going to Iraq. Expain to me what you are doing." He replied, "I have decided to set out on one of the next two days, God, the Exalted, willing." Ibn ʿAbbās said, "I ask God to protect you from that. Tell me, may God have mercy on

---

226. Although not mentioned again, al-Ḥārith b. Khālid b. al-ʿĀṣ b. Hishām appears to have been an influential person. His father had been a governor for Muʿāwiyah over Mecca. See Ṭabarī, II, 67.

227. Al-Marwah is a hill in Mecca that with another hill, al-Ṣafā, is associated with the rites of the pilgimage. See Yāqūt, Muʿjam, IV, 513.

228. Al-Ḥārith b. Kaʿb al-Wālibī is an unknown authority of Abū Mikhnaf. See Sezgin, Abū Miḥnaf, 206. For ʿUqbah the text erroneously gives ʿUtbah; see Addenda et Emendanda, DCLIII.

you. Are you going to a people who have killed their governor,   [274]
taken control of their land, and driven out their enemy? If they
have done that, then go to them. But if they have only asked you
to come to them while their governor is in control of them, and
his tax collectors are still taxing their land, then they are only
asking you to come to war and fighting. I cannot be sure that
they are not tempting you and that they will not oppose and
desert you. Indeed, they may gather to make war on you. They
may become the most violent of people against you." Ḥusayn
answered, "I will leave the choice to God and see what happens."
Ibn ʿAbbas left him.

Then Ibn al-Zubayr came and talked to him for a time. He said,
"I don't know why we have left things to these people and stood
idly by. We are the sons of the Muhājirūn (emigrants) and should
be the ones in control of this government rather than they. Tell
me what you are intending to do." Al-Ḥusayn replied, "By God! I
have reflected about going to al-Kūfah. My Shīʿah there and the
nobles of these people have written to me. I am leaving the choice
to God." Ibn al-Zubayr said, "If I had the same sort of followers as
you there, I would not seek any alternative other than them."
Then he feared that al-Ḥusayn might suspect his motive so he
added, "However, if you remain in the Ḥijāz, you could pursue
this matter here without meeting any opposition, God willing."
He rose and left him, and al-Ḥusayn said, "Nothing in the world
would please him more than my leaving the Ḥijāz for Iraq. He
realizes that he has no share in this matter while I am present, for
the people will never consider him equal to me. Therefore, he
would love me to go away from here so that he can have a free
hand."

That evening—or the next day—al-Ḥusayn went to Ibn ʿAbbās,
and the latter said, "Cousin, I invoke patience, but I do not have
it. I fear your destruction and extirpation in this enterprise. The
Iraqīs are a treacherous people. So don't go near them. Remain in
this land, for you are the leader of the people of the Ḥijāz. If the
Iraqīs want you as they claim, write to them that they should
drive out their enemies, and then you will come to them. If you   [275]
insist on leaving, then go to Yemen. There, there are fortresses
and gorges. It is a vast distant land. Your father had a Shīʿah
there, and you would be remote from the people. Then you could

write to the people, send messengers to infiltrate, and urge the people to support you. I hope that in that way what you want would come to you easily." Al-Ḥusayn answered, "Cousin, I know that you are an adviser who is anxious for me. However, I have reached my decision and I am determined to set out." Ibn ʿAbbās pleaded, "Then if you are going, do not go with your womenfolk and your children. For I fear that you will be killed just as ʿUthmān was killed, while his womenfolk and children were watching." Then Ibn ʿAbbās went on to say, "You would thrill Ibn al-Zubayr by your leaving him alone in the Ḥijāz, and by your departure from it. For now no one pays attention to him, as you are here. But by God other than Whom there is no deity! I would catch hold of your hair and your forelock until the people had gathered around you and me if I thought it would make you obey me."

Ibn ʿAbbās left him and he passed ʿAbdallāh b. al-Zubayr; he said to him, "May you be happy, Ibn al-Zubayr." Then he recited:

O what [a fortunate] lark in a flourishing country!
Now the sky is free for you, so lay eggs and hatch them,
And tap with your beak as you like.[229]

[And he explained:] "This Ḥusayn is going to Iraq, so you can take care of the Ḥijāz."

According to Abū Mikhnaf—Abū Janāb Yaḥyā b. Abī Ḥayyah—ʿAdī b. Ḥarmalah al-Asadī,[230]—ʿAbdallāh b. Sulaym[231] and al-Madhrī b. al-Mushmaʿill, both of the tribe of Asad: We went from al-Kūfah as pilgrims until we came to Mecca. We entered it on the Day of Tarwiyah. We were standing near al-Ḥusayn and ʿAbdallāh b. al-Zubayr in the middle of the morning somewhere between the Ḥijr[232] and the door of the Sacred House. As we

[276]

---

229. For this verse see Ahlwardt, *The Divans*, 185. It is also given by Balādhurī, *Ansāb*, II/2, 163.

230. Apart from his reports recorded by Abū Mikhnaf of this event, ʿAdī b. Ḥarmalah al-Asadī was otherwise unknown. See Sezgin, *Abū Miḥnaf*, 223.

231. ʿAbdallāh b. Sulaym and his colleague from the tribe of Asad were important eyewitnesses and participants in the following narrative. Both accompanied al-Ḥusayn until very near the end. Then they made separate escapes.

232. The Ḥijr was the burial spot of Ishmael and Hagar by the Kaʿbah. See *EI*[2], s.v. Kaʿba.

approached them, we heard Ibn al-Zubayr saying to al-Ḥusayn, "If you wish to stay, you could stay and take control of this affair. We will assist, aid you and give advice. We will give the oath of allegiance to you." Al-Ḥusayn replied, "My father told me, 'There will be in Mecca a ram (i.e., a leader) who will cause its sanctity to be violated,' and I do not want to be that kind of ram." Ibn al-Zubayr said, "Then stay here if you wish, and give me authority in this affair. You would be obeyed and not disobeyed." Al-Ḥusayn said, "I do not want to do that either." Then they lowered their conversation so that we could not hear, but they still continued to talk together.

Then we heard the call of the people who were going to Minā at midday. After that al-Ḥusayn performed the circumambulation of the Sacred House, and ran between al-Ṣafā and al-Marwah.[233] He had his hair trimmed[234] and left the state of consecration for the *'umrah*. He set off for al-Kūfah, but we went toward the people at Minā.

According to Abū Mikhnaf—Abū Saʿīd ʿAqīṣā[235]—one of his colleagues: I heard al-Ḥusayn b. ʿAlī, while he was standing with ʿAbdallāh b. al-Zubayr in Mecca. Ibn al-Zubayr said to him, "Listen to me, son of Fāṭimah." I tried to listen, but he whispered to him. But then al-Ḥusayn turned to us and asked, "Do you know what Ibn al-Zubayr was saying to me?" We answered, "We do not know. May God sacrifice us for you." He said, "He told me, 'Stand up in this mosque, and I shall gather the people around you.' By God! I would prefer to be killed a few inches (*shibr*) outside the sanctuary of Mecca than to be killed a few inches within it. I swear by God, even if I were in a deep snake's hole, they would pull me out in order to carry out their will. By God! They would violate me just as the Jews violated the Sabbath."

According to Abū Mikhnaf—al-Ḥārith b. Kaʿb al-Wālibī—ʿUqbah b. Simʿān: When al-Ḥusayn left Mecca, the messengers [277]

---

233. The ritual running (*saʿy*) between al-Ṣafā and al-Marwah was part of the rites of the lesser pilgrimage (*'umrah*). See *EI*[1], s.v. ʿUmra.

234. The cutting of hair took place when the pilgrim wanted to leave the state of consecration. While in the state of consecration, he was forbidden to cut his hair or nails. See *EI*[2], s.v. Iḥrām.

235. Abū Saʿīd ʿAqīṣā's name was Dīnār. He was a traditionist and a Kūfan Shīʿite. See Sezgin, *Abū Mikhnaf*, 200.

of ʿAmr b. Saʿīd b. al-ʿĀṣ met him. Yaḥyā b. Saʿīd[236] was in charge of them. They ordered him to come back from where he was going. But he refused them and continued his journey. The two groups came to blows and hit one another with whips. However, al-Ḥusayn and his followers resisted fiercely. Al-Ḥusayn continued with his journey. They called to him, "Ḥusayn, do you not fear God, lest you leave this unified people (*jamāʿah*) and split this community (*ummah*)?" In answer al-Ḥusayn recited: "My deeds are mine, and your deeds are yours. You are not accountable for my actions, nor am I accountable for yours."[237]

Al-Ḥusayn continued until he had passed al-Tanʿīm.[238] There he met a camel train that had come from Yemen. Baḥīr b. Raysān al-Ḥimyarī[239]—who was Yazīd b. Muʿāwiyah's governor of Yemen—had sent it to Yazīd. The camel train was carrying turmeric and cloth to Yazīd. Al-Ḥusayn took possession of the goods and carried them off. He said to the camel owners, "I will not force you, but whoever wants to come with us to Iraq, we will pay his hire and enjoy his company. Whoever wants to leave us at any place that we are in, we will pay his hire for the distance he has traveled." Those of them who left had their accounts settled and were paid their due. However, al-Ḥusayn paid the hire of those of them who went with him and gave them clothes.

According to Abū Mikhnaf—Abū Janāb—ʿAdī b. Ḥarmalah—ʿAbdallāh b. Sulaym and al-Madhrī: When we came to al-Ṣifāḥ[240] we met al-Farazdaq b. Ghālib,[241] the poet. He was standing in front of al-Ḥusayn and saying to him, "May God grant you your request and fulfill your hope in what you want." Al-Ḥusayn asked him, "Tell us the news of the people you have left behind you."

---

236. Yaḥyā b. Saʿīd was a brother of ʿAmr b. Saʿīd, who later became involved in his brother's attempt to gain power; he was pardoned by ʿAbd al-Malik. See Ṭabarī II, 789–804, 814.

237. Qurʾān, 10:41 (42).

238. Al-Tanʿīm was the station outside Mecca where the Meccans went in order to enter into a state of consecration for the ʿumrah. See Yāqūt, *Muʿjam*, I, 879.

239. There seems to be no further information on Baḥīr b. Raysān al-Ḥimyarī.

240. Al-Ṣifāḥ was a place to the northeast of Mecca. See Yāqūt, *Muʿjam*, III, 398.

241. Al-Farazdaq b. Ghālib was the famous Arab poet whose name was Hammām b. Ghālib; he died in 110 (728) or 112 (730). See *EI²*, s.v. al-Farazdaḳ.

Al-Farazdaq answered, "You have asked one who knows. The hearts of the people are with you, but their swords are with the Banū Umayyah. The decision will come from heaven, and God will do what He wishes." Al-Ḥusayn replied, "True. The decision is God's, and God will do what He wishes. 'Every day our Lord exercises power in [every] matter.'[242] If fate sends down what we like, we praise God for His blessings. He is the One from Whom help should be sought in order to give thanks to Him. However, although fate may frustrate their hopes, those whose intention is the truth and whose hearts are pious are not aggressors." Then al-Ḥusayn moved his mount off, saying farewell. And so the two parted.

[278]

According to Hishām (b. Muḥammad al-Kalbī)—'Awānah b. al-Ḥakam—Labaṭah b. al-Farazdaq b. Ghālib[243]—his father: I made the pilgrimage with my mother. I was driving her camel when I entered the sanctuary during the days of the pilgrimage. That was in the year 60 (680). I met al-Ḥusayn b. 'Alī leaving Mecca [accompanied by his men] with swords and shields. I asked whose caravan it was, and I was told that it was al-Ḥusayn b. 'Alī's. So I went up to him and said, "May my mother and father be your sacrifice! Son of the Apostle of God, what is making you hurry away from the pilgrimage?" He replied, "If I did not hurry away, I would be apprehended." Then he asked me who I was. I told him that I was a man from Iraq. By God! He did not question me any further about that but was satisfied with that answer. He said, "Tell me about the people you have left behind you?" I answered, "Their hearts are with you, but their swords are with the Banū Umayyah. The decision is in the hand of God." He replied that that was true. Then I asked him about matters concerning vows and pilgrimage rites. He told me about them. His voice was thick with the pleurisy that he had contracted in Iraq.[244]

I went on, and there was a large well-equipped tent pitched in the sanctuary. I went to it, and there was 'Abdallāh b. 'Amr b.

---

242. Almost identical to Qur'ān, 55:29.

243. Labaṭah b. al-Farazdaq b. Ghālib was the son of the poet. The evidence for the validity of the first report rather than this one was the verses by al-Farazdaq concerning their meeting at al-Ṣifāḥ, which are cited by Yāqūt, *Mu'jam*, III, 398.

244. This observation must refer to al-Farazdaq.

al-ʿĀṣ.[245] He questioned me and I told him about meeting al-Ḥusayn b. ʿAlī. He said to me, "Woe on you! Why don't you follow him? By God! He will be victorious, and no weapon will affect him or his followers." By God! Then I was anxious to follow him, and his words went deep into my heart. But I remembered the prophets and how they were killed. That stopped me from [279] following them. So I went to my people at ʿUsfān.[246] By God! I was with them when a camel train that had brought provisions from al-Kūfah approached. When I heard them, I went out after them until, after shouting at them and being unable to overtake them, I shouted to them, "What happened to al-Ḥusayn b. ʿAlī?" They said that he had been killed. Then I went back cursing ʿAbdallāh b. ʿAmr b. al-ʿĀṣ. The people at that time had all been like him, mentioning that "thing" and waiting for its fulfillment both day and night. ʿAbdallāh b. ʿAmr had been saying, "Neither tree nor palm nor child will grow before it is announced" (i.e., the victory of al-Ḥusayn). I said to him, "What stops you from selling the Waht?" He replied, "God curse so-and-so—meaning Muʿāwiyah—and you." I answered, "No, rather God curse you." He increased his cursing of me, and none of his coterie were around him, so I was spared their evil. I left without his recognizing me. The Waht was a grove belonging to ʿAbdallāh b. ʿAmr in al-Ṭāʾif. Muʿāwiyah had negotiated a deal with ʿAbdallāh b. ʿAmr for it and had given him a lot of money for the grove. But then ʿAbdallāh had refused to sell it for anything.

[Earlier] al-Ḥusayn had pressed on swiftly and directly until he stopped at Dhāt ʿIrq.[247]

According to Abū Mikhnaf—al-Ḥārith b. Kaʿb al-Wālibī—ʿAlī b. al-Ḥusayn b. ʿAlī b. Abī Ṭālib:[248] When we left Mecca, ʿAbd-

---

245. ʿAbdallāh was the son of ʿAmr b. al-ʿĀṣ, the conqueror of Egypt and the ally of Muʿāwiyah. He had a reputation for learning and knowing the future; he had acquired this knowledge in Egypt. See text below, p. ooo.

246. ʿUsfān was a village with palm groves and arable land about thirty-six miles from Mecca. See Yāqūt, Muʿjam, III, 673.

247. Dhāt ʿIrq is the road from Mecca to Iraq in a pass through the mountain of ʿIrq; it overlooks the northeast valley of Baṭn al-Rummah. See Yāqūt, Muʿjam, III, 651.

248. Alī b. al-Ḥusayn is the younger of the two sons of al-Ḥusayn with this name. He survived the Battle of Karbalāʾ because he was too ill to fight. He is regarded as the fourth Imām of the Shīʿah. See al-Mufīd, Irshād (trans.), 380–92 and EI[1], s.v. Zayn al-ʿĀbidīn.

allāh b. Jaʿfar b. Abī Ṭālib[249] sent a letter to al-Ḥusayn b. ʿAlī
with his two sons, ʿAwn and Muḥammad:[250] "I ask you by God
to return when you read my letter, for I am very concerned that
the direction in which you are heading will have within it your
destruction and the extirpation of your house. If you are destroyed
today, the light of the earth will be extinguished, for you are the
standard of those who are rightly guided and the hope of the
believers. Do not hurry on your journey, as I am following this
letter. Peace be with you."

ʿAbdallāh b. Jaʿfar went to ʿAmr b. Saʿīd b. al-ʿĀṣ and spoke to   [280]
him, saying, "Write a letter to al-Ḥusayn in which you offer him a
guarantee of safe-conduct. Promise to favor him with kindness
and generosity. Show trust to him in your letter. Ask him to
return, and perhaps he will be reassured by that."

ʿAmr b. Saʿīd told him to write what he wished and then to
bring it to him so that he could put the seal on it. ʿAbdallāh b.
Jaʿfar wrote the letter and took it to ʿAmr b. Saʿīd. He said to
him, "Seal it and send it with your brother, Yaḥyā b. Saʿīd. It is
more likely that al-Ḥusayn's mind will be reassured by him and
that he will realize that it is a serious endeavor on your part." He
did that. ʿAmr b. Saʿīd was Yazīd b. Muʿāwiyah's governor of
Mecca.

Yaḥyā b. Saʿīd and ʿAbdallāh b. Jaʿfar went after al-Ḥusayn.
They both left him after Yaḥyā had read him the letter. Later they
reported that they had read him the letter and that they strove to
persuade him. One of the excuses that he made to them was that
he had seen a vision in which he had seen the Apostle of God,
who confirmed that he had been ordered to do what he was doing,
whether it went against him or in his favor. They asked him what
that vision was. He answered that he had not told anyone of it and
he would not tell anyone of it until he met his Lord.

The letter of ʿAmr b. Saʿīd to al-Ḥusayn b. ʿAlī was [as follows]:
"In the name of God, the Merciful, the Compassionate, from ʿAmr
b. Saʿīd to ʿAbdallāh b. ʿAlī...I ask God to make you turn aside

---

249. ʿAbdallāh b. Jaʿfar b. Abī Ṭālib was a cousin of al-Ḥusayn and son of ʿAlī's
brother Jaʿfar.
250. Both ʿAwn and Muḥammad went on to die with al-Ḥusayn. See p. 152,
below.

from what will cause your death and to lead you to what will bring you guidance. I learnt that your destination is Iraq. I seek refuge for you in God from dissension, for I fear that your destruction is imminent. I have sent ʿAbdallāh b. Jaʿfar and Yaḥyā b. Saʿīd to you. Come to me with them. You will have a guarantee of safe-conduct from me, kindness, generosity and good-neighborly protection. God is my witness, guarantor, supervisor and trusted authority of that. Peace be with you."

[281]   Al-Ḥusayn wrote to him: "...One who calls [men] to God, the Mighty and Exalted, and to righteous actions and confesses that he is one of the Muslims does not rebel against God and His Apostle. You have invited me [to accept] a guarantee of safe-conduct, kindness and generosity. The best guarantee of safe-conduct is God's. God will never give safe-conduct on the Day of Resurrection to those who did not fear Him in this world. We ask God fearfully while in this world that His guarantee of safe-conduct be given to us on the Day of Resurrection. If you intend kindness and generosity toward me by your letter, then may you be well rewarded in this world and the next. Peace be with you."

Continuation of ʿAmmār al-Duhnī's Account from Abū Jaʿfar

According to Zakariyyā' b. Yaḥyā al-Ḍarīr—Aḥmad b. Janāb al-Maṣṣīṣī—Khālid b. Yazīd b. ʿAbdallāh al-Qasrī: ʿAmmār al-Duhnī reported that he asked Abū Jaʿfar to tell him about the killing of al-Ḥusayn so that he might think that he was present at it. Abū Jaʿfar reported: Ḥusayn b. ʿAlī set out because of Muslim b. ʿAqīl's letter that had been sent to him. When he was three miles from al-Qādisiyyah,[251] al-Ḥurr b. Yazīd al-Tamīmī[252] met him. He asked him where he was going, and al-Ḥusayn said that he was going to that town. He told him to go back, for he had not left behind him anyone who desired good for him. Al-Ḥusayn had intended to return, but the brothers of Muslim b. ʿAqīl were with

---

251. Al-Qādisiyyah was a town nineteen miles away from al-Kūfah. This was where the Muslims defeated the Persians in 16 (637). See *EI²*, s.v. al-Ḳādisīya.

252. Al-Ḥurr b. Yazīd al-Tamīmī was a leading tribesman in the tribe of Tamīm in al-Kūfah; he was in no way involved with the attempts to send for al-Ḥusayn. Later he joined al-Ḥusayn and died with him. See pp. 140–45, below.

him and they declared, "By God! We will not return until we take
our vengeance or are killed." He replied, "There would be no good
in life without you."

Al-Ḥusayn continued, and the vanguard of ʿUbaydallāh's
cavalry met him. When he saw them, he turned aside toward
Karbalāʾ.[253] He positioned himself with his rear against the
reeds and grass so that he would only have to fight from one
direction. Then he stopped and put up his tents. His followers
were forty-five horsemen and a hundred foot soldiers.

In the meantime ʿUbaydallāh had appointed ʿUmar b. Saʿd b.
Abī Waqqāṣ as governor of al-Rayy[254] and he had given him his
authority of appointment. He demanded that he give him satis-   [282]
faction against al-Ḥusayn. ʿUmar begged to be excused from that
position, but ʿUbaydallāh refused to excuse him. So ʿUmar asked
him to let him consider it during the night. He granted him the
delay, and ʿUmar considered his position. By the morning, he was
willing to carry out what he had been ordered to do. ʿUmar b.
Saʿd had set out toward al-Ḥusayn. When he reached al-Ḥusayn,
the latter said to him, "Choose one of three possibilities: Let me
go back to where I came from; let me go to Yazīd; or let me go and
join one of the frontier posts." ʿUmar accepted that, but ʿUbaydallāh wrote to him: "No, there will be no kindness until he has
submitted to me personally." Al-Ḥusayn said, "No, by God! That
will never be."

Then ʿUmar fought against him. All al-Ḥusayn's followers
were killed, among whom were more than ten young men from
his family. An arrow came and struck his [baby] son while he had
him in his lap. He began to wipe the blood from him, saying, "O
God! Judge between us and a people who asked us [to come] so
that they might help us and then killed us." He called for a striped
cloak (ḥibarah), tore it and then put it on. He took out his sword
and fought until he was killed. A man of the tribe of Madhḥij
killed him and cut off his head. He took it to ʿUbaydallāh and
said:

---

253. Karbalāʾ is on the south bank of the Euphrates due north of al-Kūfah. This
is where the battle against al-Ḥusayn took place. It is still a shrine for the Shīʿah.
See *EI*[2], Karbalāʾ.

254. Al-Rayy was a city in northern Iran; it was located five miles southeast of
modern Tehran. See *EI*[1], s.v. al-Rayy.

Fill my saddlebag with silver and gold,
For I have killed the well-guarded king.
I have killed the man of noblest parents,
And when people trace descent his is the best.[255]

He sent him to Yazīd b. Muʿāwiyah and with him he sent the head. He put his head in front of him. With him was Abū Barzah al-Aslamī.[256] Yazīd began to poke the mouth with a cane, as he recited:

[Swords] split the skulls of men who are dear
     to us; but they were more disobedient and oppressive.[257]

[283]   Abū Barzah cried out to him. "Take your cane away. By God! How often have I seen the Apostle of God kiss that mouth!"

ʿUmar b. Saʿd had sent al-Ḥusayn's womenfolk and family to ʿUbaydallāh. The only male member of the family (ahl al-bayt) of al-Ḥusayn b. ʿAlī who had survived was a young lad who had been sick and had rested with the women. ʿUbaydallāh ordered him to be killed, but Zaynab threw herself on him and said, "By God! He will not be killed until you kill me." ʿUbaydallāh had pity on her and refrained from killing the young lad. He equipped them for a journey and had them taken to Yazīd.

When they came to Yazīd, he gathered together the Syrians who used to attend on him. When the Syrians came to him and congratulated him on the victory, one of them, who was blue-eyed with a fair complexion (aḥmar), said, as he looked at one of their young women, "Commander of the Faithful, give that one to me." Zaynab said, "No, by God! There is no such honor possible for you or for him unless he leaves the religion of God." The blue-eyed man repeated his request but Yazīd said to him, "Desist from this."

---

255. These verses are also given in Abū Mikhnaf's account. See p. 162, below. Balādhurī also quotes them. See *Ansāb*, II/2, 205. In both cases the verses are recited outside ʿUmar's tent.

256. Although there are alternatives given, Abū Barzah al-Aslamī's name appears to be ʿAbdallāh b. Naḍlah al-Aslamī. He was a Companion of the Prophet. After the Prophet's death, he took part in the wars of expansion. He moved to al-Baṣrah and died in Khurāsān. See Ibn Saʿd, *Ṭabaqāt*, VII/2, 100.

257. The verse is also cited by Abū Mikhnaf and Balādhurī. See pp. 170, 174, 176, below; and *Ansāb*, II/2, 213.

Then he took them into his own family. He equipped them for a journey and had them taken to Medina. When they arrived there a woman from the Banū 'Abd al-Muṭṭalib came out to meet them untying her hair and putting her cap on her head. She was weeping and reciting:

What would you say if the Prophet asked you:
  What have you, the last of the religious communities,
Done with my offspring and my family after my departure?
  Among them are prisoners and among them are those who
  have been stained with blood.
What reward is this for me after I have given you good advice,
  that you should repay me with evil to my blood relations?[258]

According to al-Ḥusayn b. Naṣr[259]—Abū Rabī'ah[260]—Abū 'Awānah[261]—Ḥusayn b. 'Abd al-Raḥmān:[262] We were informed [284] that al-Ḥusayn. . . .

Also according to Muḥammad b. 'Ammār al-Rāzī[263]—Sa'īd b. Sulaymān[264]—'Abbād b. al-'Awwām[265]—Ḥusayn (b. 'Abd al-Raḥmān):[266] The Kūfans wrote to al-Ḥusayn b. 'Alī: "A hundred thousand are with you." He sent Muslim b. 'Aqīl to them. He came to al-Kūfah and stayed in the house of Hāni' b. 'Urwah. The people visited him, and Ibn Ziyād learnt of that.

Al-Ḥusayn b. Naṣr has [this additional information] in his account: Ibn Ziyād sent for Hāni', and the latter went to him. Ibn

---

258. The verses are also cited by Abū Mikhnaf and Balādhurī. See p. 178, below; and *Ansāb*, II/2, 221.

259. Al-Ḥusayn b. Naṣr was an authority used by Ṭabarī on rare occasions. He may be the son of the Shī'ite historian Naṣr b. Muzāhim, who died in 212 (827–28).

260. The only time Abū Rabī'ah's name seems to have occurred as a historical authority.

261. Abū 'Awānah was al-Waḍḍāḥ b. 'Abdallāh al-Yashkurī, a prolific traditionist with a special interest in historical tradition. He died in 175 (791–92) or 176 (792–93). See Ibn Ḥajar, *Tahdhīb*, XI, 116–20.

262. Ḥusayn b. 'Abd al-Raḥmān was a well-known Kūfan traditionist; he died in 136 (753–54). See Ibn Ḥajar, *Tahdhīb*, II, 381–83.

263. Muḥammad b. 'Ammār al-Rāzī was a little-known traditionist.

264. Sa'īd b. Sulaymān was a well-known traditionist, who lived in Baghdād; he died in 225 (840). See Ibn Ḥajar, *Tahdhīb*, IV, 43–44.

265. 'Abbād b. al-'Awwām was a well-known traditionist; he died between 183–87 (799–803). See Ibn Ḥajar, *Tahdhīb*, V, 99–100.

266. Balādhurī quoted the same account with the same *isnād* from Sa'īd b. Sulaymān with almost identical words. See *Ansāb*, II/2, 224–27.

Ziyād asked him, "Haven't I honored you? Haven't I favored you? Haven't I done [things] for you?" He agreed, and then Ibn Ziyād asked him, "What is the reward for that?" He replied, "The reward for it is that I give you protection." Ibn Ziyād exclaimed, "You give me protection!" He took a cane that was by him and struck Hāni' with it. Then he ordered Hāni' to be put in chains and executed.

Muslim b. ʿAqīl learnt of that and he came out with many people. When Ibn Ziyād was informed, he ordered the palace door to be locked, and a herald to call out, "Cavalry of God, ride." But no one answered him so that he suspected that Muslim was among a huge crowd of people.

According to Ḥusayn (b. ʿAbd al-Raḥmān)—Hilāl b. Yasāf:[267] I met them that night on the road by the mosque of the Anṣār. They had not gone far along any road to the right or to the left without a group of thirty or forty and the like leaving them. When the marketplace was reached—and it was then in the dark of night—they entered the mosque. Ibn Ziyād was told, "We cannot see many. We cannot hear the voices of many." He ordered the awning over the mosque to be removed. Then he ordered the reeds used for the roof to be set on fire. They began to look around and there were nearly fifty. Ibn Ziyād came in and ascended the pulpit. He told the people to separate themselves quarter by quarter. Every tribe went to the head of their quarter. A group [285] of people attacked Muslim's followers. Muslim was severely wounded, and some of his followers were killed. Muslim, himself, got away and reached one of the houses of the tribe of Kindah. Then a man [from Kindah] went to Muḥammad b. al-Ashʿath, while he was sitting with Ibn Ziyād. He whispered to Muḥammad b. al-Ashʿath that Muslim was in the house of so-and-so. Ibn Ziyād asked what the man had said to him, and Muḥammad b. al-Ashʿath told him that the man had said that Muslim was in the house of so-and-so. Ibn Ziyād told two men to go and bring the man to him. The two men came in upon Muslim while he was with a woman who had kindled a fire for him. He was washing

---

267. Hilāl b. Yasāf was a Kūfan traditionist who lived during the latter half of the first (seventh) century. See Ibn Ḥajar, *Tahdhīb*, XI, 86–87.

the blood from himself. They told him to come, as the governor
had summoned him. He asked them to give him an undertaking
for his safe-conduct; however, they said that they did not have the
right to do that. He went with them until they came to Ibn Ziyād,
who ordered him to be put in chains. Then he exclaimed, "Be
gone, be gone, son of a spinster."

According to al-Ḥusayn b. Naṣr's account, Ibn Ziyād said, "O
son of a so-and-so, did you come to take my authority away from
me?" Then he ordered him to be executed.

According to al-Ḥusayn (b. ʿAbd al-Raḥmān)—Hilāl b. Yasāf:
Ibn Ziyād ordered that the area between Wāqiṣah[268] toward the
road to Syria and toward the road to al-Baṣrah should be occupied,
and that they should allow no one to enter and no one to leave.

Al-Ḥusayn had set out without being aware of any of this until
he met some of the Bedouin. He asked them about the situation,
and they said, "No, by God! We don't know anything except that
we cannot get in and get out of al-Kūfah."

Then al-Ḥusayn began to move toward the road to Syria, toward
Yazīd. The cavalry intercepted him at Karbalāʾ. There he stopped
and began to appeal to them before God and Islam. ʿUmar b.
Saʿd, Shamir b. Dhī al-Jawshan and Ḥusayn b. Tamīm had been
sent against him. Al-Ḥusayn appealed to them before God and
Islam to let him go to the Commander of the Faithful. Then he
would put his hand in his hand. They said, "No, there is nothing
else for you to do but submit to the authority of Ibn Ziyād."
Among those who had been sent against him was al-Ḥurr b. Yazīd
al-Ḥanẓalī, of the clan of Nahshal, in command of some cavalry.
When he heard what al-Ḥusayn was saying, he said to them, "Will
you not accept what these men are offering you? By God if a Turk
or a Daylamite[269] asked this of you, it would not be lawful for you
to refuse it." However, they still refused everything except sub-
mission to the authority of Ibn Ziyād. Al-Ḥurr turned the direction   [286]
of his horse and went over to al-Ḥusayn and his followers. They
thought that he was only coming to fight them, but when he
came closer, he reversed his shield and greeted them. Later he

---

268. Wāqiṣah was on the road to Mecca, two stages from Zubālah. See Yāqūt,
Muʿjam, IV, 892.
269. Daylam is the highlands of Gīlān in northwest Iran. See *EI²*, s.v. Daylam.

attacked the followers of Ibn Ziyād and killed two of them. Then he was killed, may God have mercy on him.

It was mentioned that Zuhayr b. al-Qayn al-Bajalī[270] met al-Ḥusayn after he had been on the pilgrimage. He went forward with him. [In the battle] Ibn Abī Baḥriyyah al-Murādī[271] came out against Zuhayr and two other men, who were ʿAmr b. al-Ḥajjāj and Maʿn al-Sulamī.[272]

According to Ḥusayn (b. ʿAbd al-Raḥmān), he had seen them both.

According to Ḥusayn b. ʿAbd al-Raḥmān—Saʿd b. ʿUbaydah:[273] Old men of the Kūfans were standing on the hill [overlooking the battlefield] weeping and calling out, "O God! Send down Your aid." I said to them, "Enemies of God! Won't you go down and help him?" Then al-Ḥusayn began to speak to those whom Ibn Ziyād had sent against him. I looked toward him. He was wearing a cloak (jubbah) of streaky cloth (burūd). When he had spoken to them, he turned away. One of the Banū Tamīm called ʿUmar al-Ṭuhawī[274] shot an arrow at him. I saw the arrow sticking between his shoulders into his cloak. When they had refused him, he went back to his ranks. I looked at them. They were about a hundred men. Among them were five sons of ʿAlī b. Abī Ṭālib and sixteen members of Banū Hāshim, a man from Banū Sulaym, who was their ally, another from Banū Kinānah, who was also their ally, and Ibn ʿUmar b. Ziyād.[275]

According to Ḥusayn b. ʿAbd al-Raḥmān—Saʿd b. ʿUbaydah: We were dipping ourselves in water with ʿUmar b. Saʿd, when a man came to him and whispered, "Ibn Ziyād has sent Juwayriyah

---

270. Zuhayr b. al-Qayn al-Bajalī was a supporter of the group who opposed the Hāshimites known as ʿUthmāniyyah; he joined al-Ḥusayn en route and was killed with him. See pp. 144–45, below.

271. Ibn Abī Baḥriyyah al-Murādī seems to be unknown and his name does not occur in Abū Mikhnaf's account. According to Balādhurī, his name was Ibn Abī Ḥurayrah. See Ansāb, II/2, 225.

272. Maʿn al-Sulamī fought for Muʿāwiyah against ʿAlī. See Ṭabarī, I, 3277, 3353.

273. Saʿd b. ʿUbaydah was a well-known traditionist, who died between 101 (720) and 105 (724). See Ibn Saʿd, Ṭabaqāt, VI, 208.

274. ʿUmar al-Ṭuhawī is not mentioned in Abū Mikhnaf's account; otherwise he seems to be unknown.

275. Ibn ʿUmar b. Ziyād is not mentioned in Abū Mikhnaf's account; otherwise he seems to be unknown.

b. Badr al-Tamīmī[276] to you. He has instructed him to execute you if you do not fight the people." He jumped on his horse and rode back to the camp. There he called for his arms and put them on. On his horse he ordered the people to attack them, and they fought them. [After the battle] the head of al-Ḥusayn was taken to Ibn Ziyād. He put it in front of him and began to poke at it with his cane as he said, "Abū ʿAbdallāh's (i.e., al-Ḥusayn's) hair has grown gray."

Al-Ḥusayn's women, daughters and family were brought. The best thing that Ibn Ziyād did was to order them to be put in a house in an isolated place, to grant them a subsistence allowance (rizq) and to order them to be given expenses and clothes.   [287]

Two of their servants belonging to ʿAbdallāh b. Jaʿfar—or belonging to the son of Ibn Jaʿfar—escaped. They came to a man from the tribe of Ṭayyiʾ and sought refuge with him. However, he cut their heads off, took them and put them before Ibn Ziyād. He was about to have him executed, but instead he ordered his house to be destroyed.

According to Ḥusayn b. ʿAbd al-Raḥmān—a mawlā of Muʿāwiyah b. Abī Sufyān: When the head of al-Ḥusayn was brought to Yazīd and put before him, I saw him weep and he said, "If there had been any kinship between Ibn Ziyād and al-Ḥusayn, he would not have done this."

According to Ḥusayn (b. ʿAbd al-Raḥmān): After al-Ḥusayn was killed, it seemed as if the walls for two or three months were smeared with blood from the time of sunrise until the sun rose higher.

According to (Ḥusayn b. ʿAbd al-Raḥmān)—al-ʿAlā b. Abī ʿĀthah[277]—Raʾs al-Jālūt[278]—his father: My father told me that he never passed Karbalāʾ without making his mount gallop until he had left the place behind. I asked him the reason, and he said, "We used to talk of the son of a prophet who would be killed in

---

276. Juwayriyah b. Badr al-Tamīmī is not mentioned in Abū Mikhnaf's account; otherwise he seems to be unknown.

277. Al-ʿAlā b. Abī ʿĀthah does not seem to occur as a traditionist anywhere else.

278. Literally, Raʾs al-Jālūt means "the head of Goliath." *Jālūt* is of Hebrew origin. See *EI*², s.v. Djālūt. Perhaps this story was associated with some Jewish sect.

that place, and I was afraid that I would be that man. However, after al-Ḥusayn was killed there, we said that he was the one of whom we talked. After that, when I passed that place, I would go without galloping."

According to al-Ḥārith (b. Muḥammad)[279]—Ibn Saʿd[280]—ʿAlī b. Muḥammad (al-Madāʾinī)[281]—Jaʿfar b. Sulaymān al-Ḍabuʿī:[282] Al-Ḥusayn said, "They will not leave me until they have taken out this heart from within me. When they do that, God will dominate and humiliate them so that they will be more humiliated than a rag used by a slave girl for her menstrual blood." Then he went to Iraq and was killed at Nīnawā[283] on the Day of ʿĀshūrāʾ[284] 61 (October 10, 680).

[288]   According to al-Ḥārith (b. Muḥammad)—Ibn Saʿd—Muḥammad b. ʿUmar (al-Wāqidī): Al-Ḥusayn b. ʿAlī was killed in the month of Ṣafar in the year A.H. 61 (November, 680). At that time he was fifty-five.

According to [al-Ḥārith b. Muḥammad]—Aflaḥ b. Saʿīd[285]—Ibn Kaʿb al-Quraẓī.[286]

According to al-Ḥārith (b. Muḥammad)—Ibn Saʿd—Muḥammad b. ʿUmar (al-Wāqidī)—Abū Maʿshar:[287] Al-Ḥusayn was killed on 10 al-Muḥarram (October 10, 680).

Al-Wāqidī said this was the best confirmed report.

According to al-Ḥārith (b. Muḥammad)—Ibn Saʿd—Muḥam-

---

279. Al-Ḥārith b. Muḥammad was the author of a *musnad* and a noted scholar; he died in 282 (895–96). See al-Dhahabī, *Mīzān*, I, 442–43.

280. Ibn Saʿd was the celebrated author of *Kitāb al-ṭabaqāt al-kabīr*; he died in 230 (845). See *EI²*, s.v. Ibn Saʿd.

281. ʿAlī b. Muḥammad was a famous and prolific historian; he died in 231 (845–46). See *EI²*, s.v. al-Madāʾinī.

282. Jaʿfar b. Sulaymān al-Ḍabuʿī was a famous traditionist, who held Shīʿite inclinations; he died in 178 (794). See Ibn Ḥajar, *Tahdhīb*, II, 95–98.

283. Nīnawā was a small village near Karbalāʾ. See Yāqūt, *Muʿjam*, IV, 870.

284. The Day of ʿĀshūrāʾ was 10 Muḥarram, a day of fasting in imitation of the Jewish Day of Atonement. See *EI²*, s.v. ʿĀshūrāʾ.

285. Aflaḥ b. Saʿīd was a traditionist; he died in 156 (773). See Ibn Ḥajar, *Tahdhīb*, I, 327–28.

286. Ibn Kaʿb al-Quraẓī was Muḥammad b. Kaʿb al-Quraẓī, a respected traditionist; he died between 117–20 (735–38). See Ibn Ḥajar, *Tahdhīb*, IX, 420–22.

287. Abū Maʿshar was Nājiḥ b. ʿAbd al-Raḥmān al-Sindī, a traditionist and author of a work on the campaigns of the Prophet (*maghāzī*), who died in 170 (787). See *EI²*, s.v. Abū Maʿshar.

mad b. 'Umar (al-Wāqidī)—'Aṭā' b. Muslim[288]—the man who informed him—'Āṣim b. Abī al-Najūd[289]—Zirr b. Ḥubaysh:[290] The first head to be raised on wood was the head of al-Ḥusayn. May God be pleased with him and may God bless his soul.

According to Abū Mikhnaf—Hishām b. al-Walīd[291]—an eye-witness: Al-Ḥusayn b. 'Alī set out from Mecca with his family while Muḥammad b. al-Ḥanafiyyah was in Medina. News of al-Ḥusayn's departure reached Muḥammad b. al-Ḥanafiyyah while he was performing his ritual ablution [with water] in a bowl. He wept so that I could hear his tears dropping into the bowl.

According to Abū Mikhnaf—Yūnus b. Abī Isḥāq al-Sabī'ī: When 'Ubaydallāh b. Ziyād had learnt of the journey of al-Ḥusayn from Mecca to al-Kūfah, he sent al-Ḥusayn b. Tamīm, the commander of the police to station himself at al-Qādisiyyah, to set the cavalry between the area of al-Qādisiyyah to Khaffān[292] and the area of al-Qādisiyyah to al-Quṭquṭānah[293] and to La'la'.[294] People said, "Al-Ḥusayn is heading for Iraq."

According to Abū Mikhnaf—Muḥammad b. Qays:[295] Al-Ḥusayn went on. When he reached al-Ḥājir[296] from Baṭn al-Rummah,[297] he sent Qays b. Mushir al-Ṣaydāwī to the Kūfans. He sent a letter

---

288. 'Aṭā' b. Muslim was a Kūfan traditionist, who moved to Aleppo and died in 190 (805–6). See Ibn Ḥajar, *Tahdhīb*, VII, 211–12.

289. 'Āṣim b. Abī al-Najūd was a Kūfan traditionist; he died in 127 (744–45) or 128 (745–46). See Ibn Ḥajar, *Tahdhīb*, V, 38–40.

290. Zirr b. Ḥubaysh was an early traditionist, who heard traditions from a number of leading Companions of the Prophet and died between 81 (700) and 83 (702). See Ibn Ḥajar, *Tahdhīb*, III, 321–22.

291. Hishām b. al-Walīd was only cited by Abū Mikhnaf for this one report. Otherwise he seems to have had an interest in the lives of the caliphs, for he appears to be an authority for what seems to be a book on the subject by Ibn Shihāb al-Zuhrī. See Ṭabarī, II, 199, and p. 225, below.

292. Erroneously given as Ḥuṣayn b. Numayr in the text; see *Addenda et Emendenda*, DLLIV. Khaffān was the high ground above al-Qādisiyyah near al-Kūfah. See Yāqūt, *Mu'jam*, II, 356.

293. Al-Quṭquṭānah was near al-Kūfah on the edge of the desert. See Yāqūt, *Mu'jam*, IV, 137.

294. La'la' was a halting place between al-Kūfah and al-Baṣrah.

295. Muḥammad b. Qays was a traditionist, who only seems to have been used by Abū Mikhnaf for two reports about al-Ḥusayn. See Sezgin, *Abū Miḥnaf*, 212.

296. Al-Ḥājir was the name of any hollow in a valley; it gathers water. See Yāqūt, *Mu'jam*, II, 182.

297. Baṭn al-Rummah was a valley overlooked by the high grounds of Rummah in the Najd. See Yāqūt, *Mu'jam*, I, 66.

with him: "In the name of God, the Merciful, the Compassionate, from al-Ḥusayn b. ʿAlī to his brothers among the believers and Muslims. Peace be with you. I praise God before you, other than Whom there is no deity...Muslim b. ʿAqīl's letter came to me, informing me of your good attitude, the agreement of your leaders to support us and to seek our rights. I have asked God to make your actions good and reward you with the greatest reward. I set out to you from Mecca on Tuesday, 8 Dhū al-Ḥijjah, the Day of Tarwiyah (September 9, 680).[298] When my messenger reaches you, be urgent and purposeful in your affairs, for I am coming to you in a few days, God willing. Peace be with you and the mercy and blessings of God."

Muslim had written to al-Ḥusayn seventeen days before he was killed: "...The trusted early messenger does not lie about his own people. The majority (jamʿ) of the Kūfans are with you. Come when you read my letter. Peace be with you." Al-Ḥusayn had set out with the children and women with him without turning aside for anything.

Qays b. Mushir went toward al-Kūfah with the letter. However, when the letter reached al-Qādisiyyah, al-Ḥuṣayn b. Tamīm apprehended Qays b. Mushir and sent him to ʿUbaydallāh b. Ziyād. ʿUbaydallāh b. Ziyād ordered him, "Go up on the palace and curse the liar, the son of a liar." Qays went up and said: "People, this man, al-Ḥusayn b. ʿAlī, the best of God's creatures, the son of Fāṭimah, the daughter of the Apostle, [is nearby]. I am his messenger to you. I left him at al-Ḥājir. Answer him!" Then he cursed ʿUbaydallāh b. Ziyād and his father, and prayed for forgiveness for ʿAlī b. Abī Ṭālib. ʿUbaydallāh ordered him to be thrown from the top of the palace. They threw him; he was smashed to pieces and killed.

Al-Ḥusayn continued his journey to al-Kūfah until he came to one of the watering places of the Arabs.

ʿAbdallāh b. Muṭīʿ al-ʿAdawī was staying there. When he saw al-Ḥusayn he rose and said to him, "May my father and mother be sacrificed for you! Son of the Apostle of God, what has brought you here?" Then he helped him to dismount. Al-Ḥusayn said, "It is a result of the death of Muʿāwiyah as you would know. The

---

298. Actually a Sunday.

Iraqīs have written to me urging me to come to them." ʿAbdallāh b. Muṭīʿ said, "Son of the Apostle of God, I remind you of God and the sacredness of Islam, lest it be violated. I adjure you before God to be concerned about the veneration of the Apostle of God. I adjure you before God to be concerned about the esteem of the Arabs. By God! If you seek that which is in the hands of Banū Umayyah, they will kill you. If they kill you, they will never fear anyone after you. Then it will be the sacredness of Islam that is violated, and the veneration of Quraysh and the esteem of the Arabs. Don't do it! Don't go to al-Kūfah! do not expose yourself to the Banū Umayyah!" However, he insisted on continuing and went on until he came to the watering place above Zarūd.[299]

According to Abū Mikhnaf—al-Suddī[300]—a man from Banū Fazārah: [al-Suddī] reported: During the time of al-Ḥajjāj b. Yūsuf,[301] we were in the house of al-Ḥārith b. Abī Rabīʿah, [302] that was in the date sellers' district. This place had been given as a fief to the Banū ʿAmr b. Yashkur of Bajīlah after the death of Zuhayr b. al-Qayn. The Syrians did not dare to enter this district. We were hiding there. I said to the man of Fazārah: "Tell me on your own authority. When did you go with al-Ḥusayn b. ʿAlī?" He reported: We were with Zuhayr b. al-Qayn al-Bajalī when we came from Mecca. We were traveling alongside al-Ḥusayn. However, there was nothing more hateful to us than that we accompanied him at every halting place. When al-Ḥusayn traveled, Zuhayr stayed behind. When al-Ḥusayn halted, Zuhayr would go ahead. One day we halted in a place in which we could not avoid stopping with him. Al-Ḥusayn halted at one side of the road, and we halted at the other side of the road. While we were sitting, eating our food, a messenger of al-Ḥusayn approached, greeted us and entered our camp. He said, "Zuhayr b. al-Qayn, Abū ʿAbdallāh al-Ḥusayn b. ʿAlī has sent me to you to ask you to come to him."   [291]

---

299. Zarūd was a place with very sandy ground on the way from Mecca to al-Kūfah. See Yāqūt, *Muʿjam*, II, 927.

300. Al-Suddī's name was Ismāʿīl b. ʿAbd al-Raḥmān. He was a traditionist, who died in 128 (745–46). See Ibn Ḥajar, *Tahdhīb*, I, 313–14.

301. Al-Ḥajjāj b. Yūsuf was the distinguished governor of Iraq for the Umayyads from 75 (694) to 95 (714). See *EI*[2], s.v. al-Ḥadjdjādj b. Yūsuf.

302. Al-Ḥārith b. Abī Rabīʿah was a supporter of Ibn al-Zubayr; he was appointed governor of al-Baṣrah by him and later governor of al-Kūfah. See Ṭabarī, II, 578, 777.

Each man of us threw away what was in his hands in surprise, [and silence prevailed] as if birds had alighted on our heads.

According to Abū Mikhnaf—Dalham bt. ʿAmr, the wife of Zuhayr b. al-Qayn:[303] I said to him, "Does the son of the Messenger of God send for you, and yet you aren't going to him? Glory be to God! Won't you go to him to hear what he has to say? Then you could leave him."

Zuhayr b. al-Qayn went to him. It was not long before he returned with a cheerful shining face. He ordered his tent to be struck and called for his luggage and equipment. His tent was pulled down and taken to al-Ḥusayn. Then he said to his wife, "You are divorced, go back to your family, for I do not want anything except good to befall you because of me." Then he said to his companions, "Whoever wants to follow me may do so. Otherwise, it is the end of our association. I shall tell you a story [of something that happened to me]: We were raiding Balanjar.[304] God granted us victory, and we won [a lot of] booty. Salmān al-Bāhilī[305] said to us, 'Are you happy with the victory God has granted you and the booty you have gained?' We said, 'Yes.' Then he said, 'Therefore when you meet the young men of the family of Muḥammad be happier to fight for them than you are with the booty that you have obtained today.' Therefore, as for me, I bid you farewell."

Zuhayr remained in the first row of the people with al-Ḥusayn until he was killed.

According to Abū Mikhnaf—Abū Janāb al-Kalbī—ʿAdī b. Ḥarmalah al-Asadī—the two Asadīs, ʿAbdallāh b. Sulaym and al-Madhrī b. al-Mushmaʿill: When we had finished the pilgrimage, there was no concern more important to us than to join al-Ḥusayn on the road in order that we might see what would happen to him. We went along with our two camels trotting speedily until we joined him at Zarūd. As we approached, there was a man from al-Kūfah who had changed his route when he saw al-Ḥusayn. Al-Ḥusayn had stopped as if he wanted to speak to him, but then he

---

303. Dalham bt. ʿAmr only seems to have reported this incident.

304. Balanjar is a Khazar town in the eastern extremity of the Caucasus. See *EI*[2], s.v. Balandjar.

305. Salmān al-Bāhilī's name was Salmān b. Rabīʿah al-Bāhilī. He seems to have been an influential tribesman in al-Kūfah.

ignored him and traveled on. We journeyed toward the man. One
of us said to the other that we should go to ask this man if he had   [292]
news of al-Kūfah that we could tell al-Ḥusayn. We came up to
him and greeted him. He returned our greeting and asked for
God's mercy on us. We asked him from what tribe he came; he
answered that he was an Asadī. We said that we were also Asadīs,
and then we asked him who he was. He said that he was Bukayr b.
al-Mathʻabah;[306] then we told him our lineage. We also asked
him to tell us of the people that he had left behind. He replied that
he had only left al-Kūfah after Muslim b. ʻAqīl and Hāniʼ b.
ʻUrwah had been killed; he had seen them being dragged by their
legs into the marketplace.

We went on to join al-Ḥusayn and we were traveling close
behind him until he stopped at al-Thaʻlabiyyah[307] in the evening.
We caught up with him when he stopped; we greeted him. He
returned our greeting. We said, "May God have mercy on you, we
have news. If you wish, we will tell it to you publicly, or if you
wish, secretly." He looked at his followers and said, "Nothing is
kept secret from these men." We asked him if he had seen the
rider who was coming toward him yesterday evening? He said
that he had and that he had wanted to question him. We said,
"We have spared you the trouble of getting his news; we have
done the asking instead of you. He was a man from our tribe, of
sound judgment, honest, with merit and intelligence. He told us
that he had only left al-Kūfah after Muslim b. ʻAqīl and Hāniʼ b.
ʻUrwah had been killed; he had seen them being dragged by their
legs into the marketplace. Al-Ḥusayn said, "'We belong to God
and to Him we shall return.'[308] May God have mercy on them
both." He repeated that phrase several times. We said, "We adjure
you before God, for your own life and for your family (ahl al-bayt)
that you do not go from this place, for you have no one to support
you in al-Kūfah and no Shīʻah. Indeed, we fear that they will be
against you." At that the sons of ʻAqīl b. Abī Ṭālib[309] jumped up.

---

306. Bukayr b. al-Mathʻabah does not seem to occur in any other context.

307. Al-Thaʻlabiyyah was one of the halting places on the way from Mecca to
al-Kūfah. See Yāqūt, Muʻjam, I, 924.

308. Qurʼān, 2:156 (151).

309. ʻAqīl b. Abī Ṭālib, ʻAlī's brother, and the others were close relations of
Muslim b. ʻAqīl.

[293]

According to Abū Mikhnaf—ʿUmar b. Khālid[310]—Zayd b. ʿAlī b. Ḥusayn[311] and Dāwūd b. ʿAlī b. ʿAbdallāh b. ʿAbbās: [312] The sons of ʿAqīl declared, "By God! We will not go back until we have taken our vengeance or have tasted the death that our brother tasted."

According to Abū Mikhnaf—Abū Janāb al-Kalbī—ʿAbdallāh b. Sulaym and al-Madhrī b. al-Mushmaʿill, both of Asad: Al-Ḥusayn looked at us and said, "There is no good in life without these men." Then we knew that his decision had been taken to continue the journey. We said, "May God be good to you." He replied, "May God have mercy on you both." Then some of his followers said to him, "By God! You are not the same as Muslim b. ʿAqīl. If you go to al-Kūfah, the people will hasten to support you."

The two men of Asad reported that he waited until daybreak. Then he ordered his attendants and servants to get a lot of water, to give the people to drink and more for the journey. They set out and went on to Zubālah.

According to Abū Mikhnaf—Abū ʿAlī al-Anṣārī[313]—Bakr b. Muṣʿab al-Muzanī:[314] Al-Ḥusayn had not encountered people at any watering place without their following him. When he reached Zubālah, news of the death of his brother-in-nurture, the death of ʿAbdallāh b. Yuqṭur,[315] came to him. He had despatched him to Muslim b. ʿAqīl along the road without being aware that Muslim had already been struck down. The cavalry of al-Ḥusayn b. Tamīm met him at al-Qādisiyyah and sent him to ʿUbaydallāh b. Ziyād. ʿUbaydallāh ordered him to go up on the roof of the palace and curse the lying son of a liar. He ascended but, when he looked down on the people, he said, "People, I am the mes-

---

310. This seems to be the only report from ʿUmar b. Khālid; otherwise, he seems to be unknown. See Sezgin, *Abū Miḥnaf*, 222.

311. Zayd b. ʿAlī b. Ḥusayn was a son of ʿAlī b. al-Ḥusayn; he led a revolt against the Umayyads in which he was killed in 122 (740). See Wellhausen, *Religio-Political*, 161–67.

312. Dāwūd b. ʿAlī b. ʿAbdallāh was a grandson of Ibn ʿAbbās who died in 133 (750–51). See Sezgin, *Abū Miḥnaf*, 222.

313. Apart from this report, Abū ʿAlī al-Anṣārī seems to be otherwise unknown. See Sezgin, *Abū Miḥnaf*, 189.

314. Apart from this report, Bakr b. Muṣʿab al-Muzanī seems to be otherwise unknown.

315. ʿAbdallāh b. Yuqṭur is only mentioned with regard to this incident.

senger of al-Ḥusayn, son of Fāṭimah, son of the daughter of the Apostle of God. You can help and support him against the son of Marjānah, the [grand]son of Sumayyah, a man who claims a false [grand]father." ʿUbaydallāh ordered him to be thrown from the roof of the palace to the ground. His bones were broken but he still had a spark of life. A man called ʿAbd al-Malik b. ʿUmayr al-Lakhmī[316] went to him and cut his throat. When he was blamed for that, he said, "I only wanted to relieve his [suffering]."

According to Hishām (b. Muḥammad al-Kalbī)—Abū Bakr b.   [294]
ʿAyyāsh[317]—a man who informed him declared, "By God! It was not ʿAbd al-Malik b. ʿUmayr who went to him and cut his throat. But the man who went to him was curly-headed and tall like ʿAbd al-Malik b. ʿUmayr."

That news came to Ḥusayn while he was at Zubālah. He took out a written statement to the people and read it to them: "In the name of God, the Merciful, the Compassionate, dreadful news of the murder of Muslim b. ʿAqīl, Hāni' b. ʿUrwah and ʿAbdallāh b. Yuqṭur has reached us. Our Shīʿah has deserted us. Those of you who would prefer to leave us may leave freely without guilt." The people began to disperse from him to the right and left. The only followers left with him were those who had come with him from Medina. Al-Ḥusayn had done that because he realized that the Bedouin had only followed him because they thought that he was going to a land where the inhabitants' obedience to him had already been established. He did not want them to accompany him without being aware of what they were undertaking. He knew that when he had explained to them the possibilities, only those would accompany him who wanted to share his fate and die with him. At dawn, he ordered his attendants to provide themselves with water and some extra. Then he set out until he passed Baṭn al-ʿAqabah.[318] He stopped there.

---

316. ʿAbd al-Malik b. ʿUmayr al-Lakhmī was a well-known traditionist, who was born in 32 (652–53) and lived until 133 (750–51). See Ibn Ḥajar, *Tahdhīb*, VI, 411–13.

317. Abū Bakr b. ʿAyyāsh was a well-known traditionist, who died in 193 (808). See Ibn Ḥajar, *Tahdhīb*, XII, 34–37.

318. Baṭn al-ʿAqabah was a halting place on the way from Mecca to al-Kūfah beneath the high mountain of ʿAqabah before coming to Wāqiṣah. See Yāqūt, *Muʿjam*, III, 692.

According to Abū Mikhnaf—Lawdhān,[319] one of the Banū ʿIkrimah: One of his male relatives asked al-Ḥusayn, "Where are you heading?" He told him; then the man exhorted him, "I implore you before God not to go there. By God! You won't come to anything there except the points of spears and the edges of swords. If those who sent for you were enough to support you in battle and had prepared the ground for you, and you came to them, that would be a wise decision. However, in the light of the situation as it has been described, I do not think that you should go there." He replied, "Servant of God, wise decisions are not hidden from me. Yet the commands of God cannot be resisted." Then he departed from there.

[295]   In this year (60/680) Yazīd b. Muʿāwiyah dismissed al-Walīd b. ʿUtbah as governor of Mecca and appointed ʿAmr b. Saʿīd. That was in the month of Ramaḍān (June, 680). ʿAmr b. Saʿīd led the people in the pilgrimage. That is according to Aḥmad b. Thābit[320]—someone who mentioned it to him—Isḥāq b. ʿĪsā[321]—Abū Maʿshar.

In this year (60/680) ʿAmr b. Saʿīd was Yazīd's governor in both Mecca and Medina after al-Walīd b. ʿUtbah was dismissed. ʿUbaydallāh b. Ziyād was governor over al-Kūfah and al-Baṣrah and their districts (aʿmāl). The qāḍī of al-Kūfah was Shurayḥ b. al-Ḥārith and the qāḍī of al-Baṣrah was Hishām b. Hubayrah.[322]

---

319. This seems to be the only report from Lawdhān; he seems to be otherwise unknown. See Sezgin, *Abū Miḥnaf*, 209.

320. Aḥmad b. Thābit was a traditionist, who was alive in 255 (869). See Ibn Ḥajar, *Tahdhīb*, I, 21.

321. Isḥāq b. ʿĪsā was a traditionist, who died between 214 (829) and 216 (831). See Ibn Ḥajar, *Tahdhīb*, I, 245.

322. Hishām b. Hubayrah became qāḍī of al-Baṣrah in 58 (677–78) and remained qāḍī until 75 (694–95). See Ṭabarī, II, 188, 863.

The
Events of the Year

61

(OCTOBER 1, 680–SEPTEMBER 19, 681)

Among these events was the murder (*maqtal*) of al-Ḥusayn. He was killed on 10 al-Muḥarram (October 10) according to Aḥmad b. Thābit—someone who transmitted reports—Isḥāq b. ʿĪsā—Abū Maʿshar. This is also reported by al-Wāqidī and Hishām b. [Muḥammad] al-Kalbī. We have already mentioned the beginning of the affair of al-Ḥusayn during his journey toward Iraq and the part that took place in 60 (680). We will now give an account of what happened to him in 61 (680) and how his murder took place.

According to Hishām (b. Muḥammad al-Kalbī)—Abū Mikhnaf—Abū Jānab—ʿAdī b. Ḥarmalah—ʿAbdallāh b. Sulaym and al-Madhrī b. al-Mushmaʿill, both of Asad: Al-Ḥusayn went on from Baṭn al-ʿAqabah until he stopped at Sharaf.[323] At dawn he ordered his attendants to get water and some extra. They continued going on at a quick pace during the first part of the day until midday when one of his followers exclaimed, "God is greater (*Allāhu akbar*)." Al-Ḥusayn repeated, "God is greater." Then he asked, "Why did you say God is greater?" The man answered that he had

[296]

---

323. Sharaf was a watering place in the Najd. See Yāqūt, *Muʿjam*, III, 270.

seen palm trees. However, the two men of Asad asserted that that was a place where they had never seen a palm tree before. Al-Ḥusayn asked them what they thought that it was; they answered that they thought it was the necks of the cavalry vanguard. Al-Ḥusayn declared, "By God! I think so too. Isn't there a place where we could take refuge by putting it at our rear in order that we can face these people from one direction?" They replied, "Yes, there is Dhū Ḥusum[324] over on your left. If you reach it before them, it will be just what you want."

So he veered left toward Dhū Ḥusum; we went in that direction with him. No sooner had we done this than the necks of the cavalry vanguard appeared in front of us and we could see them clearly. We turned aside. When they saw that we had moved off the road, they moved to the side toward us. Their spears looked like palm branches stripped of their leaves; their standards were like birds' wings. We both made hastily for Dhū Ḥusum; we got there before them. Al-Ḥusayn ordered his tents to be pitched; they were erected. The people came up; there were about one thousand mounted men under the command of al-Ḥurr b. Yazīd al-Tamīmī al-Yarbūʿī. He and his cavalry stood facing al-Ḥusayn in the heat of midday. Al-Ḥusayn and his followers were all wearing their turbans and swords. He ordered his attendants to provide the people with water, to let them quench their thirst and to give their mounts water to drink little by little. The attendants stood and gave the mounts a little water at a time. But [first] the attendants stood and gave the people water to drink until they had

[297]   quenched their thirst. Then, they began filling their bowls, basins and cups; they took them to their mounts. When a mount had drunk three, four or five draughts, the water was taken away and given to another mount until they had all been watered.

According to Hishām (b. Muḥammad al-Kalbī)—Laqīṭ[325]—ʿAlī b. al-Ṭaʿʿān al-Muḥāribī:[326] I was with al-Ḥurr on that day. I was among the last of his followers to arrive. When al-Ḥusayn saw

---

324. Dhū Ḥusum was a naturally well-fortified place near Karbalāʾ. See Yāqūt, *Muʿjam*, II, 367.

325. This seems to be the only report from Laqīṭ; otherwise he seems to be unknown.

326. ʿAlī b. al-Ṭaʿʿān al-Muḥāribī is only recorded as being present in this place; otherwise, he seems to be unknown.

how thirsty both my horse and I were, he said, "Make your beast
(*rāwiyah*) kneel." To me "*rāwiyah*" meant waterskin so he said,
"Cousin, make your camel (*jamal*) kneel." I did so. Then he
said, "Drink." I did so, but when I drank, water flowed from my
waterskin. He told me, "Bend your waterskin," using the word
"*ikhnith*" that means "*iʿtif*" (bend). I did not know how to do
that. He came up and bent it. Then I drank and gave my mount to
drink.

Al-Ḥurr b. Yazīd had come from al-Qādisiyyah. ʿUbaydallāh b.
Ziyād had sent al-Ḥusayn b. Tamīm al-Tamīmī,[327] who was in
charge of his police, and ordered him to take up position at al-
Qādisiyyah, to place lookouts and to control [the area] from al-
Qādisiyyah to Khaffān. Al-Ḥurr had been sent in advance from
al-Qādisiyyah with one thousand mounted men to meet Ḥusayn.

Al-Ḥurr remained positioned opposite Ḥusayn until the time
for the midday prayer drew near. Al-Ḥusayn ordered al-Ḥajjāj b.
Masrūq al-Juʿfī[328] to give the call to prayer. When the second call
to prayer that begins the prayer (*iqāmah*)[329] was about to be made,
al-Ḥusayn came out dressed in a waistcloth (*izār*), cloak (*ridāʾ*)[330]
and wearing a pair of sandals. He praised and glorified God. Then
he said, "People, it is a true argument (*maʿdhirah*) both to God,
the Mighty and Exalted, and to you that I did not come to you
until your letters were brought to me, and your messengers came
to me saying, 'Come to us, for we have no imām. God may unite
us in the truth through you.' Since this was your view, I have   [298]
come to you. Therefore, if you give me what you guaranteed in
your covenants and sworn testimonies, I will come to your town.
If you will not and are averse to my coming, I will leave you for
the place from which I came to you."

They were silent before him. Then they said to the muezzin,
"Recite the *iqāmah*." He recited the *iqāmah*, and al-Ḥusayn asked

---

327. Erroneously given as Numayr in the text; see *Addenda et Emendanda*,
DCLIV.

328. This seems to be the only time al-Ḥajjāj b. Masrūq al-Juʿfī is mentioned.

329. The *iqāmah* repeats the same formula as in the call to prayer (*adhān*), but
is regarded as an integral part of the *ṣalāt*. See Howard, "The Development of the
Adhān and the *Iqāma* in the *Ṣalāt* in Early Islam," *Journal of Semitic Studies*,
1981.

330. The *izār* and the *ridāʾ* are traditional clothes for Islamic and pre-Islamic
worship by the Arabs. See *EI²*, s.v. *Iḥrām*.

al-Ḥurr b. Yazīd whether he wanted to lead his followers in the prayer. He replied, "No, but you pray and we will pray with you leading the prayer." After al-Ḥusayn had prayed before them, he entered his tent, and his followers gathered around him. Al-Ḥurr went back to his position and entered a tent that had been put up for him. A group of his followers gathered around him while the rest of his followers now returned to their previous positions, each of them holding the reins of his mount and sitting in the shade.

At the time for the afternoon (ʿaṣr) prayer, al-Ḥusayn ordered his followers to prepare for departure. Then he ordered the call for prayer to be made; the call for the afternoon prayer was made, and the *iqāmah* was recited. Al-Ḥusayn came forward, stood and prayed. When he had said the final greeting of peace [in the prayer], he turned his face toward al-Ḥurr's men. After praising and glorifying God, he said, "People, if you fear God and recognize the rights of those who have them, God will be more satisfied with you. We are the family (*ahl al-bayt*) of Muḥammad and as such are more entitled to the authority (*wilāyah*) of this government (*amr*) over you than these pretenders who claim what does not belong to them. They have brought tyranny and aggression among you. If you dislike us, or do not know our rights, and if your view has now changed from what came to us in your letters and what your messengers brought, then I will leave you."

Al-Ḥurr b. Yazīd declared, "By God! We know nothing of these letters and messengers that you mention." Al-Ḥusayn told one of his followers, "ʿUqbah b. Simʿān, bring out the two saddlebags in which their letters to me are kept." He brought out two saddlebags that were full of documents; he scattered them in front of them. Al-Ḥurr said, "We are not among those who wrote these letters to you, and we have been ordered that when we meet you we should not leave you until we have brought you to al-Kūfah and to ʿUbaydallāh b. Ziyād." Al-Ḥusayn told him, "Death will come to you before that." He ordered his followers to rise and mount. After they had mounted and waited for their women to be mounted, he ordered his followers to depart.

When they set out to leave, al-Ḥurr's men got in between them and the direction they were traveling. Al-Ḥusayn cried out to al-Ḥurr, "May God deprive your mother of you. What do you want?"

[299]

Al-Ḥurr answered, "By God! If any of the Arabs other than you were to say that to me, while he was in the same situation as you, I would not leave him without mentioning his mother's being deprived of him. I would say it whoever he might be. But, by God, there is no way for me to mention your mother except by saying the best things possible." Al-Ḥusayn again asked him what he wanted. He replied that he wanted to go with him to the governor, ʿUbaydallāh. Al-Ḥusayn said, "By God! I will not follow you!" Al-Ḥurr replied, "By God! I will not let you go anywhere else!" These statements were repeated three times. When their conversation was getting more intense, al-Ḥurr said, "I have not been ordered to fight you. I have only been ordered not to leave you until I bring you to al-Kūfah. If you refuse to do that, then take any road that will neither bring you into al-Kūfah nor take you back to Medina, and let that be a compromise between us; I shall write to Ibn Ziyād. You write to Yazīd b. Muʿāwiyah if you wish to write to him, or to ʿUbaydallāh b. Ziyād if you wish. Perhaps God will cause something to happen that will relieve me   [300] from being troubled in any way by your affair. Therefore, take this road here and bear to the left of the road to al-ʿUdhayb[331] and al-Qādisiyyah." There were thirty-eight miles between al-Qādisiyyah and al-ʿUdhayb. Al-Ḥusayn set off with his followers and al-Ḥurr marched by him.

According to Abū Mikhnaf—ʿUqbah b. Abī al-ʿAyzār:[332] Al-Ḥusayn preached to his followers and the followers of al-Ḥurr at al-Bīḍah.[333] After praising and glorifying God, He said: "People, the Apostle of God said: 'When anyone sees the authorities make permissible what God had forbidden, violating God's covenant, and opposing the Sunnah of the Apostle of God by acting against the servants of God sinfully and with hostility, when anyone sees all these incidents and does not upbraid them by deed or by word, it is God's decree to make that person subject to fortune.' Indeed, these authorities have cleaved to obedience to Satan and have abandoned obedience to the Merciful; they have made corruption

---

331. Al-ʿUdhayb is a watering place and one of the halting places on the way from Mecca to al-Kūfah. See Yāqūt, Muʿjam, III, 626.

332. ʿUqbah b. Abī al-ʿAyzār was a traditionist, who died during the first half of the first (eighth) century. See Sezgin, Abū Miḥnaf, 222.

333. Al-Bīḍah was a watering place between al-ʿUdhayb and Wāqiṣah.

visible; they have neglected the punishment (*ḥudūd*) laid down by God; they have appropriated the *fay'* exclusively to themselves; they have permitted what God has forbidden, and they have forbidden what He has permitted. I have the right to change more than anyone else. Your letters were brought to me, and your messengers came to me with your oath of allegiance that you would not hand me over or desert me. If you fulfill your pledge, you will arrive at true guidance, for I am al-Ḥusayn b. ʿAlī, the son of Fāṭimah, daughter of the Apostle of God. My life is with your lives, my family is with your families. In me you have an ideal model (*uswah*). However, if you will not act, but you break your covenant and renounce your responsibility for the oath of allegiance that you have given, then, by my life, it is not a thing that is unknown of you. You have done that to my father, my brother and my cousin, Muslim. Anyone who was deceived by you would be gullible. Thus have you mistaken your fortune and lost your destiny. For whoever violates his word only violates his own soul. God will enable me to do without you. Peace be with you and the mercy and blessings of God."

ʿUqbah b. Abī al-ʿAyzār reported that Ḥusayn stood up to preach at Dhū Ḥusum. After praising and glorifying God, he said, [301] "You see what this matter has come to. Indeed, the world has changed, and it has changed for the worse. Its goodness has retreated, and it regards good as bitter. Or, there remain only the dregs like the dregs in a jar, sordid nourishment like unhealthy fodder. Can you not see that truth is no longer something that men practice and falsehood is no longer desisted from, so that the believer rightly desires to meet God. I can only regard death as martyrdom (*shahādah*) and life with these oppressors as a tribulation."

Zuhayr b. al-Qayn al-Bajalī stood up amid his comrades and asked whether they would speak or should he. They told him to speak. After praising and glorifying God, he said, "We have heard God guide your words, son of the Apostle of God. By God! If our world can be eternal and we can be immortal within it and, if by helping and supporting you, we must abandon it, then we would still prefer going with you rather than staying in the world." Al-Ḥusayn prayed for him and spoke well of him.

Al-Ḥurr started to travel alongside him, while saying to him, "Ḥusayn, I remind you of God with regard to your life, for I testify

that if you fight, you will be fought, and if you are fought, you will
be killed." He replied, "Do you think that you can frighten me
with death? Could a worse disaster happen to you than killing
me? I do not know what to say to you. I can only address you as
the brother of al-Aws addressed his cousin when he met the latter
as he was going to help the Apostle of God. His cousin said to
him: 'Where are you going, for you will be killed?' He replied:

> I will depart, for there is no shame in death for a young man
>   whenever he intends right and strives as a Muslim,
> And has supported righteous men through [the sacrifice of] his
>   life,
>   abandoned the cursed and made alliance with the
> consecrated.[334]

[302]

When al-Ḥurr heard that, he drew away from him. He and his
followers traveled on one side while Ḥusayn traveled on the other,
until they reached ʿUdhayb al-Hijānāt.[335] There, the dromedaries
of al-Nuʿmān[336] used to graze. It was there, too, that a group of
four[337] approached from al-Kūfah on their camels, driving along a
horse of Nāfiʿ b. Hilāl, called al-Kāmil. They had with them their
guide, al-Ṭirimmāḥ b. ʿAdī,[338] on his horse. He was reciting:

> Camels, do not be frightened by my urging
>   but go forward quickly before the dawn rises,

---

334. These verses are also quoted by Balādhurī. See *Ansāb* II/2, 171. I have
corrected the last hemistich of the second verse, which read *yaghushshu wa-
yurghimā* to *wa-ḥālafa muḥrimā*, as in Balādhurī.

335. There were two other watering places within the area of al-ʿUdhayb. One
of them to the east of al-ʿUdhayb was called "ʿUdhayb al-Hijānāt." The area was
particularly good for grazing animals, especially horses and camels. See Yāqūt,
Muʿjam, III, 626.

336. Balādhurī gives the full name, al-Nuʿmān b. al-Mundhir. See *Ansāb*, II/2,
171. He was a famous king of the Lakhmids from A.D. 580 to 602. See P. Hittī,
History of the Arabs, 84.

337. The other three beside Nāfiʿ are given by Balādhurī: ʿAmr b. Khālid al-
Ṣaydāwī, his mawlā Saʿd, and Mujammiʿ b. ʿAbdallāh al-ʿĀʾidhī of Madhḥij. See
Ansāb, II/2, 172. None of them, including Nāfiʿ, has been mentioned before, but
they are members of the Shīʿah who managed to get to al-Ḥusayn. They eventually died fighting for him. See pp. 145, 150, below.

338. Al-Ṭirimmāḥ b. ʿAdī was a famous Arab poet whose poetry was said to be
affected by his having been a townsman. See R. A. Nicholson, *Literary History of
the Arabs*, 138.

With the best riders and the best group
    so that you may kneel down at the house of a man of high
      ancestry,
A praiseworthy man, a free man, a generous man
    whom God has sent for the best mission to fulfill.
Then may God cause him to remain for the rest of time.

When they reached al-Ḥusayn, they recited these verses to him. He replied, "By God! I hope that what waits for us will be good whether we die or be victorious."

[303]   Al-Ḥurr b. Yazīd approached and said, "These men from al-Kūfah are not among the party that came with you. I will either detain them or send them back." Al-Ḥusayn answered, "I will defend them in the same way as I would defend my own life. They are only my supporters and helpers. You gave me your word that you would not do anything against me until you received a letter from Ibn Ziyād." Al-Ḥurr insisted that they did not come with him, but al-Ḥusayn declared, "They are my followers and they are just like those who came with me. Therefore if you carry out the agreement made between us, [you will let them stay]. Otherwise, I will have to do battle with you." At that al-Ḥurr desisted.

Then al-Ḥusayn said to them, "Tell me the news of the people you have left behind you." Mujammiʿ b. ʿAbdallāh al-ʿĀʾidhī,[339] who was one of the group of four, said, "There has been much bribery among the nobles, and their coffers have been filled so that their support has been won over and their loyal support [for Ibn Ziyād] has been ensured. Now they are all united against you. As for the rest of the people, their hearts are inclined toward you, but soon their swords will be drawn against you." Al-Ḥusayn asked what they knew of his messenger to them. They asked who he was; he told them that it was Qays b. Mushir al-Ṣaydāwī. They said that al-Ḥusayn b. Tamīm[340] had captured him and sent him to Ibn Ziyād. Ibn Ziyād had ordered him to curse al-Ḥusayn and his father, but he had called for God's blessings on him and his father and cursed Ibn Ziyād and his father. Then he had urged the people to support al-Ḥusayn and told them of his coming. Ibn

---

    339. See footnote 337.
    340. Text erroneously gives al-Ḥusayn b. Numayr; see *Addenda et Emendanda*, DCLV.

Ziyād ordered him to be thrown from the wall of the palace. The eyes of al-Ḥusayn glistened with moisture, and he could not hold back the tears. He said, "'Some [of the faithful] have reached their death and some are waiting and have not changed.'[341] O God! Make paradise an abode for us [who are waiting] and for those who have reached their death. Gather us and them in a dwelling place of Your mercy and of the desirable reward that You have in store."

[304]

According to Abū Mikhnaf—Jamīl b. Marthad[342] from the Banū Maʿan—al-Ṭirimmāḥ b. ʿAdī: Al-Ṭirimmāḥ approached al-Ḥusayn and said, "I have been looking and I haven't seen anyone with you. If it was only these men whom I see traveling alongside you (i.e., al-Ḥurr's men) who would fight you, there would be enough of them to defeat you. But, before coming to you from al-Kūfah yesterday, I saw the outskirts (ẓahr) of al-Kūfah, and there were [more] people gathered together in one place than my eyes have ever seen. I asked about them; I was told that they had gathered to be inspected and that they would march against al-Ḥusayn. I adjure you before God that, if you can desist from moving only a hand's breadth (shibr) against them, you should not move. If you wish to settle in a land where God will protect you so that you can consider your position, and your activities become clear to you, then come so that I can settle you in our impregnable mountains called Ajaʾ.[343] By God! There we were protected from the Banū Ghassān, from Ḥimyar, from al-Nuʿmān b. al-Mundhir and from all types of people. By God! No humiliation has ever come to us. So I will go with you to settle you in al-Qurayyah. There we will send to the men of Ṭayyiʾ in Ajaʾ and Salmā.[344] By God! It will not be ten days before the tribe of Ṭayyiʾ brings you foot soldiers and horsemen. Stay with us for as long as it appears good to you. If anything disturbs you, I can guarantee

---

341. Qurʾān, 33:23.

342. Jamīl b. Marthad was an unknown authority of Abū Mikhnaf's whose only reports are the two presented here concerning al-Ṭirimmāḥ.

343. Ajaʾ was one of the two mountains of the tribe of Ṭayyiʾ, the other being Salmā. There was a two-day journey between the two mountains. Ajaʾ is the western one of the two. See Yāqūt, Muʿjam, I, 122.

344. See n. 343, above. Al-Qurayyah is a place between Ajaʾ and Salmā. See Yāqūt, Muʿjam, IV, 85.

for you twenty thousand Ṭāʾīs who would use their swords on your behalf. By God! No one will ever reach you while an eye still twinkles among them." Al-Ḥusayn said, "May God reward you and your people. But there is an agreement between these people and us as a result of which we cannot leave, and we do not know the final outcome of affairs between these people and us."

[305] According to Abū Mikhnaf—Jamīl b. Marthad—al-Ṭirimmāḥ b. ʿAdī: I bade him farewell and said, "May God protect you from the evil of jinn and men. I have supplies from al-Kūfah for my family and money for them. I will take them and deliver them. Then I will come back to you, God willing. If I arrive in time, by God, I will be one of your supporters." Al-Ḥusayn replied, "If you do, be quick! May God have mercy on you." I knew then, when he asked me to hurry, that he was short of men. When I reached my family, I delivered to them the things that would be useful to them. Then I gave my last instructions. My family began to say, "You are doing something that you have never done before today." I told them what I intended; I set out along the road through the territory of the Banū Thuʿal. When I was near ʿUdhayb al-Hijānāt, I met Samāʿah b. Badn,³⁴⁵ and he gave me news of al-Ḥusayn's death. So I returned.

According to [Abū Mikhnaf]: Al-Ḥusayn went on to Qaṣr Banī Muqātil.³⁴⁶ He stopped there, and a large tent had been erected.

According to Abū Mikhnaf—al-Mujālid b. Saʿīd—ʿĀmir al-Shaʿbī:³⁴⁷ Al-Ḥusayn b. ʿAlī asked, "Whose tent is this?" He was told that it belonged to ʿUbaydallāh b. al-Ḥurr al-Juʿfī.³⁴⁸ He asked them to ask ʿUbaydallāh to come to him. Someone was sent to him. The messenger went to him and said, "This is al-Ḥusayn b. ʿAlī; he asks you to come to him." ʿUbaydallāh said, "'We belong to God and to Him we shall return.'³⁴⁹ By God! I

---

345. Samāʿah b. Badn is only mentioned at this point in the narrative.

346. Qaṣr Banī Muqātil was a palace of a Christian tribe in pre-Islamic times; it was close to al-Quṭquṭānah; See Yāqūt, *Muʿjam*, IV, 121–22.

347. ʿĀmir b. Shurāḥil al-Shaʿbī, an influential jurist and traditionist, died in 105 (723–24) at the age of 73. See Ibn Saʿd, *Ṭabaqāt*, VI, 171–78.

348. ʿUbaydallāh b. al-Ḥurr al-Juʿfī was a noble Arab and poet. Although he did not give al-Ḥusayn any help, he regretted his death. He bitterly opposed al-Mukhtār's revolution, and was also hostile to Ibn al-Zubayr; he attempted to support ʿAbd al-Malik but he was killed. See Balādhurī, *Ansāb*, V, 290–97.

349. Qurʾān, 2:156 (151).

only left al-Kūfah out of dread that al-Ḥusayn would enter al-Kūfah while I was there. By God! I do not want to see him or him to see me." The messenger returned to al-Ḥusayn. Al-Ḥusayn took his sandals, put them on and went over to ʿUbaydallāh. He greeted him and sat down. Then he asked him to go with him. Ibn al-Ḥurr repeated what he had said before. Al-Ḥusayn replied, "If you are not going to help us, fear God lest you be one of those who fight against us. By God! No one will hear our cry and not help us without being destroyed." He said, "As for that, it will never happen, if God, the Exalted, wishes." Then al-Ḥusayn left him and continued his journey. [306]

According to Abū Mikhnaf—ʿAbd al-Raḥmān b. Jundab—ʿUqbah b. Simʿān: Toward the end of the night, he ordered his attendants to get provisions of water. Then he ordered us to depart. We did. When we had left Qaṣr Banī Muqātil and had gone on for a time, his head began to nod with drowsiness. He woke up, saying "'We belong to God and to Him we shall return.'[350] Praise be to God, Lord of the universe!" He did that twice or three times; then his son, ʿAlī b. al-Ḥusayn approached him and said to him, "'We belong to God and to Him we shall return.'[351] Praise be to God, Lord of the world. Father! May I be a sacrifice for you. Why are you praising God and repeating the verse of returning to Him?" He replied, "My son, I nodded off, and a horseman appeared to me, riding a horse, and he said: 'Men are traveling and the fates travel toward them.' Then I knew it was our death being announced to us." ʿAlī said, "Father, may God not show you any evil. Are we not in the right?" He said, "Indeed, by Him to Whom all servants must return!" ʿAlī said, "Then, father, we need have no concern, if we are going to die righteously." Al-Ḥusayn replied, "May God give you the best reward a son can receive from his father."

In the morning, he stopped and prayed the morning prayer. Then he hurried to remount; he began veering to the left with his followers, for his intention was to separate from al-Ḥurr's men. However, al-Ḥurr b. Yazīd came toward him to stop him and his followers. When he began to turn them toward al-Kūfah, they

---

350. Qurʾān 2:156 (151).
351. Qurʾān 2:156 (151).

strongly resisted him. So al-Ḥurr's men stopped that, but they still accompanied them in the same way until they reached Nīnawā, the place where al-Ḥusayn stopped. Suddenly, there appeared a rider on a fast mount coming from al-Kūfah. He was bearing weapons and carrying a bow on his shoulder. They all stopped and watched him. When he reached them, he greeted al-Ḥurr and his followers but he did not greet al-Ḥusayn and his followers. He handed al-Ḥurr a letter from ʿUbaydallāh b. Ziyād. It said the following: "...When this letter reaches you and my messenger comes to you, make al-Ḥusayn come to a halt. Let him stop in an open place without protection and water. I have ordered my messenger to stay with you and not to leave you until he brings me news of your carrying out my instructions. Peace be with you."

[307]

When al-Ḥurr had read the letter, he told Ḥusayn's followers, "This is a letter from the governor, ʿUbaydallāh. He has ordered me to bring you to a halt at an open place. This is his messenger; he has ordered him not to leave me until I carry out his decision and his order."

Yazīd b. Ziyād b. al-Muḥāṣir Abū al-Shaʿthāʾ al-Kindī al-Bahdalī,[352] who was with al-Ḥusayn, looked at the messenger of Ibn Ziyād and recognized him. He asked him, "Are you Mālik b. Nusayr al-Baddī?"[353] The other replied, "Yes." He was a member of the tribe of Kindah. Yazīd b. Ziyād exclamed, "May your mother be deprived of you! What is this business you have brought?" The other man retorted, "What is this that I have brought? I have obeyed my imām and remained faithful to my oath of allegiance." Abū al-Shaʿthāʾ responded, "You have been disobedient to your Lord and have obeyed your imām in bringing about the destruction of your soul. You have acquired shame and the punishment of Hell-fire. Indeed, God has said: 'We have made them imāms, who summon people to Hell-fire, and on the Day of Resurrection they will not be helped.'[354] Your imām is one of those."

---

352. Yazīd b. Ziyād is not mentioned before this event in any other context; he died fighting for al-Ḥusayn. See pp. 149–50, below.

353. Mālik b. Nusayr al-Baddī was not mentioned before, but he went on to take part in the battle against al-Ḥusayn; he attacked and struck al-Ḥusayn and took his cloak. For his part in the battle, al-Mukhtār ordered his arms and legs to be cut off, and he was left to bleed to death. See pp. 153–54, below; and Ṭabarī, II, 668.

354. Qurʾān, 28:41.

Al-Ḥurr b. Yazīd began to make the people stop in a place that was without water and where there was no village. They said, "Let us stop at this village," meaning Nīnawā, "or that one," meaning al-Ghāḍiriyyah,[355] "or that other one," meaning Shaffayyah.[356] Al-Ḥurr said, "No, by God! I cannot do that, for this man has been sent to me as a spy." Zuhayr b. al-Qayn said, "Son of the Apostle of God, fighting these people now will be easier for us than fighting those who will come against us after them. By my life! After these whom you see now, a number will come against us, and we will not have the power to fight against them." Al-Ḥusayn answered, "I will not begin to fight against them." Zuhayr b. al-Qayn said, "Go with us to that village so that you could stop there. It is well fortified and it is on the bank of the Euphrates. If they try to stop us, we can fight them. Fighting them will be easier than fighting those who will come after them." Al-Ḥusayn asked what village it was; he was told that it was called al-ʿAqr[357] (literally "wound"). He said, "O God! I seek refuge with you from al-ʿAqr." He stopped at al-ʿAqr.

[308]

That was Thursday, 2 al-Muḥarram in 61 (October 2, 680).[358] On the next day, ʿUmar b. Saʿd b. Abī Waqqāṣ came against them from al-Kūfah with four thousand men. The reason for Ibn Saʿd's coming out against al-Ḥusayn was that ʿUbaydallāh had commissioned him with four thousand Kūfans to go with them to Dastabā.[359] The people of al-Daylam had come against Dastabā and overrun this place. So Ibn Ziyād had written ʿUmar b. Saʿd a letter of appointment over al-Rayy and ordered him to set out. He had gone out to an encampment with the men at Ḥammām Aʿyan.[360] When the affair of al-Ḥusayn developed, and the latter had set out for al-Kūfah, Ibn Ziyād recalled ʿUmar b. Saʿd. He told him, "Go against al-Ḥusayn and when you have finished our business with him, you can go to your governorate." ʿUmar b. Saʿd pleaded, "If you would consider, may God have mercy on

---

355. Al-Ghāḍiriyyah was a small village to the northeast of Karbalāʾ.

356. Shaffayyah was a village near Karbalāʾ.

357. Al-ʿAqr was a village near Karbalāʾ. See Yāqūt, *Muʿjam*, III, 695.

358. Actually a Tuesday.

359. Dastabā was a large district between al-Rayy and Hamadhān. See Yāqūt, *Muʿjam*, II, 573.

360. Ḥammām Aʿyan was close to al-Kūfah; it seems to have been used as a military camp for campaigns to the east. See Yāqūt, *Muʿjam*, II, 329

you, relieving me, do so." ʿUbaydallāh said, "Yes, if you give us back our letter of appointment." ʿUmar b. Saʿd asked him to give him a day's respite to think. When he had said that to him, ʿUmar went away; he consulted men who would give him sincere advice. He did not find one who did not advise him to refuse. Ḥamzah b. al-Mughīrah b. Shuʿbah,[361] who was his sister's son, came to him and said, "Uncle, I adjure you before God not to go against al-Ḥusayn, for you would be committing a crime before your Lord and breaking the bonds of your kinship with him. By God! It is better that you should abandon all your world, the wealth and the earthly authority that you have than that you should meet God with the blood of al-Ḥusayn on your hands." ʿUmar b. Saʿd replied, "God willing, I will do that."

[309]

According to Hishām (b. Muḥammad al-Kalbī)—ʿAwānah b. al-Ḥakam—ʿAmmār b. ʿAbdallāh b. Yasār al-Juhanī[362]—his father:[363] I went to ʿUmar b. Saʿd when he had been ordered to go against al-Ḥusayn. He said to me, "The governor has ordered me to go against al-Ḥusayn and I have refused to do that for him." I said to him, "May God keep you in the right and guide you. Withdraw and do not do it; do not go against al-Ḥusayn." Then I left him. Someone came to me and told me, "This ʿUmar b. Saʿd is urging the people against al-Ḥusayn." I went to him, and he was sitting down. When he saw me, he turned his face away. I knew, then, that he had decided to go against al-Ḥusayn. ʿUmar b. Saʿd had gone to Ibn Ziyād and said, "May God make the governor prosperous; you appointed me to the governorship. You wrote me a letter of appointment, and the people have heard about it. If you thought it right to send me to this governorship, then act accordingly and send some of the Kūfan nobles with this army, for I am not more suitable to fight for you against him than...." Then he named some people to him. Ibn Ziyād retorted, "Don't teach me about the Kūfan nobles. I am not asking you to tell me about whom I want to send. If you will go with your troops, [well

---

361. Ḥamzah's father, Mughīrah b. Shuʿbah, had been governor of al-Kūfah; he had an influential position.

362. ʿAmmār b. ʿAbdallāh was only quoted on this one occasion; otherwise he seems to be unknown.

363. ʿAbdallāh b. Yasār al-Juhanī, a Kūfan traditionist, was contemporary with the events. See Ibn Ḥajar, *Tahdhīb*, VI, 84–85.

and good]. If not, then return me your letter of appointment."
'Umar b. Sa'd said that he would go when he saw that Ibn Ziyād
was insisting. He went with four thousand men and reached al-
Ḥusayn the day after al-Ḥusayn had stopped at Nīnawā.

'Umar b. Sa'd wanted to send 'Azrah b. Qays al-Aḥmasī to al-
Ḥusayn. He said, "Go to al-Ḥusayn and ask him what brought
him; ask him what he wants." 'Azrah was one of those who had
written to al-Ḥusayn; he was ashamed to go to him. The same
was the case with all the leaders who had written to him; all
of them refused and were unwilling. Kathīr b. 'Abdallāh al-
Sha'bī[364] stood up—he was a brave horseman who was never
daunted by anything and said, "I will go to him. By God! If you
wish, I will finish him." 'Umar said, "I don't want you to finish
him, but go to him and ask him what has brought him here." As
Kathīr was approaching him, Abū Thumāmah al-Ṣā'idī saw him
and said to al-Ḥusayn, "May God make you prosperous, Abū
'Abdallāh, the wickedest man on earth, the one who has shed the
most blood and the boldest of them all in attack is coming toward
you." Then Abū Thumāmah stood facing him and said, "Put
down your sword." He replied, "No, by God! There is no reason
for that, for I am only a messenger. If you will listen to me, I will
tell you what I have been sent to ask you. If you refuse, I will go
away." Abū Thumāmah said, "I will hold the hilt of your sword,
and you can say what you need to." He retorted, "No, by God!
You will not touch it." Abū Thumāmah said, "Then tell me what
you have brought, and I will inform al-Ḥusayn for you. But I will
not let you go near him, for you are a charlatan." They both
cursed each other. Kathīr went back to 'Umar b. Sa'd and gave
him a report about what occurred.

'Umar summoned Qurrah b. Qays al-Ḥanẓalī[365] and said to
him, "Shame upon you Qurrah! Go and meet al-Ḥusayn and ask
him what brought him and what he wants." Qurrah began to
approach him. When al-Ḥusayn saw him approaching, he asked,
"Do you know that man?" Ḥabīb b. Muẓāhir replied, "Yes, he is

[310]

---

364. Kathīr b. 'Abdallāh al-Sha'bī only seems to have been mentioned at the
Battle of Karbalā'.
365. Qurrah b. Qays al-Ḥanẓalī only seems to have been mentioned at the
Battle of Karbalā'.

from the Ḥanẓalah clan of Tamīm. He is the son of our sister. I used to know him as a man of sound judgment. I would not have thought that he would be present at this scene." He came and greeted al-Ḥusayn. Then he informed him of ʿUmar b. Saʿd's message. Al-Ḥusayn said, "The people of this town of yours wrote to me that I should come. However, if they have now come to dislike me, then I will leave them." Ḥabīb b. Muẓāhir said "Shame upon you Qurrah b. Qays! How could you return to those unjust men. Support this man through whose fathers God granted you and us favor." Qurrah replied, "I will return to my leader with the answer to his message and then I will reflect what to do." He went back to ʿUmar b. Saʿd and gave him his report. ʿUmar said, "I hope that God will spare me from making war on him and fighting against him."

[311]

According to Hishām (b. Muḥammad al-Kalbī)—Abū Mikhnaf—al-Naḍr b. Ṣāliḥ b. Ḥabīb b. Zuhayr al-ʿAbsī[366]—Hassān b. Fāʾid b. Bakr al-ʿAbsī:[367] I testify that the letter of ʿUmar came to ʿUbaydallāh b. Ziyād while I was with him. It was as follows: "In the name of God, the Merciful, the Compassionate.... From where I positioned myself near al-Ḥusayn, I sent my messenger to him and asked him what brought him and what he wanted. He answered: 'The people of this land wrote to me and their messengers came to me asking me to come; I have done so. However, since they have come to dislike me and had new ideas other than what their messengers brought to me, I will go away from them.'"

When the letter was read to Ibn Ziyād, he recited:

Now when our claws cling to him,
    he hopes for escape but now is not the time for escape.[368]

He wrote to ʿUmar b. Saʿd: "In the name of God, the Merciful, the Compassionate...your letter has reached me and I have understood what you have mentioned. Offer al-Ḥusayn the opportunity for him and all his followers to give the oath of al-

---

366. Al-Naḍr b. Ṣāliḥ b. Ḥabīb b. Zuhayr al-ʿAbsī was an otherwise unknown authority of Abū Mikhnaf. See Sezgin, *Abū Miḥnaf*, 214.

367. Ḥassān b. Fāʾid b. Bakr al-ʿAbsī was a traditionist who reported traditions from ʿUmar b. al-Khaṭṭāb. He must have lived until the end of the first (seventh) century. See Sezgin, *Abū Miḥnaf*, 215.

368. A similar verse is quoted by Balādhurī. See *Ansāb*, II/2, 177.

legiance to Yazīd. If he does that, we will then see what our judgment will be." When the answer reached 'Umar b. Sa'd, he said "I was afraid that 'Ubaydallāh would not go easy."

According to Abū Mikhnaf—Sulaymān b. Abī Rāshid—Ḥumayd b. Muslim al-Azdī:[369] There came [another] letter from Ibn Ziyād: "...Prevent al-Ḥusayn and his followers from getting water. Do not let them taste a drop of it just as was done with the pious, chaste and wronged caliph 'Uthmān b. 'Affān." 'Umar b. Sa'd sent 'Amr b. al-Ḥajjāj with five hundred horsemen to take position along the river and to prevent al-Ḥusayn and his followers from getting a drop of water. That was three days before the battle against al-Ḥusayn.

'Abdallāh b. Ḥusayn al-Azdī,[370] who was numbered among Bajīlah, called out to him, "Ḥusayn, don't you see that the water is as hard to get as the middle of heaven! By God! You will not taste a drop of it until you die of thirst." Al-Ḥusayn cried out, "O God! Make him die of thirst and never forgive him."

Ḥumayd b. Muslim reported: By God! Later I visited him when he was ill. By God, other than Whom there is no deity! I saw him drinking water without being able to quench his thirst, and then he vomited. Again he drank water without being able to quench his thirst. This went on until his breath, that is his life, came to an end.

When the thirst of al-Ḥusayn and his followers became severe, al-Ḥusayn summoned his brother al-'Abbās b. 'Alī b. Abī Ṭālib[371] and sent him together with thirty horsemen and twenty foot soldiers. He sent them with twenty waterskins. They went forward to approach the watering place by night. At their head with the standard was Nāfi' b. Hilāl al-Jamalī. 'Amr b. al-Ḥajjāj al-Zubaydī cried out, "Who goes there? What have you come for?" Nāfi'[372] replied, "We have come to drink from this water that you

[312]

[313]

---

369. Ḥumayd b. Muslim al-Azdī was an eyewitness of the events; he later supported those who demanded vengeance for al-Ḥusayn. See Wellhausen, *Religio-Political*, 124.

370. 'Abdallāh b. Ḥusayn al-Azdī was not mentioned elsewhere but for this battle and his own death.

371. Al-'Abbās b. 'Alī b. Abī Ṭālib was the half-brother of al-Ḥusayn; his mother was Umm al-Banīn. See p. 111, below.

372. Balādhurī supplies Nāfi''s name. See *Ansāb*, II/2, 181.

are trying to keep from us." He said, "Drink to your health." Nāfiʿ said, "No, by God! I will not drink a drop of it while Husayn is thirsty and those of his followers whom you can see." Then the rest reached him. ʿAmr b. al-Hajjāj said, "There is no way for these men to get water. We have only been stationed in this place to prevent them from getting water." When the rest of his followers reached Nāfiʿ, he ordered the foot soldiers, "Fill your waterskins." The foot soldiers hurried and filled their waterskins. ʿAmr b. al-Hajjāj and his followers rose against them. Al-ʿAbbās b. ʿAlī and Nāfiʿ b. Hilāl attacked them and kept them back. They went to the foot soldiers and told them to go while they remained behind to protect them. ʿAmr b. al-Hajjāj and his followers turned toward them, and they charged at each other for a short time. A man from the tribe of Sudda', who was a follower of ʿAmr b. al-Hajjāj, was stabbed by Nāfiʿ b. Hilāl. He thought it was nothing, but later complications developed; he died of his wound. The followers of Husayn returned with the waterskins and took them to him.

According to Abū Mikhnaf—Abū Janāb—Hāni' b. Thubayt al-Hadramī,[373] who was an eyewitness of the killing of al-Husayn: Al-Husayn sent ʿAmr b. Qarazah b. Kaʿb al-Ansārī[374] to ʿUmar b. Saʿd [to say] that he wanted to meet him at night between the two camps. ʿUmar b. Saʿd came out with about twenty horsemen as did Husayn. When they met, Husayn ordered his followers to go aside and so did ʿUmar b. Saʿd. We stayed away from them insofar as we could not hear their voices and their conversation. They talked together for a long time until a [great] part of the night had gone. Then each of them went back to his own camp with his followers. The people made guesses about what had occurred between them. The suggestion that they put forward [314] was that Husayn had said to ʿUmar b. Saʿd, "Come with me to Yazīd b. Muʿāwiyah, and let us leave the two armies." ʿUmar replied, "Then my house will be destroyed." Al-Husayn said, "I will rebuild it for you." ʿUmar answered, "Then my estates will

---

373. Hāni' b. Thubayt al-Hadramī was a participant in the Battle of Karbalā' against al-Husayn but his name does not occur anywhere else.

374. ʿAmr b. Qarazah b. Kaʿb al-Ansārī fought and died with al-Husayn, but he is not mentioned elsewhere. See p. 135, below.

be seized." Al-Ḥusayn said, "I will give you better property than that in Ḥijāz." However, ʿUmar was still unwilling to go with Ḥusayn. The people talked about this event; it spread among the people without their ever having heard the conversation or knowing anything about what actually was discussed.

According to Abū Mikhnaf—al-Mujālid b. Saʿīd, al-Ṣaqʿab b. Zuhayr al-Azdī and others—which is what the majority (jamāʿah) of the transmitters hold: Al-Ḥusayn said, "Choose one of three courses for me: First, that I should return to the place from which I came; second, that I should put my hand in the hand of Yazīd b. Muʿāwiyah, and he should make his own judgment about what is between him and me; or, third, that you should send me to any one of the Muslims' border stations you wish, where I can be one of its inhabitants with the same rights and responsibilities."

According to Abū Mikhnaf—ʿAbd al-Raḥmān b. Jundab—ʿUqbah b. Simʿān: I accompanied Ḥusayn [all the time]. I left Medina for Mecca with him, and Mecca for Iraq. I did not leave him until he died. There was no one who addressed a word to him, either in Medina, in Mecca, on the road, in Iraq, or in the camp, until the day of his death, without my hearing the conversation. By God! He neither gave the promise, which the people claim to recall when they allege that he would put his hand in the hand of Yazīd b. Muʿāwiyah or that they should send him to any one of the Muslims' border stations. Rather he said, "Leave me, and I will travel this broad land so that we may see how the people's affair develops."

According to Abū Mikhnaf—al-Mujālid b. Saʿīd al-Hamdānī and al-Ṣaqʿab b. Zuhayr: The two men—Ḥusayn and ʿUmar b. Saʿd—met three or four times. Then ʿUmar b. Saʿd wrote to ʿUbaydallāh b. Ziyād: "...God has extinguished hatred, brought about unity of opinion, and set right the affairs of the community. This man, al-Ḥusayn, has given me a promise that he will return to his former place; either we can send him to one of the border outposts—he will become like any of the Muslims with the same rights and duties as they—or he will go to Yazīd, the Commander of the Faithful, offer him his hand, and see his view with regard to the differences between them. This will satisfy you, and benefit the community." [315]

When ʿUbaydallāh read the letter, he said, "This is the letter of a sincere man to his governor, one who is anxious for his people. Yes, I accept." However, Shamir b. Dhī al-Jawshan jumped up and said, "Are you going to accept this from him when he has encamped nearby on your land? By God! If he left your land, without putting his hand in yours, he would be in a position of power and strength and you would be in a position of weakness and impotence. Do not give this concession, for it would be a mark of weakness. Rather let him and his followers submit to your authority. Then if you punish them, you are the one who administers the punishment. You have the right, however, to forgive them. By God! I have been told that Ḥusayn and ʿUmar b. Saʿd have been sitting between the camps talking all the night." Ibn Ziyād said, "What you have suggested is good. Your view is correct."

According to Abū Mikhnaf—Sulaymān b. Abī Rāshid—Ḥumayd b. Muslim: ʿUbaydallāh b. Ziyād summoned Shamir b. Dhī al-Jawshan and said, "Take this message to ʿUmar b. Saʿd and let him offer al-Ḥusayn and his followers the option of submitting to my authority. If they agree, let him send them to me in peace. If they refuse, he should fight them. If ʿUmar b. Saʿd acts according to my instructions, then heed him and obey him. However, if he refuses to fight them, then you are the commander of the people; attack Ḥusayn, cut his head off and send it to me."

According to Abū Mikhnaf—Abū Janāb al-Kalbī: Then ʿUbaydallāh b. Ziyād wrote to ʿUmar b. Saʿd: "...I did not send you to Ḥusayn to hold off from fighting him, to give him time, to promise him peace and preservation, or to be an intercessor on his behalf with me. Therefore, see that, if Ḥusayn and his followers submit to my authority and surrender, you can send them to me in peace. If they refuse, then march against them to kill and disfigure them, for they deserve that. If Ḥusayn is killed, make the horses trample on his chest and back, for he is a disobedient rebel, an evil man who splits the community. Not that I think he would feel any harm once he is dead, but I have vowed to do this to him if I killed him. If you carry out our order concerning him, we will give you the reward due to one who heeds and obeys. If you refuse, then withdraw from our command and our army. Leave the army to Shamir b. Dhī al-Jawshan. We have given him our authority. Peace be with you."

According to Abū Mikhnaf—al-Ḥārith b. Ḥaṣīrah[375]—ʿAbd-allāh b. Sharīk al-ʿĀmirī:[376] When Shamir b. Dhī al-Jawshan took hold of the letter, he rose to go with ʿAbdallāh b. Abī Muḥill. The latter's paternal aunt was Umm al-Banīn bt. Ḥizām,[377] who had been married to ʿAlī b. Abī Ṭālib and who had borne him al-ʿAbbās, Jaʿfar and ʿUthmān. ʿAbdallāh b. Abī Muḥill b. Ḥizām b. Khālid b. Rabīʿah b. al-Waḥīd b. Kaʿb b. ʿĀmir b. Kilāb had said to ʿUbaydallāh b. Ziyād, "May God make the governor prosperous. The sons of our sister are with al-Ḥusayn. If you would consider it good, write that they be given a guarantee of safe-conduct. Please, do so." He said that he would be happy to do so. He ordered his secretary to write a guarantee of safe-conduct for them. It was sent by ʿAbdallāh b. Abī Muḥill with his mawlā, who was called Kuzmān.[378] When the latter approached them, he called to them and said, "Here is a guarantee of safe-conduct that your maternal uncle has sent." The young men replied, "Give our greetings to our uncle and tell him that we have no need of your guarantee of safe-conduct, for God's guarantee of safe-conduct is better than the guarantee of safe-conduct of Ibn Sumayyah."

[317]

Shamir b. Dhī al-Jawshan brought ʿUbaydallāh b. Ziyād's letter to ʿUmar b. Saʿd. After he had brought it and read it, ʿUmar said to him, "Shame upon you! What is this to you? May your home never be close! May God make abominable what you have brought to me! By God! I think that you must have personally stopped him from accepting what I had written to him and ruined for us a matter that we had hoped to set right. By God! Ḥusayn will not surrender, for there is a proud spirit in his body." Shamir demanded, "Tell me what you are going to do. Are you going to carry out the governor's command and kill his enemy? Other-

---

375. Al-Ḥārith b. Ḥaṣīrah was a traditionist from al-Kūfah. He is said to be a follower of the sixth Imām Jaʿfar al-Ṣādiq; he died in 148 (765). See Sezgin, *Abū Mihnaf*, 205.

376. ʿAbdallāh b. Sharīk al-ʿĀmirī was Shīʿite traditionist, who became a follower of al-Mukhtār; he died in the first half of the second (eighth) century. See Sezgin, *Abū Mihnaf*, 205.

377. Umm al-Banīn was a wife of ʿAlī. Her three sons went with al-Ḥusayn and were killed at Karbalāʾ. Her nephew ʿAbdallāh b. Abī Muḥill fought for ʿUbaydallāh b. Ziyād.

378. Kuzmān is not mentioned elsewhere.

wise, leave the command of the army to me." He answered, "No, there will be no advantage to you. I will carry that out instead of you." Shamir told him, "Go ahead, you lead the men."

ʿUmar b. Saʿd prepared to do battle with al-Ḥusayn on the evening of Thursday, 9 al-Muḥarram (October 9).[379] Shamir went out and stood in front of the followers of al-Ḥusayn calling out, "Where are our sister's sons?" Al-ʿAbbās, Jaʿfar and ʿUthmān, sons of ʿAlī b. Abī Ṭālib, came forward and demanded, "What is your business? What do you want?" Shamir said, "Sons of my sister, you are given a guarantee of safe-conduct." The young men replied, "God curse you and curse the guarantee of safe-conduct! If you are our uncle, how could you offer us a guarantee of safe-conduct while the son of the Apostle of God has no guarantee of safe-conduct?" ʿUmar b. Saʿd called out, "Cavalry of God, mount

[318]   with good hope." He rode among the people and he approached [the supporters of al-Ḥusayn] after the afternoon (ʿaṣr) prayer.

Meanwhile, Ḥusayn was sitting in front of his tent leaning on his sword when he nodded off with his head on his knees. His sister Zaynab heard the clamor. She came up to him and said, "My brother, don't you hear the sounds that are getting nearer?" As he raised his head, he said, "I have just seen the Apostle of God in my sleep. He said to me: 'You are coming to us.'" His sister struck at her face and cried out, "O Woe to me!" He told her, "Woe is not for you, sister. Be quiet, may God have mercy on you."

Al-ʿAbbās b. ʿAlī called out, "Brother, the people have advanced against you." Al-Ḥusayn rose and said, "Al-ʿAbbās, you, brother, [I would give] my soul for you. Ride out yourself to meet them. Talk to them about what their views are and what has changed them.[380] Ask them about what has brought them against us." Al-ʿAbbās went toward them with about twenty horsemen, among whom was Zuhayr b. al-Qayn and Ḥabīb b. Muẓāhir. Al-ʿAbbās asked them, "What has changed your view? What are you intending?" They answered, "The command of the governor has

---

379. Actually a Tuesday.

380. The Arabic *mā badā lakum* lit. means "what [different thing] has seemed good to them." The term is used by Shīʿite theologians for God's changing his mind. See *EI²*, s.v. *Badāʾ*.

arrived that we should offer you the option of submitting to his authority, or we should attack you." Al-ʿAbbās said, "Do not hurry to do anything until I have gone back to Abū ʿAbdallāh (i.e., al-Ḥusayn) and told him what you have said." They stopped where they were and told him, "Go to him and inform him! Bring back what he says."

Al-ʿAbbās went galloping back to al-Ḥusayn to give him the information, while his companions stood speaking to the people. Ḥabīb b. Muẓāhir said to Zuhayr b. al-Qayn, "If you wish, you speak to the people, or if you wish, I will speak to them." Zuhayr told him, "You began this. So you be the one to speak to them." Ḥabīb b. Muẓāhir, then, addressed them, "How wretched will it be in the eyes of God for people who come to Him after having killed the offspring of His Prophet, his progeny, his family (ahl baytihi), and the devoted worshipers among the people of this town, who strive in prayer until the close of night and who men- [319] tion God frequently." ʿAzrah b. Qays retorted, "You ascribe as much purity to your soul as you can." Zuhayr called to him, "ʿAzrah, God is the one Who purified and guided that soul. Fear God, ʿAzrah, I am one of those who give you sincere advice. ʿAzrah, I adjure you before God not to be one of those who give help to those who have gone astray or kill pure souls." He replied, "Zuhayr, according to us you were not from the Shīʿah of this family (bayt). You used to be a supporter of the party of ʿUthmān." Zuhayr said, "Aren't you presuming from my position that I am one of them? By God! I did not ever write to him; I did not ever send messengers to him; I did not ever promise him my help. However, the road brought us together. When I saw him, I was reminded by him of the Apostle of God and of his position with regard to the Apostle of God. I knew his enemies and your party whom he was going toward. Then, I saw that it was right that I should help him, be in his party, and put my life forward to protect his because of the truth of God and the truth of His Apostle, which you have abandoned."

Al-ʿAbbās b. ʿAlī came galloping back to them. He said, "Fellows, Abū ʿAbdallāh (i.e., al-Ḥusayn) asks you to go back this evening so that he can consider the matter. For this is a matter in which no discussion between you and him has taken place. In the morning, we shall meet, God willing. Either we will be satisfied and then we will accept this demand which you are asking for and offering; or we will be unwilling and will reject it." Al-Ḥusayn only intended by this explanation to keep them off him for that evening in order that he might give orders concerning his affairs and advise his family.

When al-ʿAbbās b. ʿAlī had brought them that reply, ʿUmar b. Saʿd asked, "What do you think, Shamir?" He replied, "What do you think yourself? You are the general, and the decision is yours." ʿUmar said, "I wish that I wasn't." Then he went to the people and asked, "What do you think?" ʿAmr b. al-Ḥajjāj b. Salamah al-Zubaydī exclaimed, "Glory be to God! If they were from al-Daylam and they asked you for this postponement, you would have to grant it to them." Qays b. al-Ashʿath urged, "Yes, give them what they demand. Then, by my life, let morning be the time for you to fight." ʿUmar b. Saʿd said, "By God! Even if I knew that they would do that, I would not have postponed the fight tonight."

When al-ʿAbbās had brought back to Ḥusayn the proposal of ʿUmar b. Saʿd, al-Ḥusayn had said, "Go back to them. If you can, delay them until the morning and keep them away from us during this evening. Then, perhaps, we may be able to pray to our Lord during the night, to call upon Him and seek his forgiveness. He knows that I have always loved His prayer, the recitation of His book, making many invocations to Him, and seeking His forgiveness."

According to Abū Mikhnaf—al-Ḥārith b. Ḥaṣīrah—ʿAbdallāh b. Sharīk al-ʿAmirī—ʿAlī b. al-Ḥusayn: A messenger from ʿUmar b. Saʿd came to us. He stood where his voice could be heard and he said, "We will grant you a delay until tomorrow. Then, if you surrender, we will send you to our governor ʿUbaydallāh b. Ziyād but if you refuse we will not leave you."

According to Abū Mikhnaf—ʿAbdallāh b. ʿĀṣim al-Fāʾishī[381]—al-Ḍaḥḥāk b. ʿAbdallāh al-Mishraqī,[382] (Mishraq) being a clan of

[320]

---

381. ʿAbdallāh b. ʿĀṣim al-Fāʾishī was an unknown authority of Abū Mikhnaf's, who cites him several more times in his account of the martyrdom of al-Ḥusayn. See Sezgin, *Abū Miḥnaf*, 192.

382. Al-Ḍaḥḥāk b. ʿAbdallāh al-Mishraqī was an eyewitness of the events at Karbalāʾ; he only left al-Ḥusayn at the end. See Sezgin, *Abū Miḥnaf*, 192, 200–1; and pp. 148–49, below.

Hamdān, reported: Al-Ḥusayn gathered his followers around him.

According to Abū Mikhnaf—al-Ḥārith b. Ḥaṣīrah—ʿAbdallāh b. Sharīk al-ʿĀmirī—ʿAlī b. al-Ḥusayn and al-Ḍaḥḥak b. ʿAbdallāh: Al-Ḥusayn gathered his followers after ʿUmar b. Saʿd had withdrawn, which was toward evening.

According to ʿAlī b. al-Ḥusayn: I went near to hear what he would say to them even though at that time I was sick. I heard my father say to his followers, "I glorify God, the Blessed and Exalted, with the most perfect glorification and I praise Him in happiness and misfortune. O God, I praise You for blessing us with prophethood, teaching us the Qurʾān and making us understand the religion. You have given us ears, eyes, and hearts. You have not made us be among the polytheists. I know of no followers more fitting and more virtuous than my followers, nor of any family (ahl al-bayt) more pious and more caring about family relationships than my family. May God reward you well on my behalf. Indeed, I think that our final day will come tomorrow through these enemies. I have thought about you. All, go away with the absolution from your oath, for there will be no obligation on you from me. This is a night that will give cover to you with its darkness. Use it as a camel to ride away through it." [321]

According to Abū Mikhnaf—ʿAbdallāh b. ʿĀṣim al-Fāʾishī, Fāʾish is a clan of Hamdān—al-Ḍaḥḥāk b. ʿAbdallāh al-Mishraqī: Malik b. al-Naḍr al-Arḥabī[383] and I went up to al-Ḥusayn. We greeted him and then we sat down with him. He returned our greetings and welcomed us. He asked us why we had come to him. We answered, "We have come to you to greet you, to ask God's safety for you, to establish a relationship with you, and to give you news of the people. We tell you that they have determined to fight you, so reconsider your situation." He replied, "God is sufficient for me. How excellent a guardian He is!" So we kept his pledge; we greeted him and we prayed to God for him. But then he asked, "What is stopping you from helping me?" Mālik b. al-Naḍr said, "I have debts and a family." I said, "I also have debts and a family, but if you would give me your permission to go when I do not see any other fighter, I will fight for you as

---

383. Mālik b. al-Nadr al-Arḥabī is not mentioned elsewhere.

long as it is of benefit to you and protects you." He answered, "You have my permission." And so I stayed with him.

At night al-Ḥusayn said, "This night will give cover to you with its darkness. Use it as a camel to ride away through it. Every one of you take the hand of a man from my family. Then scatter in your lands of the Sawād[384] and your towns until God relieves you. The people only want me. If they find me, they will cease searching for anyone else."

[322]

His brothers and sons, the sons of his brother and the two sons of ʿAbdallāh b. Jaʿfar said, "Why should we do that? Is it in order to remain alive after you? May God never see us do that." Al-ʿAbbās b. ʿAlī was the first of them to make this declaration. Then they declared this or something like it. Al-Ḥusayn said, "Sons of ʿAqīl, by losing Muslim enough of your family has been killed. So go away as I have permitted you." They replied, "What would the people say? They would say that we deserted our shaykh, our leader, our cousins and the best of uncles; that we had not shot any arrows alongside them; that we had not thrust any spears alongside them; that we had not struck any swords alongside them; and that we do not know what they did. No, by God! We will not do that. Rather we will offer for your safety our lives, property, and families. We will fight with you until we reach your destination. How abominable is life after you!"

According to Abū Mikhnaf—ʿAbdallāh b. ʿĀṣim (al-Fāʾishī)—al-Ḍaḥḥāk b. ʿAbdallāh al-Mishraqī: Then Muslim b. ʿAwsajah al-Asadī arose and spoke, "Could we leave you alone? How should we excuse ourselves before God concerning doing our duty to you? By God! Not before I thrust with my spear until I break it in their chests. Not before I strike them with my sword as long as its hilt is in my hand. I will not leave you. If I have no weapon to fight them with, I will throw stones at them to defend you until I die with you."

Then Saʿīd b. ʿAbdallāh Ḥanafī[385] said, "By God! We will never leave you until God knows that we have upheld the honor of the

---

384. The Sawād stretched from the head of the Persian Gulf to Mosul in the north and from the border of the Syrian-Iraqi desert to Ḥulwān in the east. See Shaban, *Islamic History*, I, 46.

385. Text erroneously gives Saʿd b. ʿAbdallāh; see *Addenda et Emendanda*, DCLV.

absent Apostle of God in you. By God! If I knew that I would die, and then be revived, and then burnt alive, and then scattered, and that that would be done to me seventy times, I would never leave you until I met my death in defense of you. So how could I not do it when there can only be one death, which is a great blessing that can never be rejected?" [323]

Zuhayr b. al-Qayn spoke, "By God! I would prefer to be killed and then recalled to life, and then be killed a thousand times in this manner, and that through this death I should protect your life and the lives of these young men of your family."

All his followers spoke in similar vein, one after the other. They said, "By God! We will not leave you. Rather our lives will be sacrificed for you; we will protect you with our necks, our heads and our hands. If we are killed, we will have fulfilled and accomplished what we promised."

According to Abū Mikhnaf—al-Ḥārith b. Ka'b and Abū al-Ḍaḥḥāk[386]—'Alī b. al-Ḥusayn b. 'Alī: I was sitting on that evening before the morning in which my father was killed; with me was my aunt, Zaynab, who was nursing me, when my father retired with his followers into his tent. With him was Ḥuwayy,[387] the mawlā of Abū Dharr al-Ghifārī,[388] who was preparing his sword and putting it right. My father recited:

Time, shame on you as a friend!
     At the day's dawning and the sun's setting,
How many a companion or seeker will be a corpse!
     Time will not be satisfied with my substitute.
The matter will rest with the Mighty One,
     and every living creature will have to journey along the
     path.[389]

---

386. Abū al-Ḍaḥḥāk was a traditionist who reported from Abū Hurayrah. He died in 110 (729). See Sezgin, *Abū Miḥnaf*, 188.

387. Ḥuwayy was not mentioned elsewhere.

388. Abū Dharr al-Ghifārī was an early Companion of the Prophet, who came to be regarded as an ascetic. The Shī'ah have a very high regard for him. He was exiled to al-Rabadhah by 'Uthmān where he died in 32 (652–53). See *EI*[2], s.v. Abū Dharr.

389. These verses are also found in Balādhurī, *Ansāb*, II/2, 185, and al-Ya'qūbī, *Ta'rīkh*, II, 230.

He repeated it twice or three times so that I understood it and realized what he meant. Tears choked me, and I pushed them back. I kept silent and knew that tribulation had come upon us. As for my aunt, she heard what I heard, but she is a woman, and weakness and grief are the [qualities] of women; she could not control herself. She jumped up, tearing at her clothes. Unveiled she went to him. She said to him, "I will lose a brother. Would that death had deprived me of life today! My mother Fāṭimah is dead, and my father ʿAlī, and my brother al-Ḥasan. O! You are the successor (khalīfah) of those who have passed away and the guardian of those who remain!" Al-Ḥusayn said to her as he looked at her, "O sister! Don't let Satan take away your forbearance." She replied, "By my father and mother, O Abū ʿAbdallāh (i.e., al-Ḥusayn)! You have exposed yourself to death. May God accept my life for yours!" Choking back his grief and with his eyes full of tears, he said, "If the sand grouse are left at night, they will sleep."[390] She lamented, "O my grief! Your life will be violently wrenched from you, and that is more wounding to my heart and harsher to my soul." She struck at her face and bent down to her dress and tore it. Then she fell down in a faint. Al-Ḥusayn got up and bathed her face with water. Then he said to her, "Sister, fear God and take comfort in the consolation of God. Know that the people of the earth will die and the inhabitants of heaven will not continue to exist forever, '...for everything will be destroyed except the face of God,'[391] Who created earth by His power, Who sends forth creatures and causes them to return, Who is unique and alone. My father was better than I, my mother was better than I, and my brother was better than I. I and every Muslim have an ideal model in the Apostle of God." By this and the like he tried to console her and he said, "Sister, I swear to you—so keep my oath—that you must not tear your clothes, nor scratch your face, nor cry out with grief and loss when I am destroyed." Then he brought her and made her sit with me. He went out to his followers and ordered them to bring their tents closer together

[324]

---

390. An Arabic proverb meaning that when one is aroused to action, then one must allow this arousal to take effect. The sand grouse got all its water and food for its young at night. See Ibn Manẓūr, Lisān, s.v. qṭw.

391. Qurʾān, 28:88.

so that the tent pegs came within the area of each other's tents, and so that if they remained among their tents, the enemy could only approach them from one side.

According to Abū Mikhnaf—'Abdallāh b. 'Āṣim (al-Fā'ishī)—al-Daḥḥāk b. 'Abdallāh al-Mishraqī: When evening came, Ḥusayn and his followers spent the whole night in performing the prayer, in calling on God's forgiveness and in making invocations and humble entreaties. Some of their cavalry kept passing us to keep watch on us. Ḥusayn, himself, recited, "Let not those who disbelieve think that our giving them a delay is better for their souls. We give them a delay only that they might increase their wickedness. They shall have disgraceful torture. God does not leave the believers in the situation you are in until he has made the evil distinct from the good."[392] One of those horsemen, who was keeping watch over us, heard Ḥusayn. He cried out, "By the Lord of the Ka'bah! We are the good, we have been distinguished from you." I recognized him and I asked Burayr b. Ḥuḍayr[393] whether he knew that man. He said that he did not. I told him, "That is Abū Ḥarb al-Sabī'ī 'Abdallāh b. Shahr.[394] He is given to amusement and laughter. Yet he was honest, brave, and ruthless. Sa'īd b. Qays[395] had occasionally imprisoned him for criminal acts." Burayr b. Ḥuḍayr cried out, "O terrible sinner! Would God make you one of the good?" He shouted back, "Who are you?" Burayr said, "I am Burayr b. Ḥuḍayr." He replied, "We belong to God. It grieves me that you are coming to a bad end, Burayr." Burayr retorted, "Are you ready to repent to God for your terrible sins, Abū Ḥarb? By God! We are the good and you are the evil." Burayr added, "I am a witness of that." I (i.e., al-Mishraqī) called out to him, "Woe upon you! Doesn't knowledge help you?" He retorted, "May I offer my soul for you who used to be the drinking com-

[325]

---

392. Qur'ān, 3:178–79 (172–73).

393. This is the first time Burayr b. Ḥuḍayr has been mentioned. From his position among the followers of al-Ḥusayn, he seems to have been a leading member of the Kūfan Shī'ah. He died fighting for al-Ḥusayn. See pp. 132–33 below.

394. 'Abdallāh b. Shahr is not mentioned elsewhere.

395. Sa'īd b. Qays was a leader of Hamdān; formerly he was governor of al-Rayy for 'Uthmān, fought for 'Alī at Ṣiffīn and was one of the witnesses of the arbitration document between 'Alī and Mu'āwiyah. See Ṭabarī, I, 2927 and 3337.

panion of Yazīd b. ʿUdhrah al-ʿAnzī[396] of the clan ʿAnz b. Wāʾil?" He said, "Here he is with me." The other answered, "May God show his disapproval of your views in every circumstance! You are stupid!" Then he withdrew from us. One of those who was in the cavalry guarding us was ʿAzrah b. Qays al-Aḥmasī, who was in charge of the cavalry.

After ʿUmar b. Saʿd had performed the morning prayer on Saturday—it is also reported that it was Friday[397]—the Day of ʿĀshūrāʾ, he came out with the people who were with him.

Al-Ḥusayn mobilized his followers after he had prayed the morning prayer with them. He had with him thirty-two horse-men and forty foot soldiers. He put Zuhayr b. al-Qayn in charge of his right wing and Ḥabīb b. Muẓāhir in charge of his left wing; he gave his standard to his brother, al-ʿAbbās b. ʿAlī. They positioned themselves with their tents at their rear. He ordered the firewood and cane that was behind the tents to be set on fire, fearing that his enemies would attack from the rear. Al-Ḥusayn had brought cane and firewood to lower ground behind them, which was like the bed of a stream. For some time during the night, they had dug it and made it like a ditch. Then they threw into the ditch the firewood and cane. They had said, "When they come against us to fight us, we will set fire to it so that we will not be attacked from behind; we can fight the people from one side." They did that and it was of some advantage to them.

According to Abū Mikhnaf—Fuḍayl b. Khadīj al-Kindī[398]—Muḥammad b. Bishr—ʿAmr al-Ḥaḍramī:[399] When ʿUmar b. Saʿd came out with the people, on that day ʿAbdallāh b. Zuhayr b. Sulaym al-Azdī[400] was in charge of the quarter of the people of Medina; ʿAbd al-Raḥmān b. Abī Sabrah al-Juʿfī[401] was in charge of the quarter of Asad and Madhḥij; Qays b. al-Ashʿath b. Qays was in charge of the quarter of Rabīʿah and Kindah; and al-Ḥurr

[326]

---

396. Yazīd b. ʿUdhrah al-ʿAnzī is not mentioned elsewhere.

397. Actually a Wednesday.

398. Fuḍayl b. Khadīj was a traditionist as well as being an authority of Abū Mikhnaf. See Sezgin, *Abū Miḥnaf*, 201–2.

399. ʿAmr al-Ḥaḍramī is not mentioned elsewhere.

400. ʿAbdallāh b. Zuhayr b. Sulaym al-Azdī is one of the leaders of Azd; he killed on the frontiers. See Ṭabarī, II, 1429.

401. ʿAbd al-Raḥmān b. Abī Sabrah al-Juʿfī is not mentioned elsewhere; however, he is obviously an influential tribal leader.

b. Yazīd al-Riyāḥī was in charge of the quarter of Tamīm and Hamdān. All these men were present at the killing of al-Ḥusayn. However, al-Ḥurr b. Yazīd went over to al-Ḥusayn and was killed with him. ʿUmar put ʿAmr b. al-Ḥajjāj al-Zubaydī in command of his right wing and Shamir b. Dhī al-Jawshan b. Shuraḥbīl b. al-Aʿwar b. ʿUmar b. Muʿāwiyah—he was al-Ḍibāb b. Kilāb—in command of his left wing. He put ʿAzrah b. Qays al-Aḥmasī in command of the cavalry and Shabath b. Ribʿī al-Yarbūʿī in command of the foot soldiers. He gave the standard to Dhuwayd, his mawlā.[402]

According to Abū Mikhnaf—ʿAmr b. Murrah al-Jamalī[403]— Abū Ṣāliḥ al-Ḥanafī,[404]—servant[405] of ʿAbd al-Raḥmān b. ʿAbd [327] Rabbih al-Anṣārī:[406] I was with my patron (mawlā) when the people were ready and began to move against al-Ḥusayn. Al-Ḥusayn ordered a tent to be erected and he ordered musk to be dissolved in a big bowl or dish. Then he went into that tent and was anointed with perfume.[407] My patron (mawlā), ʿAbd al-Raḥmān b. ʿAbd Rabbih, and Burayr b. Ḥuḍayr al-Hamdānī were shoulder to shoulder at the door of the tent; they both struggled to be the first to use the perfume after him. Burayr began to tease ʿAbd al-Raḥmān. He told him to leave him alone as this was not a time for empty words. Burayr replied, "By God! My people know that I have never loved empty words whether as a youth or as a mature man. Yet, by God, I feel happy for what we shall soon meet, for, by God, if all there is between us and the maidens of Paradise (al-ḥūr al-ʿayn) is that these people should come against us with their swords, then I want them to come against us with their swords."

When al-Ḥusayn had finished, we went in and anointed ourselves. Al-Ḥusayn mounted his animal and called for a copy of the Qurʾān, which he put in front of him. His followers fought

---

402. Dhuwayd is not mentioned elsewhere.
403. ʿAmr b. Murrah al-Jamalī is not mentioned elsewhere.
404. Abū Ṣāliḥ al-Ḥanafī is not mentioned elsewhere.
405. This servant is not identified.
406. ʿAbd al-Raḥmān b. ʿAbd Rabbih al-Anṣārī is not mentioned elsewhere.
407. Anointing with perfume is an indication that al-Ḥusayn was preparing for death. Corpses being prepared for burial are often anointed in this manner. See A. S. Tritton "Muslim Funeral Customs," *Bulletin of the School of Oriental Studies*, 1937–39, 653–61.

fiercely in front of him, and when I saw that the people (i.e., al-Ḥusayn's followers) were being killed, I slipped away and left them.

According to Abū Mikhnaf—one of his colleagues—Abū Khālid al-Kāhilī:[408] When the cavalry began to approach al-Ḥusayn, he raised his hands and said, "O God! It is You in Whom I trust amid all grief. You are my hope amid all distress. You are my trust and provision in everything that happens to me, no matter how much the heart may seem to weaken, ingenuity to fail, the friend to desert and the enemy to rejoice. I have received it through You and I complain to You out of my desire for You, You alone. May You dispel it for me and relieve me of it. You are the Master of all grace, the Possessor of all goodness and the Ultimate Resort of all desire."

[328] According to Abū Mikhnaf—ʿAbdallāh b. ʿĀṣim (al-Fāʾishī)—al-Ḍaḥḥāk al-Mishraqī: When they began to move toward us and saw the fire burning the firewood and cane, which we had lit so that they could not attack us from behind, one of them came galloping toward us on a horse, which was completely covered with armor. He did not address us until he had gone past our tents. Then he looked toward our tents, but he could not see anything except the fire blazing in the firewood. He began to ride back and he called out at the top of his voice, "Al-Ḥusayn, are you hurrying toward Hell-fire in this world before the Day of Resurrection?" Al-Ḥusayn asked, "Who is that? It is like Shamir b. Dhī al-Jawshan." They answered, "Yes, may God make you prosperous." He shouted at him, "Son of a goat herdess! You are more worthy to be burnt by that." Muslim b. ʿAwsajah said, "May I offer my soul for you, son of the Apostle of God, let me shoot at him. Now it is possible, for an arrow would not miss. He is a sinner and one of the great tyrants." Al-Ḥusayn replied, "Do not shoot at him, for I am unwilling to begin the fighting against them."

Al-Ḥusayn had a horse called Lāḥiq that his son ʿAlī b. al-Ḥusayn was riding. When the people began to come nearer to him, he called for his mount and mounted. Then he called out at

408. Abū Khālid al-Kāhilī is not mentioned elsewhere.

the top of his voice. So loud was the tone of his voice that most of the people heard, "People, listen to my words and do not hurry me so that I may remind you of the duties you have toward me and so that I may give you the reasons for my coming to you. If you accept my reasons, believe my words and give me justice, you will become happier through that, and you will not have any cause against me. If you do not accept my reasons and give me justice of your own accord as individuals, 'Then agree upon your affair and call your associates. Let not your affair be in darkness to you. Then carry it out against me and do not delay any further.'[409] 'Indeed my guardian is God, Who sent down the Book. He takes care of the righteous.'"[410]

When his sisters heard these words of his, they shrieked and wept, and his daughters cried and raised their voices. He sent his brother, al-'Abbās b. 'Alī, and his son, 'Alī, back to them. He told them both, "Quiet them, for, by my life, their weeping will be excessive." When the two had gone back to quiet them, al-Ḥusayn said, "May Ibn 'Abbās not perish." We think he only said that when their weeping was heard because Ibn 'Abbās had told him not to take them with him. When the women were silent, he praised and glorified God and mentioned what God is entitled to. He called for blessings on Muḥammad, on His angels and on the prophets. In that context, he mentioned what God knows and other matters that would be too numerous to mention here. By God! I have never heard a speaker, before or after him, more eloquent in his speech than he was. He said: "...Trace back my lineage and consider who I am. Then, look back at yourselves and remonstrate with yourselves. Consider whether it is right for you to kill me and desecrate my inviolability. Am I not the son of the daughter of your Prophet, the son of the executor of his will (*waṣī*)[411] and his cousin, the first of the believers in God and the man who [first] believed in what His Apostle brought from his Lord? Was not Ḥamzah, the lord of the martyrs,[412] my uncle? Was

[329]

---

409. Qur'ān, 10:71 (72).

410. Qur'ān, 7:196 (195).

411. The use of the term *waṣī* has specific implications for 'Alī's status as successor of the Prophet among the Shī'ah.

412. Ḥamzah was an uncle of the Prophet and hero of the early battles of the Prophet against the Meccans. See *EI*[2], s.v. Ḥamza b. 'Abd al-Muṭṭalib.

not Jaʿfar, who flies with two wings in heaven,[413] my uncle?
Have you not heard the words that circulate among you that the
Prophet of God said concerning myself and my brother: 'These
are the two lords of the youths of the inhabitants of heaven'?[414] If
you believe what I am saying—and it is the truth, for, by God, I
have never told a lie since I learned that God hated people who told
them and that those who opposed Him grieved Him.... If you
still regard me as a liar, then there are among you those who,
if you asked them, would tell you. Ask Jābir b. ʿAbdallāh al-
Anṣārī,[415] Abū Saʿīd al-Khudrī,[416] Sahl b. Saʿd al-Sāʿidī,[417] Zayd
b. Arqam[418] and Anas b. Mālik[419] to tell you that they heard these
words from the Apostle of God concerning myself and my brother.

[330]   Is this not sufficient to prevent your shedding my blood?"

Shamir b. Dhī al-Jawshan interrupted saying, "Consider me as
one who worships God very shakily on the edge, if I understand
what you say."[420] Ḥabīb b. Muẓāhir said, "I think that you worship God [very shakily] on seventy edges, for I testify that you are
truthful by saying that. You do not understand what he is saying,
for God has sealed your heart."

Al-Ḥusayn told them, "If you are in any doubt about this, do
you have the slightest doubt that I am the son of the daughter of
your Prophet? By God! There is no son of a prophet other than
me among you and among the other peoples from east to west.
Indeed, I am the son of your Prophet. Tell me, are you seeking
retribution from me for one of your dead whom I have killed, or
for property of yours that I have expropriated, or for a wound that

---

413. Jaʿfar b. Abī Ṭālib, brother of ʿAlī, was the person whom the Prophet dreamt
of as flying to heaven on two bloody wings amid a band of angels. See *EI²*, s.v.
Djaʿfar b. Abī Ṭālib.

414. See A. J. Wensinck, *Handbook of Early Muhammadan Traditions*, 94.

415. Jābir b. ʿAbdallāh al-Anṣārī was a Companion of the Prophet; he died
between 73 (692) and 78 (698). See Ibn Ḥajar, *Tahdhīb*, II, 42–43.

416. Abū Saʿīd al-Khudrī was a Companion of the Prophet, who died between
63 (682) and 74 (694). See Ibn Ḥajar, *Tahdhīb*, III, 479–80.

417. Sahl b. Saʿd al-Sāʿdī was a Companion of the Prophet, who died between
88 (707) and 91 (710). See Ibn Ḥajar, *Tahdhīb*, IV, 252–53.

418. Zayd b. Arqam was a Companion of the Prophet, who died in 68 (687–89).
See Ibn Saʿd, *Ṭabaqāt*, VI, 10.

419. Anas b. Mālik was a Companion of the Prophet, who died in 93 (711–12).
See Ibn Saʿd, *Ṭabaqāt*, VII/1, 10–16.

420. See Qurʾān, 22:11.

I have inflicted?" They did not say anything to him. Then he called, "Shabath b. Rib'ī, Ḥajjār b. Abjar, Qays b. al-Ash'ath,[421] Yazīd b. al-Ḥārith, didn't you write: 'The fruit has ripened; the Janāb has grown green; the waters have overflowed; you will come to an army which has been gathered for you, come'?" They said that they had not, and he declared, "Glory be to God! By God! Indeed, you did. People, since you dislike me, let me leave you for a place in the land where I may be safe." Qays b. al-Ash'ath asked, "Won't you submit to the authority of your kinsmen? They will always treat you as you would like. Nothing hateful will ever come to you from them." Al-Ḥusayn replied, "You are your brother's brother. Do you want the Banū Hāshim to seek vengeance from you for more than the blood of Muslim b. 'Aqīl? No, by God! I will neither give them my hand like a man who has been humiliated, nor will I flee like a slave.[422] Servants of God, 'I take refuge in my Lord and your Lord, from your stoning.'[423] 'I take refuge in my Lord and your Lord, from every haughty man who does not believe in the Day of Reckoning.'"[424] He made his mount kneel and ordered 'Uqbah b. Sim'ān to tie its reins. The Kūfans began to advance toward him.

According to Abū Mikhnaf—'Alī b. Ḥanẓalah b. As'ad al-Shāmī[425]—a man of his tribe who witnessed the killing of al-Ḥusayn at the time he was killed, whose name was Kathīr b. 'Abdallah al-Sha'bī: When we advanced toward al-Ḥusayn, Zuhayr b. al-Qayn came out toward us on his horse with a fine tail, carrying arms. He said, "People of al-Kūfah, here is a warning to you of God's punishment, a warning insofar as it is the duty of a Muslim to advise his brother Muslim—and we are still brothers in one religion and one faith as long as the sword does not strike between you and us. Therefore you are still appropriate persons to receive advice from us. When the sword strikes, the protection

[331]

---

421. Qays b. al-Ash'ath was not among those who wrote that letter to al-Ḥusayn. See pp. 24–26, above.

422. Emending *uqirru iqrār al-'abīd* to *afirru ifrār al-'abīd* as in Balādhurī, *Ansāb*, II/2, 188.

423. Qur'ān, 44:20 (19).

424. Qur'ān, 40:26 (27).

425. 'Alī b. Ḥanẓalah b. As'ad al-Shāmī was only used as an authority by Abū Mikhnaf for this one account. He seems to be otherwise unknown.

will be cut asunder. We will be a community, and you will be a community. God has tested us and you through the offspring of Muḥammad so that God may see what you and we are doing. We summon you to help them and to desert the tyrant, ʿUbaydallāh b. Ziyād. You will never attain anything from Yazīd and ʿUbaydallāh except evil through their rule; they will both poke out your eyes with hot irons, cut off your hands and legs, mutilate you and hang you on the trunks of palm trees; they will kill the ideal men among you and your Qurʾānic reciters (qurrāʾ), men like Ḥujr b. ʿAdī[426] and his followers, Hāniʾ b. ʿUrwah and others like him."

Then they cursed him and praised and prayed for ʿUbaydallāh b. Ziyād. They called out to Zuhayr, "By God! Soon we will kill your leader and those with him or we will send him and them peacefully to the governor, ʿUbaydallāh b. Ziyād." Zuhayr said to them, "Servants of God, the offspring of Fāṭimah, may God's happiness be hers, are more entitled to love and help than the son of Sumayyah. If you will not help them, then I seek refuge with God for you that you do not kill them. Do not prevent this man from going to his cousin, Yazīd b. Muʿāwiyah. By my life! Yazīd will be satisfied with your obedience without killing al-Ḥusayn." Shamir b. Dhī al-Jawshan yelled out as he shot an arrow at him, "Shut up! May God silence you by death, you have wearied us with your lengthy speech." Zuhayr retorted, "O son of one who urinates at both ends! I am not addressing you. You are merely an animal. By God! I doubt whether you understand two verses of the Book of God. Therefore I give you tidings of retribution on the Day of Resurrection and of dread torture." Shamir replied, "God will be the one who kills you and your master soon." Zuhayr answered, "Are you trying to terrify me with death? By God! What death has is preferable to me than living forever with you." Then he advanced toward the people, raising his voice and saying, "Servants of God, do not let this rude devil and his like seduce you from your religion. By God! The intercession of Muḥammad will not be given to a people who shed the blood of his offspring and his family (ahl al-bayt) and who kill those who aid them and

[332]

---

426. Ḥujr b. ʿAdī was a member of the Shīʿah, who led a revolt against Muʿā-wiyah b. Abī Sufyān in al-Kūfah in 51 (671); after this incident, he was executed. See Wellhausen, Religio-Political, 95–101.

protect their womenfolk." A man called out to him, "Abū ʿAbd-allāh (i.e., al-Ḥusayn) says: 'Come back. By my life! If the believer of the people of Pharaoh gave advice to his people and was eloquent in pleading, so have you given advice and spoken to these people, if there is any advantage in advice and information.'"

According to Abū Mikhnaf—Abū Janāb al-Kalbī—ʿAdī b. Ḥarmalah: When ʿUmar b. Saʿd began to march forward, al-Ḥurr b. Yazīd said to him, "May God make you prosperous, are you going to fight this man?" He replied, "Yes, by God! It will be a battle, the least part of which will be heads falling and severed hands flying." Al-Ḥurr said, "Aren't you satisfied with one of the three proposals that he offered you?" ʿUmar b. Saʿd answered, "If the matter rested with me, I would accept, but your governor has refused." Al-Ḥurr went and stood apart from the people. With him was a man from his tribe called Qurrah b. Qays. He said, "Qurrah, have you watered your horse today?" Qurrah said, "No." He said, "Don't you want to water it?" [333]

Qurrah reported later: I thought that al-Ḥurr was going to leave the battle and did not want to be present at it, but was unwilling that I should see him when he did that, for he was afraid that I might find fault with him for that. So I said, "I have not watered it and I am going to water it." Then I left him where he was. By God! If he had told me what he was intending to do, I would have gone with him to al-Ḥusayn.

He began to approach al-Ḥusayn little by little. One of his tribe called al-Muhājir b. Aws[427] asked him, "What do you want, Ibn Yazīd? Do you want to attack?" He was silent but a great shudder came over him. Al-Muhājir said, "By God! Ibn Yazīd, your behavior is suspicious. By God! I have never seen you act like this before. If I was asked who was the bravest of the Kūfans, I would not ignore you. What is this I see in you?" Al-Ḥurr answered, "By God! I am giving my soul the choice between heaven and the fire of hell. By God! I will not choose anything before heaven, even though I am cut to pieces and burnt."

He whipped his horse and joined Ḥusayn. He said, "May God accept my soul for you, son of the Apostle of God. I was your companion who stopped you from returning. I accompanied you

---

427. Al-Muhājir b. Aws was only mentioned with regard to the Battle of Karbalāʾ.

along the road and made you stop in this place. By Him other than Whom there is no deity! I did not think that the people would refuse to respond to what you have offered them and that they would ever come to this position with regard to you. I had said to myself: I do not care if I obey these people in some of their authority (*amr*) while they do not consider that I have discarded totally their obedience, for in the long run they will accept these proposals that Ḥusayn offers them. By God! If I had thought that they would not accept them from you, I would not have joined them against you. I have come repenting to my Lord for what I have done, and offering you my life as consolation so that I may die before you. Will you accept that as repentance from me?" Al-Ḥusayn replied, "Yes. God will accept your repentance and forgive you. What is your name?" He said, "I am al-Ḥurr b. Yazīd." Al-Ḥusayn said, "You are the free man (*al-ḥurr*) as your mother named you. You are a free man (*al-ḥurr*) in this world and the next, God willing. So dismount." He replied, "I would be better for you as a horseman than I would as a foot soldier. I will fight them on my horse for a while. Dismounting will be my ultimate end." Al-Ḥusayn said, "Do whatever you deem wise. May God grant you mercy."

[334]

He advanced in front of his followers and called out, "People, aren't you going to accept one of the three proposals that Ḥusayn proposed to you so that god may grant you release from making war against him and fighting him?" They answered, "The general here is ʿUmar b. Saʿd. Speak to him." He spoke to him in the same way as he had spoken to him before and in the same way as he had spoken to his followers. ʿUmar answered, "I am anxious. If I could find a way to do that, I would do it." Then al-Ḥurr said, "People of al-Kūfah, may your mothers be deprived of their sons and may tears come to their eyes. You summoned him. Then, when he had come to you, you handed him over. You claimed that you would fight with your own lives for him, and then you have begun to attack him in order to kill him. You have laid hold of his life; you have seized his throat; you have encircled him on every side in order to prevent his returning to God's broad land, where he may be secure and where his family (*ahl baytihi*) may be secure. He has come into your hands like a prisoner who no longer can attract benefit to himself and cannot secure himself against harm. You have prevented him, his womenfolk, his children, and his followers from the water of the flowing Euphrates, which Jews, Magians, and Christians may drink, and which the pigs and dogs of Sawād wallow in. Now they are likely to die of thirst. How wickedly you have treated the offspring of Muḥammad! May God not give you water to drink on the Day of Thirst, if you do not repent and do not desist from what you are set upon this day and this hour." Some of the foot soldiers attacked him by shooting arrows at him. He went and stood in front of al-Ḥusayn. [335]

According to Abū Mikhnaf—al-Ṣaʿqab b. Zuhayr and Sulaymān b. Abī Rāshid—Ḥumayd b. Muslim: ʿUmar b. Saʿd advanced toward them. Then he called out, "Dhuwayd, bring forward your standard." He brought it forward. ʿUmar put an arrow in his bow and let fly. He said, "Be witnesses that I was the first to shoot."

According to Abū Mikhnaf—Abū Janab al-Kalbī: One of our men called ʿAbdallāh b. ʿUmayr[428] of the Banū ʿUlaym[429] had settled in al-Kūfah and had taken a house beside the well of the clan of al-Jaʿd of Hamdān. With him was his wife who was from the clan of al-Namir b. Qāsiṭ[430] called Umm Wahb bt. ʿAbd.[431] He saw the people at al-Nukhaylah[432] being drawn up to be sent against al-Ḥusayn. He asked about them and was told, "They are being sent against Ḥusayn, son of Fāṭimah, the daughter of the Apostle of God." He said, "By God! I was anxious to make holy war (jihād) against the polytheists. I hope that making holy war against these people, who are attacking the son of the daughter of their Prophet, will be no less rewarded with God than His reward would be to me for making holy war against the polytheists." He went to his wife and told her about what he had heard, and he informed her of what he was intending to do. She said, "You are right. May God make you achieve the most wise of your affairs. Do it but take me with you." He went with her by night until he came to Ḥusayn and stayed with him.

---

428. ʿAbdallāh b. ʿUmayr was only mentioned with regard to the Battle of Karbalāʾ.

429. The Banū ʿUlaym were a clan of the tribe of Kalb. See Ṭabarī, II, 478.

430. Al-Namir b. Qāsiṭ was a clan of the tribe of Tamīm. See Ṭabarī, I, 3315.

431. Umm Wahb bt. ʿAbd is only mentioned with regard to the Battle of Karbalāʾ.

432. Al-Nukhaylah was close to al-Kūfah on the road to Syria. See Yāqūt, Muʿjam, IV, 771.

When ʿUmar b. Saʿd came toward al-Ḥusayn and shot the arrow, the people began to shoot at each other. While they were shooting at each other, Yasār,[433] a mawlā of Ziyād b. Abī Sufyān, and Sālim,[434] a mawlā of ʿUbaydallāh b. Ziyād, came forward. They called out, "Which of you will come forward to fight against us?" Ḥabīb b. Muẓāhir and Burayr jumped up but Ḥusayn said to [336] them, "Sit down." Then ʿAbdallāh b. ʿUmayr al-Kalbī arose. He said, "Abū ʿAbdallāh (i.e., al-Ḥusayn), may God have mercy on you, permit me to go out against them." Ḥusayn saw a tall dark man, strong in arm and with broad shoulders. He said, "I think he will be deadly enough for those opponents. Go forward if you wish." He went forward to meet them. They asked him who he was, and ʿAbdallāh b. ʿUmayr al-Kalbī gave them his lineage. They answered, "We do not know you. Let Zuhayr b. al-Qayn, Ḥabīb b. Muẓāhir or Burayr b. Ḥuḍayr come out against us." Yasār got ready in front of Sālim, and ʿAbdallāh b. ʿUmayr al-Kalbī retorted, "Son of an adulteress! You wanted to do single combat with one of the people. So one of the people has come forward against you. In any case he is better than you." With that ʿAbdallāh b. ʿUmayr struck Yasār with his sword until he had silenced him. While he was occupied with striking against him with his sword, Sālim attacked. They cried out in warning, "The other servant is closing in on you." ʿAbdallāh b. ʿUmayr did not notice Sālim until the latter was upon him. With his left hand, he warded off Sālim's blow but the fingers of his hand were cut off. Then he turned on Sālim, struck him and killed him. After he had killed them both, he came forward and recited:

If you do not know me, I am a son from the tribe of Kalb.
  Sufficient for me is my status (bayt) among ʿUlaym; it is
    sufficient for me.
I am a man of strength and muscles.
  I am not a weakling in the face of disaster.
I promise you, Umm Wahb,
  that I will go forward stabbing and striking among them,
Just as does a servant who believes in the Lord.

---

433. Yasār was only mentioned at the Battle of Karbalāʾ.
434. Sālim was only mentioned at the Battle of Karbalāʾ.

Umm Wahb seized a tent pole and went toward her husband, saying to him, "I give up my father and mother for you and fight to protect the good, the offspring of Muḥammad." He began to send her back to the women. She held on to his clothes and she said, "I will never leave you unless I die with you." Ḥusayn called out to her, "May you as a good family be well rewarded. May God have mercy on you, go back to the women and sit with them. It is not for women to fight." So she went back to them.

'Amr b. al-Ḥajjāj, who was on the right wing, launched an attack against al-Ḥusayn's right wing. When they drew near Ḥusayn, the followers of al-Ḥusayn knelt down and pointed their spears at them. Their horses would not come forward against the spears; they swung round to retreat. The followers of al-Ḥusayn began to shoot arrows at them, killing some of them and wounding others.

According to Abū Mikhnaf—Ḥusayn Abū Ja'far:[435] One of the Banū Tamīm called 'Abdallāh b. Ḥawzah[436] came and stood, opposite al-Ḥusayn. He called out, "Ḥusayn, Ḥusayn!" He answered, "What do you want?" 'Abdallāh b. Ḥawzah said, "Do you expect Hell-fire!" Al-Ḥusayn declared, "No, I am advancing to a merciful Lord and an intercessor who is listened to." He asked his followers, "Who is that?" They told him that it was Ibn Ḥawzah. Al-Ḥusayn prayed, "O my Lord! Drive him into the fire." Then his horse upset him in its stride and made him fall. His leg was stuck in the stirrups, and his head fell to the ground. The horse bolted and dragged him along, making his head strike every stone and clod of earth until he died.

According to Abū Mikhnaf—Suwayd b. Ḥayyah:[437] When 'Abdallāh b. Ḥawzah's horse fell, his left leg stuck in the stirrups and his right leg went flying up. His horse galloped off with him with his head striking every stone and tree trunk until he died.

According to Abū Mikhnaf—'Aṭā' b. al-Sā'ib[438]—'Abd al-Jabbār

[337]

---

435. Ḥusayn Abū Ja'far was an authority of Abū Mikhnaf who seems to be otherwise unknown. See Sezgin, *Abū Miḥnaf*, 207.

436. 'Abdallāh b. Ḥawzah is only mentioned in connection with this incident.

437. Suwayd b. Ḥayyah was an authority of Abū Mikhnaf who seems to be otherwise unknown. See Sezgin, *Abū Miḥnaf*, 218–19.

438. 'Aṭā' b. al-Sā'ib was a traditionist, who died in 137 (153). See Sezgin, *Abū Miḥnaf*, 200–1.

[338]

b. Wāʾil al-Ḥaḍramī,[439]—his brother, Masrūq b. Wāʾil:[440] I was among the first horsemen who came against al-Ḥusayn. I had told myself, "I will be one of the first of them; perhaps I may strike the head of al-Ḥusayn and by that attain a position of rank with ʿUbaydallāh b. Ziyād." As we came toward Ḥusayn, one of the people called Ibn Ḥawzah went forward. He called out, "Is Ḥusayn among you?" Ḥusayn was silent. He called again, and still he was silent. When there was the third call, al-Ḥusayn said to them, "Yes, here is Ḥusayn. What do you want?" Ibn Ḥawzah said, "Ḥusayn, do you expect Hell-fire!" Al-Ḥusayn replied, "You lie, rather I am advancing to a forgiving Lord and an intercessor who is listened to. Who are you?" He answered, "Ibn Ḥawzah." Ḥusayn raised his arms so that we could see the white of his armpits above his clothes and he prayed, "O God! Drive him into the fire." Ibn Ḥawzah became angry and he spurred his horse toward al-Ḥusayn. Between the two there was the bed of a stream, and while one foot was stuck in the stirrup, the horse dragged him along until he fell from the horse. One foot, leg, and thigh were pulled off while the other remained hanging in the stirrup.

Masrūq added that the cavalry left him behind.

ʿAbd al-Jabbār reported that he questioned Masrūq, and the latter said, "I have seen [of the wonders] of the Prophet's family (*ahl al-bayt*) enough to deter me from ever fighting them."

Then the battle flared up.

According to Abū Mikhnaf—Yūsuf b. Yazīd—ʿAfīf b. Zuhayr b. Abī al-Akhnas,[441] who witnessed the killing of al-Ḥusayn: Yazīd b. Maʿqil[442] of the Banū ʿAmīrah b. Rabīʿah, an ally of the Banū Salīmah of ʿAbd al-Qays, came forward and called out, "Burayr b. Ḥuḍayr, how do you think God has treated you?" Burayr replied, "By God! God has treated me well and treated you badly." He answered, "You are a liar. Even before today you were always a

---

439. ʿAbd al-Jabbār b. Wāʾil al-Ḥaḍramī was a traditionist, who died in 112 (731). See Sezgin, *Abū Miḥnaf*, 201.

440. Masrūq b. Wāʾil was an elder brother of the traditionist ʿAbd al-Jabbār b. Wāʾil, who was present at the Battle of Karbalāʾ; he does not seem to have been mentioned elsewhere.

441. ʿAfīf b. Zuhayr b. Abī al-Akhnas was an eyewitness at the Battle of Karbalāʾ; he seems to be otherwise unknown.

442. Yazīd b. Maʿqil is only mentioned with regard to the Battle of Karbalāʾ.

liar. Do you remember when I used to go with you among the Banū Lawdhān? Then you used to say that 'Uthmān b. 'Affān was a man who indulged himself excessively, that Mu'āwiyah b. Abī Sufyān was one who was in error and who caused people to go astray, and that the imām of guidance and truth was 'Alī b. Abī Ṭālib." Burayr retorted, "I testify that this is my opinion and belief." Yazīd b. Ma'qil replied, "And I testify that you are one of those who are in error." Burayr called out, "Then I challenge you to a contest of curses. Let us call on God that the liar be cursed and the spreader of falsehoods be killed. Then come out for combat." They both advanced and raised their hands to God, calling upon Him to curse the liar and that the one who was truthful should kill the one who was false. Each of them came forward against the other. They exchanged blows. Yazīd b. Ma'qil struck Burayr b. Ḥuḍayr a light blow that did not do him any harm. Burayr b. Ḥuḍayr struck Yazīd b. Ma'qil a blow that cut through his helmet and penetrated his brain. He fell prostrate just as if he had been hurled from a mountain, and the sword of Ibn Ḥuḍayr was stuck in his head. As I looked at Burayr, he was pulling it out of Yazīd's head when Raḍī b. Munqidh al-'Abdī[443] attacked him and grappled with him. They fought together for a time. Then Burayr sat on his chest. Raḍī called out, "Where are the people to fight and to defend?" At this Ka'b b. Jābir b. 'Amr al-Azdī[444] went to attack Burayr. I said to him, "This man, Burayr b. Ḥuḍayr, is the reciter of the Qur'ān (qāri'). He often recited the Qur'ān to us in the mosque." But Ka'b attacked with his spear and struck him in the back. When Burayr felt the contact of the spear, he grappled with him and bit into his face, cutting off the edge of his nose. Then Ka'b b. Jābir stabbed him until he had flung Burayr down from him. The point of Ka'b's spear was hidden in Burayr's back. Then Ka'b came at him, striking him with his sword until he killed him.

'Afīf reported: It is as if I see Raḍī b. Munqidh al-'Abdī, who had been lying prostrate, rising, shaking the dust from his clothes,

[339]

---

443. Raḍī b. Munqidh al-'Abdī is only mentioned with regard to this incident in the Battle of Karbalā' and his view concerning the event.

444. Ka'b b. Jābir b. 'Amr al-Azdī is only mentioned with regard to this incident in the Battle of Karbalā' and the consequences concerning the event.

and saying to Kaʿb b. Jābir al-Azdī, "Thank you brother of al-Azd, I will never forget that."

Yūsuf b. Yazīd reported that he asked ʿAfīf whether he saw that, and he replied that he had seen it with his own eyes and heard it with his own ears. He added: When Kaʿb b. Jābir returned, his wife or his sister, al-Nawār bt. Jābir,[445] said to him, "You have given help against the son of Fāṭimah and you have killed the leader of the reciters of the Qurʾān. You have brought great disgrace. By God! I will never speak a word to you." Kaʿb b. Jābir recited:

[340]

Ask that you be told about me—and you are blameworthy—
    at the battle against Ḥusayn, while the spears were pointed.
Have I not gone to the farthest point of your dislike? Was not
    what I did on the day of terror appropriate to me?
I had with me a spear from Yazan,[446] whose joints had not
    betrayed it,
    and a white sword which was sharpened, and both edges of it
    were cutting.
I singled him out amid a group whose religion was not
    my religion, for I am satisfied with Ibn Ḥarb (i.e., Yazīd).
My eyes did not see their like in their time,
    nor anyone among the people before them since I was a
    young man.
For there were none fiercer in striking with the sword in battle.
    Indeed everyone who protects his honor comes to fight.
They have endured without protection, stabbing and striking.
    They would have attacked had all this been of any advantage.
Tell ʿUbaydallāh, if you meet him,
    that I am obedient and attentive to the Caliph.
I killed Burayr. I brought help to
    Abū Munqidh[447] when he called, "Who will fight?"

According to Abū Mikhnaf—ʿAbd al-Raḥmān b. Jundab: During the governorship of Muṣʿab b. al-Zubayr,[448] I heard Kaʿb b. Jābir

---

445. Whether Nawār bt. Jābir is Kaʿb's wife or sister cannot be ascertained, as she is not mentioned elsewhere.
446. Yazan were a clan of Ḥimyar. See al-Bustānī, *Muḥīṭ*, s.v. *yzn*.
447. He means Raḍī b. Munqidh.
448. Between the years 67 (687) and 72 (691–92).

saying, "O Lord! We have been loyal. O Lord! Do not treat us like those who have been treacherous." My father said to him, "True! God is true to His word and generous, but you have earned evil for yourself." He retorted, "No. I have not earned evil for myself; rather I have earned good."

They claimed that later Raḍī b. Munqidh al-ʿAbdī gave a reply to the words of Kaʿb b. Jābir. He said:

If my Lord had wished, I would not have been present at their
    battle,
    and Ibn Jābir would not have done me any favors.
That day was shameful and disgraceful,
    for which the sons who come after these people will
    denounce them.
I wish that I had been dead before his death
    and, at the battle against Ḥusayn, I had been in the grave.

ʿAmr b. Qarazah al-Anṣārī[449] came forward to fight in the de-   [341]
fense of Ḥusayn. He was reciting:

May the battalion of helpers know
    that I will defend the nature of honor,
With the blow of a boy who is no broken arrow, who sells his
    soul for paradise.
In protection of Ḥusayn, I offer my life and my house.

According to Abū Mikhnaf—Thābit b. Hubayrah:[450] ʿAmr b. Qarazah b. Kaʿb was killed. He had been with al-Ḥusayn, while his brother ʿAlī[451] was with ʿUmar b. Saʿd. ʿAlī b. Qarazah called out, "Ḥusayn, you lying son of a liar, you have led my brother astray and tempted him so that he has been killed." Al-Ḥusayn retorted, "God did not lead your brother astray. Rather He guided your brother and led you astray." ʿAlī b. Qarazah declared, "May God kill me if I do not kill you, or I will die before I get to you."

---

449. ʿAmr b. Qarazah al-Anṣārī is mentioned here for the first time as a follower of al-Ḥusayn; he is not mentioned elsewhere. His father was a supporter and official of ʿAlī b. Abī Ṭālib. See Ṭabarī, I, 3173, 3423.

450. Thābit b. Hubayrah was an authority of Abū Mikhnaf who seems to be otherwise unknown. See Sezgin, *Abū Miḥnaf*, 222.

451. ʿAlī is not mentioned elsewhere. His attitude is obviously opposed to his brother and father. Balādhurī gives him the name al-Zubayr. See *Ansāb*, II/2, 192.

He launched an attack against Ḥusayn. But Nāfiʿ b. Hilāl al-Murādī intercepted him, stabbed him and brought him down. ʿAlī b. Qaraẓah's comrades rescued ʿAlī. Later he was treated until he recovered.

According to Abū Mikhnaf—al-Naḍr b. Ṣāliḥ Abū Zuhayr al-ʿAbsī: When al-Ḥurr b. Yazīd joined Ḥusayn, a man from Banū Tamīm, of the clan of Banū Shaqirah, who are the Banū al-Ḥārith b. Tamīm—he was called Yazīd b. Sufyān[452]—called out, "By God, if I had seen al-Ḥurr b. Yazīd, I would have followed him with my spear to stab him."

Meanwhile the people were driving against each other and fighting, and al-Ḥurr was advancing to attack the people, reciting the words of ʿAntarah.[453]

I kept hurling my horse against them, neck
  and breast, until it was clothed with blood.

His horse was struck on its ears and nose, and blood was flowing from it. Al-Ḥusayn b. Tamīm was in command of the police of ʿUbaydallāh and was sent by him to al-Ḥusayn. He was with ʿUmar b. Saʿd, and ʿUmar had put him in charge of the armored police. Al-Ḥusayn now said to Yazīd b. Sufyān, "This is al-Ḥurr b. Yazīd, the man you wanted." He admitted that and went out toward him saying, "Ḥurr b. Yazīd, are you ready to fight in single combat?" Al-Ḥurr replied, "Yes, if you wish." He came forward toward him.

I (the narrator, al-Naḍr) have heard al-Ḥusayn b. Tamīm say, "By God! As Yazīd went out to fight, it was as if his soul were in al-Ḥurr's hand. No sooner had he gone out against him than al-Ḥurr killed him."

According to Hishām b. Muḥammad (al-Kalbī)—Abū Mikhnaf—Yaḥyā b. Hāniʾ b. ʿUrwah: Nāfiʿ b. Hilāl was fighting on that day, reciting:

I am al-Jamalī. I believe in the religion of ʿAlī.

---

452. Yazīd b. Sufyān is not mentioned except in the Battle of Karbalāʾ; he was killed in the battle.

453. ʿAntarah was a warrior poet of the sixth century, See *EI²*, s.v. ʿAntarah. For the verse of ʿAntarah, see Ahlwardt, *The Divans*, 48.

A man called Muzāhim b. Ḥurayth[454] came against him, crying, "I follow the religion of ʿUthmān." Nāfiʿ replied, "Rather you follow the religion of Satan." Then he attacked and killed him.

ʿAmr b. al-Ḥajjāj cried out to his men, "You stupid fellows, don't you realize whom you are fighting? These horsemen of the town are people who are seeking death. Don't let any of you go forward to fight them in single combat. They are only few, and their time is running out. By God! If you only threw stones at them, you would kill them." ʿUmar b. Saʿd said to him, "True, you have come to the right conclusion." Then he sent to the commanders that none of their own men should fight one of their men in single combat.

According to Abū Mikhnaf—al-Ḥusayn b. ʿUqbah al-Murādī[455] —a Zubaydī tribesman: He heard ʿAmr b. al-Ḥajjāj, when he approached the followers of al-Ḥusayn, saying, "People of al-Kūfah, stay steadfast in your obedience and unity (jamāʿah). Do not have any doubts about fighting against those who have strayed from the true religion and have opposed the imām." Al-Ḥusayn retorted, "ʿAmr b. al-Ḥajjāj, are you urging the people against me? Are we the ones who have strayed from the true religion, and you the ones who have remained firm in it? By God! If our souls were taken, and you died with your actions, you would know which of us has strayed from the true religion and who was more worthy to be roasted by Hell-fire."

ʿAmr b. al-Ḥajjāj with the right wing of ʿUmar b. Saʿd launched an attack against al-Ḥusayn from the direction of the Euphrates. They fought together fiercely for a time. Muslim b. ʿAwsajah al-Asadī was struck down, but ʿAmr and his men withdrew and the dust lifted. There was Muslim, stretched out dying. Al-Ḥusayn walked toward him while Muslim was on the point of death. He said, "Muslim b. ʿAwsajah, may your Lord have mercy on you. 'Of them [the believers] is he who has accomplished his vow [by death in battle], and of them is he who waits: they have not changed at all.'"[456] Ḥabīb b. Muẓāhir approached and said, [343]

---

454. Muzāhim b. Ḥurayth is only mentioned at the Battle of Karbalāʾ.

455. Al-Ḥusayn b. ʿUqbah al-Murādī is an unknown authority of Abū Mikhnaf. See Sezgin, *Abū Miḥnaf*, 207.

456. Qurʾān, 33:23.

"Muslim, your death is hard for me to bear but rejoice that Heaven is your abode." He replied in a weak voice, "May God bring you the same luck." Ḥabīb said, "I know that I am following you at this very moment. Otherwise I would have liked you to entrust me to carry out everything that concerns you, so that I might preserve for you what you are worthy of through kinship and religion." He answered, "Indeed, I do entrust to you. May God have mercy on you to do this." And pointing toward al-Ḥusayn, he added, "To die with this man." He said, "I do this, by the Lord of the Kaʿbah."

No sooner had he died in their midst than a maidservant of his cried out, "O Ibn ʿAwsajah! O master!" The followers of ʿAmr b. al-Ḥajjāj called to each other, "We have killed Muslim b. ʿAwsajah." Shabath (b. Ribʿī) said to some of his followers around him, "May your mothers be bereft of you. You have only killed yourselves with your own hands, and you have humiliated yourselves for someone else. Do you rejoice at killing a man like Muslim b. ʿAwsajah? Indeed, it was due to him that I embraced Islam. Many a noble stand have I seen him make among the Muslims! I saw him at the battle of the plain of Ādharbayjān[457] kill six polytheists before the horsemen of the Muslims all arrived. Could you be happy while a man among you like him is killed?"

[344]   Those who killed Muslim b. ʿAwsajah were Muslim b. ʿAbdallāh al-Ḍibābī[458] and ʿAbd al-Raḥmān b. Abī Khushkārah al-Bajalī.[459]

With his left wing Shamir b. Dhī al-Jawshan attacked the people of al-Ḥusayn's left wing. But the latter stood firm and forced Shamir and his followers away with their spears. Al-Ḥusayn and his followers were attacked on every side. [ʿAbdallāh b. ʿUmayr] al-Kalbī was killed. He had killed another two men after the first two. He had fought fiercely, but Hāniʾ b. Thubayt al-Ḥaḍramī and

---

457. The Arab conquest of Ādharbayjān took place between 18 (639) and 22 (643). See *EI²*, s.v. Ādharbaydjān.

458. Muslim b. ʿAbdallāh al-Ḍibābī was present at the Battle of Ṣiffīn fighting for ʿAlī with his tribal leader Shamir b. Dhī al-Jawshan. He was with Shamir when the latter was killed by al-Mukhtār but he escaped. See Ṭabarī, I, 3305, II, 661–62.

459. ʿAbd al-Raḥmān b. Abī Khushkārah al-Bajalī was killed by al-Mukhtār. See Ṭabarī, II, 669.

Bukayr b. Ḥayy al-Taymī of Taym Allāh b. Thaʿlabah[460] attacked him and killed him. He was the second of the followers of al-Ḥusayn to be killed.

The followers of al-Ḥusayn fought fiercely. Then their cavalry began to attack, and even though they were only thirty-two horsemen, they did not attack any side of the Kūfan cavalry without putting it to flight. When ʿAzrah b. Qays, who was in command of the Kūfan cavalry, saw that his cavalry was being put to flight on every side, he sent ʿAbd al-Raḥmān b. Ḥiṣn[461] to ʿUmar b. Saʿd to tell him, "Don't you see what my cavalry is receiving today from this small number? Send the foot soldiers and archers against them." ʿUmar asked Shabath b. Ribʿī, "Will you not go against them?" He replied, "Glory be to God! Are you turning to the shaykh of Muḍar and of the people of this town generally to send him with the archers because you cannot find anyone who will volunteer for this? Surely someone else other than me will be sufficient for you?" They could see Shabath's reluctance to fight against Ḥusayn.

According to Abū Zuhayr al-ʿAbsī (al-Naḍr b. Ṣāliḥ): During the governorship of Muṣʿab (b. al-Zubayr),[462] I heard Shabath saying: "God will neither give the people of this town any good nor will He direct them toward true guidance. Are you not amazed that we should fight for ʿAlī b. Abī Ṭālib and his son after him against the clan of Abū Sufyān for five years, and then make war on his other son and fight for the clan of Muʿāwiyah and the son of Sumayyah, the harlot, against the best man on earth? Error! O what error!" [345]

ʿUmar b. Saʿd summoned al-Ḥusayn b. Tamīm and sent the armored police with him and five hundred of the archers. They advanced until they came near al-Ḥusayn and his followers. They shot arrows at al-Ḥusayn's followers until soon they had wounded their horses; they all were on foot.

According to Abū Mikhnaf—Numayr b. Waʿlah—Ayyūb b. Mishraḥ al-Khaywānī:[463] By God! I wounded the horse of al-Ḥurr

---

460. Bukayr b. Ḥayy al-Taymī is not mentioned elsewhere.
461. ʿAbd al-Raḥmān b. Ḥiṣn is not mentioned elsewhere.
462. Muṣʿab was governor between the years 67 (687) and 72 (691–92).
463. Ayyūb b. Mishraḥ al-Khaywānī is not mentioned elsewhere except for his later justification.

b. Yazīd. I shot an arrow in its belly. At once the horse shook, turned over, and fell prostrate. Al-Ḥurr jumped from his horse like a lion; with his sword in his hand he recited:

If you wound my horse, then I am son of a free man,
   braver than any lion with mane.

I have never seen anyone accomplish what he accomplished.

The shaykhs of the tribe told Ayyūb b. Mishraḥ, "You killed him." He replied, "No, I did not kill him. Someone else killed him. I do not want it to be thought that I killed him." Abū Waddāk asked him, "Why?" He said, "They claim that he was one of the righteous. Even though what I had done was a sin, I would rather that I met God with the sin of wounding rather than that I should meet him with the sin of killing." Abū Waddāk replied, "I can only see that you will meet God with the sin of killing them all. Surely, you can see that if you shot at this man, wounded this man, fired at this man, took up a position, attacked him and urged on your comrades—while you increased the number of your comrades—and when there was an attack against you, you were reluctant to flee, and the others of your comrades did as you, and others, and others, it can be considered that such a man and his comrades killed al-Ḥurr b. Yazīd and his horse? You are partners in their blood, all of you." He said, "O Abū Waddāk, you would drive us to despair of the mercy of God, if you were the custodian of our account on the Day of Resurrection. May God not forgive you, if you do forgive us." He answered, "It is the way that I am telling you."

They fought against them in the fiercest battle God created, until midday. They could only come against them from one direction because of the way they had gathered their tents close to each other. When ʿUmar b. Saʿd saw that, he sent men to pull them down from the right and the left; they wanted to surround them. Three or four of al-Ḥusayn's followers went back through the tents in order to attack any man who was pulling down the tents and plundering them, and so that they could not only fight and shoot at him from close range but also wound him. At that, ʿUmar b. Saʿd ordered his men to set fire to the tents. He said, "Set fire to them. Don't go into a tent or plunder it." Then they set the tents on fire. Ḥusayn said, "Leave them. Let them burn them. If they set them on fire, they will not be able to come through them against you." That was how it was. They could still only attack them from one direction.

The wife of ['Abdallāh b. 'Umayr] al-Kalbī went out to her husband. She sat by his head rubbing it with earth, saying, "May you enjoy heaven." Shamir b. Dhī al-Jawshan said to a servant called Rustam, "Beat her head with a tent pole." He struck her head and smashed it. She died where she was.

Shamir b. Dhī al-Jawshan came up to al-Ḥusayn's tent. He struck against it and called out, "Bring me fire so that I can burn this tent and the people inside it." The women screamed and rushed out of the tent. Al-Ḥusayn called out to him, "Ibn Dhī al-Jawshan are you calling for fire to burn down my tent and my family? May God burn you in Hell-fire!"

According to Abū Mikhnaf—Sulaymān b. Abī Rāshid—Ḥumayd b. Muslim: I said to Shamir b. Dhī al-Jawshan, "Glory be to God! [347] This is not appropriate for you. Do you want to impose on yourself two evil qualities for which you will be punished by God? You are killing women and children. By God! It is by your killing of men that you will satisfy your commander." He asked me, "Who are you?" I replied, "I will not tell you who I am." For, by God, I was afraid that if he knew me, he would harm my position with the authorities. Then a man called Shabath b. Rib'ī came to him; he was more obedient to him than I was. He told him, "I have neither heard any words more evil than yours nor seen any behavior more disgraceful than yours. Have you become a man who terrorizes women?" At that I testify that Shamir became ashamed and began to withdraw.

Zuhayr b. al-Qayn launched an attack against him with ten of his comrades. So fierce was his attack on Shamir b. Dhī al-Jawshan and his followers that he drove them from the tents so that they all withdrew from them. They brought down Abū 'Azzah al-Ḍibābī and killed him. He was one of the followers of Shamir.[464] The people clustered round Zuhayr and his comrades; they outnumbered them considerably. Each man of the followers of al-Ḥusayn continued to fight until he was killed. However, when a man or two among them was killed, it was apparent,

___

464. Abū 'Azzah al-Ḍibābī is not mentioned elsewhere.

while, since the others were numerous, it was not apparent how many were killed. When Abū Thumāmah ʿAmr b. ʿAbdallāh al-Ṣāʾidī saw the violence, he said to al-Ḥusayn, "O Abū ʿAbdallāh! To you I sacrifice my soul. I see that these men are getting closer to you. No, by God! You will get killed unless I am killed defending you, if God is willing. I would love to meet my Lord when I have already prayed the prayer; the time for performance has now drawn near." Al-Ḥusayn raised his head and said, "You mentioned the prayer. May God make you always one of those who pray and mention His name. Yes, it is now the first time for that prayer." Then he said, "Ask them to desist from us so that [348] we may pray." Al-Ḥusayn b. Tamīm told them that the prayer would not be acceptable. Ḥabīb b. Muẓāhir said to him, "You have claimed that it is not acceptable. Is the prayer of the family of the Apostle of God not acceptable, while your prayer is acceptable, you donkey?" Ḥusayn b. Tamīm launched an attack against them, and Ḥabīb b. Muẓāhir came out against him. Ḥabīb struck his horse's face with his sword. The horse pranced, and Ḥusayn fell from it. His followers carried him away and rescued him. Ḥabīb began to recite:

I swear if we had the numbers you have
    or even half of you, you would turn your backs.
You the worst people of lineage and of deeds.

    On that day he began to recite:

I am Ḥabīb, my father is Muẓāhir,
    a horseman of battle and war that is kindled.
You are more numerous than we,
    but we are more loyal and steadfast than you.
Ours is stronger logic and clearer
    right. We are of greater piety and freer from blame than you.

Ḥabīb fought fiercely. A man from the Banū Tamīm attacked him, but Ḥabīb struck him on the head with his sword and killed him. The man was called Badīl b. Ṣuraym of the Banū ʿUqfān.[465] Another from the Banū Tamīm attacked him and stabbed him. Ḥabīb fell. He started to rise, and al-Ḥusayn b. Tamīm struck him

---

465. Badīl b. Ṣuraym is not mentioned elsewhere.

on the head with his sword. He fell, and the Tamīmī stooped
down and cut off his head. Al-Ḥusayn told him, "I am your partner
in killing him." The other declared, "By God! No one except me
killed him." Al-Ḥusayn ordered, "Give his head to me. I will hang
it on the neck of my horse so that the people may see and know
that I participated in killing him. Then you will take it and go
with it to ʿUbaydallāh b. Ziyād, for I have no need of what you
will be given for killing him." The man refused him, but then his   [349]
people persuaded him to settle their dispute in that way. So he
handed al-Ḥusayn the head of Ḥabīb b. Muẓāhir, and al-Ḥusayn
went around the army with it hung on the neck of his horse. After
that, he handed it back to the Tamīmī.

When they returned to al-Kūfah, the other man took the head of
Ḥabīb and hung it on the withers of his mare. Then he took it to
Ibn Ziyād in the palace. Ḥabīb's son, al-Qāsim b. Ḥabīb, caught
sight of the head. At that time he was still an adolescent. He
followed that horsemen wherever he went; he never left him.
Whenever he went into the palace, al-Qāsim went in with him.
When he left, al-Qāsim left with him. The latter became
suspicious and asked, "My son, what is wrong with you that you
follow me?" Al-Qāsim answered, "Nothing." He said, "Yes, there
is, my son. Tell me." Al-Qāsim told him, "This head that you
have is the head of my father. Will you give it to me so that I may
bury it?" He answered, "My son, the governor would not be
pleased if it were buried, and I want the governor to give me a
good reward for killing him." The boy cried out, "But God will
only give you an evil reward. My God! You have killed one who is
better than you." Then he burst into tears. The boy waited until
the time when he was grown up. Then his only concern was to
track down his father's killer, to find him unprepared, and to kill
him for his father. In the time of Muṣʿab b. al-Zubayr while
Muṣʿab was attacking Bājumayrā,[466] al-Qāsim b. Ḥabīb went into
Muṣʿab's camp; there he found his father's murderer in his tent.
He began to come frequently in order to look for him; he sought

---

466. This campaign at Bājumayrā, which is near Takrīt in the region of Mosul
in Iraq (See Yāqūt, *Muʿjam*, I, 454–55), probably went on for three seasons; the
eventual battle between Muṣʿab and ʿAbd al-Malik book place in either 71 (690–
91) or 72 (691–92). See Wellhausen, *Arab Kingdom*, 188–95.

for a moment when he was unprepared. He visited him while he was taking his midday siesta. He struck him with his sword until he was dead.

According to Abū Mikhnaf—Muhammad b. Qays: When Habīb b. Muzāhir was killed, it overwhelmed Husayn and at that he said, "I will dedicate my life and my brave companions to God."

Al-Hurr began to recite:

I swear that I will not be killed until I have killed.
    Today I will only be struck advancing
[350] While I strike them with a biting blow from my sword.
    I will not be cowardly before them, nor will I run away.

He also recited:

I will strike my sword against their men of good repute
    on behalf of the best man who settled at Minā and al-Khayf.

He and Zuhayr b. al-Qayn fought fiercely against them. When one of them attacked, if he became surrounded by fighters, the other attacked until he freed him. They both did that for some time. Then foot soldiers attacked al-Hurr b. Yazīd and killed him. Abū Thumāmah al-Ṣāʾidī was also killed. His cousin was his opponent.

Then they prayed the midday prayer. Al-Husayn prayed the prayer of fear with them.[467] They fought again after midday. Their battle was very fierce and it reached al-Husayn. However, [Saʿīd b. ʿAbdallāh][468] al-Hanafī came forward in front of him. He was exposed to them while they shot arrows to his right and left. He stood in front of al-Husayn while he continued to be shot at until he fell.

Zuhayr b. al-Qayn fought fiercely while reciting:

I am Zuhayr. I am the son of al-Qayn.
    I will drive them away from Husayn with my sword.

He began to tap Husayn on the shoulder while he said:

---

467. This form of prayer was said to have been introduced by the Prophet at al-Hudaybiyyah. The people divide into two groups. One group performs the prayer while the other group acts as guard; then the two groups change roles. See Wāqidī, *Maghāzī*, II, 573.

468. Saʿīd b. ʿAbdallāh was added from Balādhurī. See *Ansāb*, II/2, 195.

Forward, you have been guided as one who guides, who is rightly
    guided (*mahdī*).
Today, you will meet your grandfather, the Prophet,
And al-Ḥasan, and him whom God is pleased with, ʿAlī,
    and the iron-clad young man with two wings[469]
And the lion of God, the martyr who still lives.[470]

Kathīr b. ʿAbdallāh al-Shaʿbī and Muhājir b. Aws attacked him and
killed him.

Nāfiʿ b. Hilāl al-Jamalī had written his name on the tips of his
arrows. He began to shoot them when they were marked while
declaring:

I am al-Jamalī. I believe in the religion of ʿAlī.

Nāfiʿ b. Hilāl al-Jamalī killed twelve of the followers of ʿUmar   [351]
b. Saʿd beside those he wounded. He struck out until both his
upper arms were broken and he was taken prisoner. Shamir b.
Dhī al-Jawshan apprehended him. He had with him some of his
followers, who drove Nāfiʿ along until he was brought before
ʿUmar b. Saʿd. ʿUmar b. Saʿd said to him, "Woe upon you Nāfiʿ!
What made you do what you have done to yourself?" He answered,
"My Lord has taught me what I should want." Blood was flowing
onto his beard as he continued, "By God! I have killed twelve of
you beside those I have wounded. I do not blame myself for the
effort. If there remained to me an upper arm and a forearm, you
would not have captured me." Shamir, said to ʿUmar, "Kill him,
may God make you prosperous." ʿUmar replied, "You brought
him. You kill him if you want to." Shamir drew his sword. Nāfiʿ
said to him, "By God! If you were one of the Muslims, how
terrible you would feel to meet God with our blood on your hands.
Praise be to God, Who has ordained that our fate should come
through the wicked ones of His creatures." Then Shamir killed
him.
Shamir began to launch an attack against them while he recited:

Escape, enemies of God, escape from Shamir,
    who will strike you with his sword and does not flee.
He is a bitter pill, a poison and bitter herb for you.

---

469. Jaʿfar b. Abī Ṭālib. See *EI²*, s.v. Djaʿfar b. Abī Ṭālib.
470. Ḥamzah b. ʿAbd al-Muṭṭalib. See *EI²*, s.v. Hamza b. ʿAbd al-Muṭṭalib.

When the followers of al-Ḥusayn realized that the enemy had become numerous and that they would no longer be able to defend Ḥusayn, or themselves, they vied with each other to be killed in front of him. ʿAbdallāh and ʿAbd al-Raḥmān, the two sons of ʿAzrah,[471] both of Ghifār, declared, "Abū ʿAbdallāh (i.e., al-Ḥusayn), the enemy have driven us back to you. We want to be killed in front of you while we protect and defend you." He replied, "Welcome to you both. Come closer to me." They went close to him. Then they began to fight close beside him while one of them recited:

Banū Ghifār, Banū Nizār, and
    Khindif after them know truly

[352] That we will strike against dissolute men
    with every sharp-edged cutting sword.
People, defend the sons of free men
    with swords and brandished spears.

Two young men of Jābir, Sayf b. al-Ḥārith b. Surayʿ and Mālik b. ʿAbd b. Surayʿ, paternal cousins and half-brothers through their mother,[472] came and drew near Ḥusayn; they were weeping. Al-Ḥusayn said, "Cousins, what is making you cry? By God! I hope that in a short time you will both be joyful." They replied, "May God accept our lives for yours; it is not for ourselves that we weep, but we weep for you, for we see you surrounded and we cannot defend you." He said, "May God reward you with the best reward of the pious for your grief for that and for your giving up your own lives for me."

Ḥanẓalah b. Asʿad al-Shibāmī[473] advanced in front of Ḥusayn and began to call out, "'O my people! I fear for you the same as happened on the Day of the Allies, the same as happened to the people of Noah, and ʿĀd and Thamūd, and those who came after them, but God does not want injustice for His servants. O my people! I fear for you on the Day of Summoning, a day when you will turn back retreating; there will be no protector for you from

---

471. ʿAbdallāh and ʿAbd al-Raḥmān are mentioned for the first time.
472. Sayf b. al-Ḥārith b. Surayʿ and Mālik are mentioned for the first time.
473. Ḥanẓalah b. Asʿad al-Shibāmī is mentioned for the first time.

God. Whoever God causes to err, has no guide."[474] People, do not kill Ḥusayn, '...for God will destroy you with punishment. He who forges a lie will be disappointed.'"[475] Ḥusayn said to him, "May God have mercy on you, Ibn Asʿad. Indeed, they have brought punishment on themselves when they refused the right that you summoned them to. They have come against you to destroy you and your companions. Therefore, how is it to be for them now when they have killed your righteous brothers?" He said, "You have spoken truly, may I sacrifice my life for you. You are more knowledgeable than I and more correct. Shall we not go to the next world and join our brothers?" Al-Ḥusayn replied, "You will go to a better place than this world and what it comprises, to a kingdom that will never be worn out." Ḥanẓalah said, "Peace be with you, Abū ʿAbdallāh, and may God bless you and your family. May He make us know you in His Heaven." Al-Ḥusayn answered, "Amen, amen." Then Ḥanẓalah advanced and fought until he was killed.

[353]

The two young sons of Jābir came forward looking toward Ḥusayn and saying, "Peace be with you, son of the Apostle of God." He replied, "Peace be with you both and the mercy of God." They fought until they were killed.

Next ʿĀbis b. Abī Shabīb al-Shākirī came forward. With him was Shawdhab,[476] mawlā of Shākir. ʿĀbis had said to him, "What do you intend to do?" He said, "What I will do is fight alongside you on behalf of the son of the daughter of the Apostle of God until I am killed." ʿĀbis told him, "That is what I thought about you. But no. Go forward in front of Abū ʿAbdallāh (i.e., al-Ḥusayn) so that he may dedicate you to God as he has done with his other followers and so that I, too, may dedicate you to God. If anyone had been with me for a time, for whom I had such responsibility as I have for you, it would please me that he should come in front of me so that I should dedicate him to God. On this day, it is appropriate for us to seek the reward with all our power, for there will be no works to earn God's favor after today, only the Day of Reckoning." Shawdhab went forward, greeted al-Ḥusayn. He went

---

474. Qurʾān, 40:30–33 (31–34).
475. Qurʾān, 20:64 (65).
476. Shawdhab is mentioned for the first time.

on and fought until he was killed. Then ʿĀbis b. Abī Shabīb said, "Abū ʿAbdallāh, there has not been on the face of the earth anyone, either close or distant relative, who is dearer to me and more loved by me than you. If I were able to defend you from oppression and murder with something more precious to me than my own life and blood, I would do it. Peace be with you, Abū ʿAbdallāh. I bear witness to God that I have ever been subject to your guidance and the guidance of your father." Then he walked toward them, [354] unsheathing his sword, and tapped his forehead with it.

According to Abū Mikhnaf—Numayr b. Waʿlah—a man of Banu ʿAbd of Hamdān called Rabīʿ b. Tamīm,[477] who witnessed that battle: When I saw ʿĀbis advancing, I recognized him, for I had seen him in the campaigns. He was the bravest of men. I said, "People, this is the lion of lions. This is Ibn Shabīb. Let none of you go out against him." ʿĀbis began to call out, "Will no man fight me man to man?" ʿUmar b. Saʿd ordered stones to be thrown at him. Stones began to be thrown at him from all sides. When he saw that, he threw off his breastplate and his helmet; he charged against the people. By God, I saw him driving away more than two hundred men. Then they surrounded him on every side; he was killed. I saw his head in the hands of several men. One would claim, "I killed him." Then another would say, "I killed him." They went to ʿUmar b. Saʿd who said, "Don't dispute about this. No one spear killed him." He separated them through these words.

According to Abū Mikhnaf—ʿAbdallāh b. ʿĀṣim—al-Ḍaḥḥāk b. ʿAbdallāh al-Mishraqī: I saw that the followers of al-Ḥusayn had been struck down and [now the battle] had reached him and his family (ahl baytihi). The only others who were left with him were Suwayd b. ʿAmr b. Abī al-Muṭāʿ al-Khathʿamī,[478] and Bushayr b. ʿAmr al-Ḥaḍramī.[479] I said to al-Ḥusayn, "Son of the Apostle of God, you know the agreement between you and me. I told you that I would fight for you as long as I saw another fighter. Since I do not see any fighter alongside you, I am free to go. You

---

477. Rabīʿ b. Tamīm is mentioned for the first time; this is his only report.

478. Suwayd b. ʿAmr b. Abī al-Muṭāʿ al-Khathʿamī is mentioned for the first time with regard to his role in the battle.

479. Bushayr b. ʿAmr al-Ḥaḍramī is mentioned for the first time.

agree." He replied, "You have spoken truly, but how will it be possible for you to escape? Yet, if you can do that, you are free to go." I went to my horse. When I had seen the horses of our comrades wounded, I brought my horse and took it inside one of the large tents among the tents of our comrades; I began to fight on foot. On that day, I killed two men in front of al-Ḥusayn and cut off the hand of another. On that day, al-Ḥusayn said to me several times, "May God never wither or cut off your hand. May God reward you well on behalf of the family of your Prophet." After he had given me permission to go, I brought out my horse from the tent. I settled myself on its back. I struck it so that, as it reared up on the front of its hooves, I galloped on toward the people. They moved out of my way. Fifteen of them chased after me until I reached Shufayyah, a village on the bank of the Euphrates. When they got close to me, I turned against them. Kathīr b. ʿAbdallāh al-Shaʿbī, Ayyūb b. Mishraḥ al-Khaywānī and Qays b. ʿAbdallāh al-Ṣāʾidī[480] recognized me. They said, "This is al-Ḍaḥḥāk b. ʿAbdallāh al-Mishraqī. He is our cousin, we adjure you before God to leave him." Three members of Banū Tamīm who were with them agreed saying, "By God! Let us agree to our brothers; the people are entitled to ask us to refrain from their colleague when they want us to." When the members of Banū Tamīm agreed with my colleagues, the rest left me. Thus, God saved me.

According to Abū Mikhnaf—Fuḍayl Khadīj al-Kindī: Yazīd b. Ziyād—that is Abū al-Shaʿthāʾ al-Kindī of Banū Bahdalah—went down on both knees in front of al-Ḥusayn and shot a hundred arrows and hardly five missed. As he was shooting, he would say, "I am a son of Bahdalah, the horsemen of al-ʿArjulah." Al-Ḥusayn would say, "O God! Make his aim be straight when he shoots and make his reward heaven." After he had shot them, he stood up and said, "Only five of the arrows have missed and it is clear to me that I have killed five men." He was among the first who were killed. On that day he recited:

I am Yazīd. My father is Muhāṣir.
  I am braver than a lion lurking in its covert.

---

480. Qays b. ʿAbdallāh al-Ṣāʾidī is mentioned for the first time.

O Lord, I am a supporter of al-Ḥusayn,
  and one who has abandoned and left Ibn Saʿd.

Yazīd b. Ziyād b. al-Muhāṣir had been one of those who had come with ʿUmar b. Saʿd against al-Ḥusayn. When they had rejected the conditions made by al-Ḥusayn, he had gone across to him and fought alongside him until he had been killed.

In the case of ʿAmr[481] b. Khālid al-Ṣaydāwī, Jābir b. al-Ḥārith al-Salmānī, Saʿd, the mawlā of ʿAmr b. Khālid, and Mujammiʿ b. ʿAbdallāh al-ʿĀʾidhī,[482] they had fought at the beginning of the battle and had been at the forefront of the attack with their swords against the people. However, when they had penetrated too deeply, the people turned on them, began to gain the advantage over them and cut them off from their colleagues, who were not far away. Al-ʿAbbās b. ʿAlī attacked the people and rescued them. They returned but they had been wounded. When their opponents got near them, they attacked them with their swords. They had fought at the very beginning of the battle until they were killed at the same place.

According to Abū Mikhnaf—Zuhayr b. ʿAbd al-Raḥmān b. Zuhayr al-Khathʿamī: The last of his followers left with al-Ḥusayn was Suwayd b. ʿAmr b. Abī al-Mutāʿ al-Khathʿamī.

On that day, the first of Banū Abī Ṭālib to be killed was ʿAlī al-Akbar b. al-Ḥusayn b. ʿAlī. His mother was Laylā bt. Abī Murrah b. ʿUrwah b. Masʿūd al-Thaqafī.[483] He attacked the people, while declaring:

I am ʿAlī b. Ḥusayn b. ʿAlī.
  By the House of God! We are those with better claim to the
  Prophet.
By God! The son of an illegitimate son will not judge us!

---

481. Following the Constantinople ms. and reading ʿAmr as in Balādhurī, *Ansāb*, II/2, 172.

482. ʿAmr, his *mawlā* Saʿd and Mujammiʿ were three of the group of four who came to al-Ḥusayn with al-Ṭirimmāḥ. See Balādhurī, *Ansāb*, II/2, 172. Jābir's name occurs for the first time; he is otherwise unknown.

483. Laylā was a wife of al-Ḥusayn. ʿAlī al-Akbar was the only child she bore al-Ḥusayn. See Mufīd, *Irshād* (trans.), 379. Her father, Abū Murrah, is otherwise unknown.

He declared these words several times, and the Kūfans were afraid   [357]
to kill him. Then Murrah b. Munqidh b. al-Nuʿmān al-ʿAbdī[484]
saw him. He said, "If I do not deprive his father of him, may the
felonies of the Arabs come on me if he passes me doing the same
as he has been doing." ʿAlī b. al-Ḥusayn continued to attack the
people, but then Murrah b. Munqidh came against him and stabbed
him. He was struck down and the people fell upon him, cutting
him with their swords.

According to Abū Mikhnaf—Sulaymān b. Abī Rāshid—Ḥumayd
b. Muslim al-Azdī: On that day I heard al-Ḥusayn saying, "May
God kill the people who killed you, my son. How courageous they
are against the Merciful God and in violating the inviolable kin of
the Apostle of God! After you the world means nothing for me."
Then I saw a woman like the rising sun come out, hurrying. She
was crying, "My brother, my nephew!" I asked who she was and
was told that it was Zaynab, daughter of Fāṭimah, daughter of the
Apostle of God. She came and threw herself on him. Al-Ḥusayn
went, took her by the hand and then led her back to the tent.
Then he went to his son, and his young men went to him. He
said, "Carry your brother back." They carried him and put him
before the tent that they had been fighting in front of.

ʿAmr b. Ṣubayḥ al-Ṣaddāʾī[485] shot an arrow at ʿAbdallāh b.
Muslim b. ʿAqīl.[486] As ʿAbdallāh put up his hand to guard his
brow, [the arrow struck his hand and penetrated through to his
brow, and fixed his hand to his forehead]. He was not able to move
his hand.[487] Then another arrow was directed at him that split his
heart in two.

The people began to drive against them from every side. ʿAbd-

---

484. Murrah b. Munqidh b. al-Nuʿmān al-ʿAbdī fought at the Battle of the
Camel for ʿAlī. See Ṭabarī, I, 3202. The supporters of al-Mukhtār tried to kill him
in vengeance for his part in this battle but, although he was wounded, he escaped
and joined their enemies. See Ṭabarī, II, 667.

485. It is also claimed that Zayd b. Ruqād shot the arrow. See Ṭabarī, II, 667.
Anyway for his part in the battle, ʿAmr b. Ṣubayḥ al-Ṣaddāʾī was stabbed to death
by al-Mukhtār's followers in vengeance for the death of al-Ḥusayn. See Ṭabarī, II,
678.

486. ʿAbdallāh is one of the sons of Muslim b. ʿAqīl. His mother was Ruqayyah,
who was a slave wife of ʿAlī b. Abī Ṭālib. See Iṣfahānī, Maqātil, 62.

487. The text is clearly defective. I have added the sentence in brackets from
Mufīd, Irshād, 223, and emended kaffayhi to read kaffahu.

[358] allāh b. Quṭbah al-Ṭāʾī al-Nabhānī[488] attacked ʿAwn b. ʿAbdallāh b. Jaʿfar b. Abī Ṭālib and killed him. ʿĀmir b. Nahshal al-Taymī[489] attacked Muḥammad b. ʿAbdallāh b. Jaʿfar b. Abī Ṭālib and killed him. ʿUthmān b. Khālid b. Usayr al-Juhanī and Bishr b. Sawṭ al-Hamdānī al-Qābiḍī[490] launched themselves against ʿAbd al-Raḥmān b. ʿAqīl b. Abī Ṭālib,[491] and killed him. ʿAbdallāh b. ʿUrwah al-Khathʿamī[492] shot at Jaʿfar b. ʿAqīl b. Abī Ṭālib[493] and killed him.

According to Abū Mikhnaf—Sulaymān b. Abī Rāshid—Ḥumayd b. Muslim: A young lad came out against us. His face was young like the first splinter of the moon, and there was a sword in his hand. He was wearing a shirt and a waistcloth, and a pair of sandals, one of whose straps was broken—as I remember, it was the left. ʿAmr b. Saʿd b. Nufayl al-Azdī said to me, "By God! Let me attack him." I said, "Praise be to God! What do you want to do that for? Is it not enough for you that these people who, you see, have surrounded them should do the killing?" But he insisted, "By God! Let me attack him." So he rushed against him and did not turn back until he had struck his head with his sword. The young lad fell face downward as he called out, "O uncle!" Al-Ḥusayn showed himself just like the hawk shows itself. He launched into attack like a raging lion and struck ʿAmr [b. Saʿd b. Nufayl] with his sword. That man tried to fend off the blow with his arm, but his arm was cut off from the elbow; he gave a great shriek. As al-Ḥusayn turned away from him, the cavalry of the Kūfans attacked in order to save ʿAmr [b. Saʿd b. Nufayl] from

---

488. ʿAbdallāh b. Quṭbah al-Ṭāʾī al-Nabhānī is not mentioned elsewhere.

489. ʿĀmir b. Nashhal al-Taymī is not mentioned elsewhere.

490. Both ʿUthman and Bishr were killed by the supporters of al-Mukhtār; then their bodies were burned in vengeance for their part in this battle. See Ṭabarī, II, 669–70.

491. ʿAbd al-Raḥmān was a son of ʿAqīl, who was ʿAlī b. Abī Ṭālib's brother. His mother was a slave wife. See Iṣfahānī, Maqātil, 61.

492. Following the Constantinople ms. and reading ʿUrwah for ʿAzrah as in Balādhurī, Ansāb, II/2, 200. See also Iṣfahānī, Maqātil, 61; and Ṭabarī, II, 678. ʿAbdallāh b. ʿUrwah al-Khathʿamī claimed that, although he shot arrows at them, he missed. Nevertheless, he escaped the followers of al-Mukhtār and joined their enemies. His house was destroyed by them. See Ṭabarī, II, 678.

493. Jaʿfar was a son of ʿAqīl; his mother was Umm al-Thaghr. See Iṣfahānī, Maqātil, 61.

Ḥusayn. Their horses collided against ʿAmr with their chests, their hooves kicked out and they galloped with their riders over him so that they trampled him to death. The dust fell; there[494] was al-Ḥusayn standing by the head of the young lad; the lad had his feet stretched out on the ground. Ḥusayn was saying, "May the people who killed you perish, for the one who will oppose them on the Day of Resurrection on your behalf will be your grandfather. By God! It is hard on your uncle that you called him and he did not answer you, or rather he answered but your cry did not help you, for, by God, those who kill his relatives are many but those who help him are few." Then he carried him.

It is just as if I can see the two feet of the boy leaving tracks in the ground while Ḥusayn held his breast close to his own. I asked myself what he would do with him. He brought him and put him with his son ʿAlī b. al-Ḥusayn and the other members of his family who had been slain. I asked about the boy and was told that he was al-Qāsim b. al-Ḥasan b. ʿAlī b. Abī Ṭālib.[495]

Al-Ḥusayn remained there for a long time during that day. Whenever one of the people came against him, he would turn aside from him and was unwilling to be responsible for his death and such a dreadful sin. A man from the Banū Baddāʾ of Kindah called Mālik b. al-Nusayr came against him and struck him on the head with his sword. Al-Ḥusayn was wearing a hooded cloak. The sword cut through [the hood of] the cloak and wounded his head. The cloak became covered with blood. Al-Ḥusayn declared. "Because of that may you never eat and drink with your hand. May God gather you on the [Day of Judgment] with those people who are wrongdoers." He threw down the cloak and called for a cap. He put on the cap and wound a turban around it. He was tired and had become less active.

The man from Kindah had managed to take the cloak, which was made of silk. Later, when he brought it to his wife, Umm ʿAbdallāh bt. al-Ḥurr—she was the sister of Ḥusayn b. al-Ḥurr

[359]

---

494. *Anā* has been omitted as in Iṣfahānī, *Maqātil*, 58.
495. Al-Qāsim was a nephew of al-Ḥusayn; his mother was either Umm al-Salīl or a slave wife. See Iṣfahānī, *Maqātil*, 58; Mufīd, *Irshād* (trans.), 290; and p. 180, below.

al-Baddī[496]—he began to wash the blood from the cloak. His wife said to him, "Have you brought plunder from the son of the daughter of the Apostle of God into my house? Take it away from me." His colleagues mentioned that he remained poor as a result of the wicked action until he died.[497]

[360]   When al-Ḥusayn sat down, he was brought his young child. He sat the babe on his knee. They claim that the child was ʿAbdallāh b. al-Ḥusayn.[498]

According to Abū Mikhnaf—ʿUqbah b. Bashīr al-Asadī[499] said: Abū Jaʿfar Muḥammad b. ʿAlī b. al-Ḥusayn told me that the blood of his family was on the hands of us from Banū Asad. I said to him, "Is it my fault? May God have mercy on you." Then I asked him what our guilt was. He answered, "Al-Ḥusayn was brought his young child; he was on his knee. Then one of you, Banū Asad, shot an arrow that slaughtered the child. Al-Ḥusayn caught the blood [in his hand]. When the palm of his hand was full, he poured the blood onto the ground and said, "O Lord, if it be that You have kept the help of heaven from us, then let it be because Your purpose is better than [immediate] help. Take vengeance for us on these oppressors."

ʿAbdallāh b. ʿUqbah al-Ghanawī[500] shot an arrow at Abū Bakr b. al-Ḥasan b. ʿAlī[501] and killed him. The poet, Ibn Abī ʿAqib (al-Laythī), said [of it]:

---

496. Neither Umm ʿAbdallāh bt. al-Ḥurr or the man of Kindah is mentioned elsewhere.

497. According to Ṭabarī, II, 668, the followers of al-Mukhtār cut his legs off and beat him to death in vengeance for his part in the battle.

498. ʿAbdallāh b. al-Ḥusayn's mother was al-Rabāb daughter of Imruʾ al-Qays. See Iṣfahānī, *Maqātil*, 59.

499. ʿUqbah b. Bashīr al-Asadī is an otherwise unknown reporter of Abū Mikhnaf. See Sezgin, *Abū Miḥnaf*, 223.

500. In his youth, ʿAbdallāh b. ʿUqbah al-Ghanawī had been a Khārijite rebel with Mustawrid. See Wellhausen, *Religio-Political*, 29ff. Later he escaped from the followers of al-Mukhtār, who destroyed his house for his part in this battle. See Ṭabarī, II, 678. He was killed in Ibn al-Ashʿath's rebellion at the Battle of Dayr Jamājim in 82 (701). See Ṭabarī, II, 59, and Sezgin, *Abū Miḥnaf*, 195.

501. Abū Bakr b. al-Ḥusayn has been corrected to Abū Bakr b. al-Ḥasan, as later in Ṭabarī, II, 387. See also Balādhurī, *Ansāb*, II/2, 201; and Mufīd, *Irshād* (trans.), 224. Abū Bakr's name was ʿUmar; see Mufīd, *Irshād* (trans.), 295, where ʿUmar is named as one of the three sons of al-Ḥasan who was killed. According to Ṭabarī, II, 387, his mother was a slave wife.

With the tribe of Ghanī is a drop of our blood,
    and another is with the tribe of Asad. It will be counted and
    remembered.[502]

They claim that al-ʿAbbās b. ʿAlī said to his brothers on his
mother's side, ʿAbdallāh, Jaʿfar and ʿUthmān, "My brothers
through my mother, go forward so that I may be your heir. For
you have no children." They did and they were killed. Hāniʾ b.
Thubayt al-Ḥaḍramī attacked ʿAbdallāh b. ʿAlī b. Abī Ṭālib and
killed him. Then he attacked Jaʿfar b. ʿAlī and killed him. He
brought back his head. Khawalī b. Yazīd al-Aṣbaḥī[503] shot an arrow
at ʿUthmān b. ʿAlī b. Abī Ṭālib. Then a man from Banū Abān b.
Dārim attacked him and killed him. Another man from Banū
Abān b. Dārim shot at Muḥammad b. ʿAlī b. Abī Ṭālib[504] and
killed him. He took away his head.

According to Hishām (b. Muḥammad al-Kalbī)—Abū al-
Hudhayl,[505] one of the clan of Sakūn: I saw Hāniʾ b. Thubayt al-
Ḥaḍramī sitting among a group of Ḥaḍramīs in the time of Khālid
b. ʿAbdallāh.[506] He was then a very old man. I heard him claim   [361]
that he was among those who had witnessed the killing of al-
Ḥusayn and he reported: By God! I was one of ten, all of whom
were on horseback. The horses were circling around and prancing
in fear, as a young man from the family of al-Ḥusayn came out
clutching a stick from the tents and wearing a waistcloth (*izār*)
and a shirt. He was very frightened and looked to the right and
left. I saw two pearls in his ears swinging whenever he turned. A
man approached. Riding until he was close to him, he leaned

---

502. This verse is cited in Balādhurī, *Ansāb*, II/2, 201; Ṭabarī, II, 678; and
Iṣfahānī, *Maqātil*, 57.

503. For his part in this battle, Khawalī b. Yazīd al-Asaḥī was killed and his
body burned in vengeance for his having helped to kill al-Ḥusayn. See Ṭabarī, II,
671.

504. There is some confusion over the identity of this son of ʿAlī. Mufīd made
his *kunyah* Abū Bakr and said he was a son of Laylā bt. Masʿūd. See Mufīd, *Irshād*
(trans.), 168. Hishām b. Muḥammad al-Kalbī maintained that he was the son of
Asmāʾ, daughter of Umays al-Khathʿami. See Ṭabarī, I, 3471. The greater evidence
is that he was the son of a slave wife. See Ṭabarī, I, 3471, and Iṣfahānī, *Maqātil*, 56.

505. Perhaps Abū al-Hudhayl was Ghālib b. Hudhayl al-Kūfī, a traditionist,
who died between 140 (757) and 150 (767). See Sezgin, *Abū Miḥnaf*, 44.

506. Khālid b. ʿAbdallāh became governor of Iraq in 105 (724) and remained in
the post until 120 (738). See *EI²*, s.v. Khālid b. ʿAbd Allāh al-Ḳasrī.

down from his horse. Then he overcame the boy and cut him down with his sword.[507]

According to Hishām (b. Muḥammad al-Kalbī)—the Sakūnī said: Hāniʾ b. Thubayt was the man who had killed the youth. When he was blamed for it, he attributed it to someone other than himself.

According to Hishām (b. Muḥammad al-Kalbī)—ʿAmr b. Shamir[508]—Jābir (b. Yazīd) al-Juʿfī:[509] Al-Ḥusayn's thirst became so great that he approached in order to drink water. Ḥuṣayn b. Tamīm shot an arrow at him, and it landed in his mouth. The blood spurted from his mouth, and he brushed it away into the air. Then he praised and glorified God. He brought his hands together and said, "O God! Count their number, destroy their power and do not let one of them remain on the earth."

According to Hishām (b. Muḥammad al-Kalbī)—his father, Muḥammad b. al-Sāʾib[510]—al-Qāsim b. al-Aṣbagh b. Nubātah[511] —one of those who was a witness in the camp of al-Ḥusayn: When Ḥusayn's camp was overrun, he rode toward the dam, trying to reach the Euphrates. One of the Banū Abān b. Dārim shouted, "Woe upon you! Prevent him from getting to the water. Don't let his Shīʿah get to him." He whipped his horse, and the people followed him so that they prevented al-Ḥusayn from getting to [362] the Euphrates. Then al-Ḥusayn cried out, "O God! Make him thirsty!" The Abānī took out an arrow and lodged it in al-Ḥusayn's throat. Al-Ḥusayn pulled out the arrow and held out the palms of his hands. Both were filled with blood. Then al-Ḥusayn

---

507. The youth is not identified in the text. It may have been either ʿAbdallāh b. ʿAlī or Jaʿfar b. ʿAlī, whom Hāniʾ has just been reported to have killed.

508. ʿAmr b. Shamir was a follower of the sixth Shīʿite Imām Jaʿfar al-Ṣādiq who died in 148 (765). He was regarded by the Shīʿah as an unreliable transmitter; he chiefly reported from Jābir b. Yazīd al-Juʿfī. See Najāshī, *Rijāl*, 220.

509. Jābir (b. Yazīd) al-Juʿfī was a follower of both the fifth Shīʿite Imām, Muḥammad al-Bāqir, and the sixth Imām, Jaʿfar al-Ṣādiq. He was regarded by the Shīʿah as having mixed with extremists. Although he wrote many books, they regard them as suspect. He wrote an account of the death of al-Ḥusayn; he died in 128 (745–46). See Najāshī, *Rijāl*, 99–100.

510. Muḥammad b. al-Sāʾib was an authority on genealogy and the Qurʾān; he died in al-Kūfah in 146 (763). See Ibn al-Nadīm, *Fihrist*, ed. and trans. Bayard Dodge, I, 205–6.

511. Al-Qāsim's father, al-Aṣbagh b. Nubātah, was a well-known Shīʿite and supporter of ʿAlī. Al-Aṣbagh wrote a book on the death of al-Ḥusayn. Perhaps this report is from his father's book. See al-Ṭūsī, *Fihrist*, 63.

said, "O God! I complain to you about what is being done to the son of the daughter of your Prophet."

By God! The man from Banū Abān b. Dārim only waited a short time before God cast down on him a thirst that he could never quench.

According to al-Qāsim b. al-Aṣbagh: You could have seen me among those who used to visit that man. There would be cold water with date wine in it, glasses with milk in them, and earthenware bottles with water, and yet he would say, "Woe upon you! Give me a drink, for the thirst is killing me." Then he would be given the earthenware bottle or the glass, which would have quenched the thirst of a whole family. He would drink it. When he took it away from his mouth, he would rest for a moment. Then he would say, "Woe upon you! Give me a drink, for the thirst is killing me." By God! It was not long before his belly was split open as if it were a camel's belly.

According to Abū Mikhnaf's account: Shamir b. Dhī al-Jawshan advanced with a group of about ten Kūfan foot soldiers opposite the place where al-Ḥusayn had put his baggage and his family. Al-Ḥusayn moved toward it but they cut him off from his baggage. Al-Ḥusayn cried out, "Shame on you! If you have no religion and do not fear the Day of Return, then [at least] in matters of your world be freeborn men, who have some qualities of nobility, and prevent the mean and ignorant among you from getting to my baggage and my family." Ibn Dhī al-Jawshan retorted, "That is your task, son of Fāṭimah." He advanced against him with the foot soldiers. Among them were: Abū al-Janūb—his name was ʿAbd al-Raḥmān al-Juʿfī, al-Qashʿam b. ʿAmr b. Yazīd al-Juʿfī,[512] Ṣāliḥ b. Wahb al-Yazanī,[513] Sinān b. Anas al-Nakhaʿī,[514] and Khawalī b. Yazīd al-Aṣbaḥī.[515] Shamir b. Dhī al-Jawshan began to urge them on. He went past Abū al-Janūb,

---

512. Balādhurī gave his name as al-Qashʿam b. ʿAmr b. Nadhīr and added that he was among those who held back from supporting ʿAlī. See *Ansāb*, II/2, 202. He is not mentioned with regard to any other incident.

513. Ṣāliḥ b. Wahb al-Yazanī is not mentioned with regard to any other incident.

514. It is reported that in the days of al-Ḥajjāj b. Yūsuf, Sinān b. Anas al-Nakhaʿī's tongue used to stick in his throat; he became mad and, whenever he ate, he had to defecate, because of the part he played in killing al-Ḥusayn. See Ṭabarī, III, 2333.

515. Khawalī b. Yazīd al-Aṣbaḥī also took al-Ḥusayn's head. See text p. 161, below; and Balādhurī, *Ansāb*, II/2, 202.

[363] who was fully armed and told him, "Advance against him." Abū al-Janūb retorted, "What is stopping you from advancing against him?" Shamir said, "Are you saying that to me?" Abū Janūb demanded, "Are you saying it to me?" They cursed each other and Abū al-Janūb—he was a brave man—said, "By God! I am tempted to dash the point of my spear into your eye." Shamir went away from him, declaring, "By God! If I have the power to harm you, I will harm you."

Then Shamir b. Dhī al-Jawshan advanced with the foot soldiers toward al-Ḥusayn. Al-Ḥusayn began to attack them and they drew back from him. They surrounded him completely. A boy from his family came toward al-Ḥusayn. His aunt, Zaynab, daughter of ʿAlī, caught hold of him to stop him. Al-Ḥusayn told her to keep him with her but the boy refused. He rushed forward to al-Ḥusayn and stood at his side.[516] Baḥr b. Kaʿb b. ʿUbaydallāh of the Banū Taym Allāh b. Thaʿlabah b. ʿUkābah[517] rushed toward al-Ḥusayn with a sword. The young lad said to him, "Son of an impure woman, are you trying to kill my uncle?" Baḥr struck at him with his sword. The boy tried to fend off the blow with his arm. The sword cut through it to the skin; there was the arm hanging. The boy cried out, "O my mother!" Al-Ḥusayn took hold of him and embraced him. He said to him, "My nephew, try to bear what has come to you and consider the good in it, for God will unite you with your righteous ancestors, with the Apostle of God, with ʿAlī b. Abī Ṭālib, Ḥamzah, Jaʿfar and al-Ḥasan b. ʿAlī."

According to Abū Mikhnaf—Sulaymān b. Abī Rāshid—Ḥumayd b. Muslim: On that day I heard al-Ḥusayn say, "O God! Keep the drops of rain from the sky from them. Deny them the blessings of the earth. Even as You have made [life] pleasant for them for a

[364] time, divide them into factions, and make them follow the ways of factions and let their rulers never be pleased with them. They summoned us so that they might support us and then they became hostile to us and killed us." He struck out against the foot soldiers until they drew back from him.

---

516. It is unclear who the boy was; Baḥr was not listed as having killed any of al-Ḥusayn's nephews.

517. Baḥr b. Kaʿb b. ʿUbaydallāh is unknown apart from his part in this battle and the consequence for him of it. See pp. 159, 161, below.

When al-Ḥusayn was left with only a group of three or four, he called for a pair of well-woven trousers (*sarāwīl*) in which the edge, which was of well-woven Yemenī cloth, glittered. He tore them and split them open so that he should not have them plundered. One of his followers said to him, "You should wear underbreeches (*tubbān*)[518] under them." He answered, "Those are lowly clothes, and it is not appropriate for me to wear them." When he was killed, Baḥr b. Kaʿb plundered him of [the trousers] and left him naked.

According to Abū Mikhnaf—ʿAmr b. Shuʿayb[519]—Muḥammad b. ʿAbd al-Raḥmān:[520] The hands of Baḥr b. Kaʿb were so wet in winter that they used to sprinkle water and they were so dry in summer that they were like sticks.

According to Abū Mikhnaf—al-Ḥajjāj (b. ʿAlī)—ʿAbdallāh b. ʿAmmār b. ʿAbd Yāguth al-Bāriqī:[521] Afterwards, ʿAbdallāh b. ʿAmmār was blamed for being present at the killing of al-Ḥusayn but ʿAbdallāh b. ʿAmmār maintained, "I have done a favor to the Banū Hāshim." We asked, "What favor have you done them?" He answered, "I attacked Ḥusayn with my spear. I came toward him. By God! I could have stabbed him if I had wanted to. Then I turned aside from him but not too far away, for I said to myself, 'What will I achieve by taking his killing on myself? Let someone else kill him.'"

Then ʿAbdallāh b. ʿAmmār reported: The foot soldiers attacked him from right and left. He launched himself against those to his right until they dispersed. Then he launched himself against those to his left until they dispersed. He was wearing one of his shirts of silk and a turban. By God! I have never seen such persistence. His sons, his family and his followers had been killed, Yet he was stronger in heart. Neither was anyone sharper in spirit than he, nor bolder in advancing. By God! I have not seen his like before or   [365]

---

518. *Tubbān* are described as small trousers; they cover the private parts, and they are worn by sailors. See Ibn Manẓūr, *Lisān*, s.v. *tbn*.

519. ʿAmr b. Shuʿayb was a well-known traditionist, who died in 118 (736). See Ibn Ḥajar, *Tahdhīb*, VIII, 48−55.

520. Muḥammad b. ʿAbd al-Raḥmān is not mentioned with regard to any other incident.

521. ʿAbdallāh b. ʿAmmār was at one time a follower of ʿAlī; however, he had a considerable change of heart. See Sezgin, *Abū Miḥnaf*, 204.

since. If the foot soldiers were there, they would retreat from his right and his left as the goats retreat when the wolf comes upon them. By God! He was just like that when Zaynab, daughter of Fāṭimah, came out. I could see her earrings bobbing between her ears and her shoulders. She was saying, "I wish that the sky would come down on the earth." ʿUmar b. Saʿd had come closer to Ḥusayn and she called out, "ʿUmar b. Saʿd, is Abū ʿAbdallāh being killed while you watch?" I could see ʿUmar's tears flowing down his cheeks and beard as he turned his face away from her.

According to Abū Mikhnaf—al-Ṣaqʿab b. Zuhayr—Ḥumayd b. Muslim: Al-Ḥusayn was wearing a shirt (jubbah) of silk and a turban that had been dyed with woad. I heard him say before he was killed, while he was fighting on foot like a brave horseman, avoiding blows, taking advantage of gaps [in the ranks] and attacking the cavalry, "Are you urging one another to kill me? By God! After me you will not kill another servant of God, for God will be more displeased with you for killing than He will be with me. By God! I hope that God will favor me by making you lowly. Then may He grant me vengeance on you without your perceiving it. By God! If you kill me, God will send misfortune among you and cause the shedding of your blood. Nor will God be satisfied until He has multiplied the dread torture for you."

There was a long delay through the day. If the people had wanted to kill him, they could have done so but each of them was averting the action; each hoped the other would kill al-Ḥusayn. Each of them preferred that the others should do the deed. Then Shamir shouted among the people, "Shame on you! Why are you waiting for the man? Kill him, may your mothers be deprived of you!" So an attack was launched against him on every side. A blow was struck against his left hand by Zurʿah b. Sharīk al-Tamīmī.[522] It hit him on his shoulder. They withdrew while he was falling and stumbling. As he was in that plight, Sinān b. Anas b. ʿAmr al-Nakhaʿī attacked him and stabbed him with his spear. He fell. Sinān told Khawalī b. Yazīd al-Aṣbaḥī to cut off his head. The latter wanted to do so but he was weak; he trembled. Sinān b. Anas said to him, "May God crush your arms and take away your

[366]

---

522. Zurʿah b. Sharīk al-Tamīmī is not mentioned with regard to any other incident.

hands." He bent down, killed him and cut his head off. It was, then, handed to Khawalī b. Yazīd.

Before that al-Ḥusayn had been struck by [many] swords.

According to Abū Mikhnaf—Jaʿfar b. Muḥammad b. ʿAlī:[523] When al-Ḥusayn was killed, there were thirty-three stab wounds and thirty-four blows.

[Ḥumayd] continued: Sinān b. Anas did not let anyone go near al-Ḥusayn without attacking him, out of fear that he might be deprived of al-Ḥusayn's head. Then he took al-Ḥusayn's head and handed it to Khawalī. The body of al-Ḥusayn was plundered as it was. Baḥr b. Kaʿb took his trousers. Qays b. al-Ashʿath took his cloak. It was silken, and he was afterward called Qays of the cloak. One of Banū Awd called al-Aswad took his sandals, and one of the Banū Nahshal b. Dārim took his sword. Later it came into the possession of the family of Ḥabīb b. Budayl.[524]

The people turned to the turmeric, the garments and the camels (in al-Ḥusayn's camp); they plundered them. The people turned to the womenfolk of al-Ḥusayn, his baggage, and equipment. The women had their clothes ripped off their backs, they were forcibly deprived of them and they were taken away from them.

According to Abū Mikhnaf—Zuhayr b. ʿAbd al-Raḥmān al-Khathʿamī: Suwayd b. ʿAmr b. Abī al-Muṭāʿ had been brought [367] down and was covered with wounds. He had fallen wounded amid those killed. As he recovered consciousness, he heard them saying that al-Ḥusayn had been killed. He had a knife but his sword had been taken. So he fought against them with the knife for a time, but then he was killed. ʿUrwah b. Biṭār al-Taghlibī[525] and Zayd b. Ruqād al-Janbī[526] killed him. He was the last to be killed.

According to Abū Mikhnaf—Sulaymān b. Abī Rashīd—Ḥumayd b. Muslim: I came to ʿAlī al-Aṣghar b. al-Ḥusayn b. ʿAlī. He was

---

523. Jaʿfar b. Muḥammad b. ʿAlī was a great-grandson of al-Ḥusayn and the sixth Imām of the Shīʿah, who died in 148/765. See *EI²*, s.v. Djaʿfar al-Ṣādiḳ.

524. Ḥabīb b. Budayl became governor of al-Rayy in 131 (748). See Ṭabarī, III, 2–3.

525. Balādhurī gave ʿUrwah's name as ʿAzrah b. Biṭān. See *Ansāb* II/2, 204. Under either name he is otherwise unknown.

526. Zayd b. Ruqād al-Janbī is also claimed to have been responsible for the killing of ʿAbdallāh b. Muslim b. ʿAqīl. He was burned to death by the supporters of al-Mukhtār in vengeance for his part in the battle. See Ṭabarī, II, 667–68.

stretched out on his bed and he was ill. There was Shamir b. Dhī al-Jawshan with some foot soldiers who were asking him, "Shall we not kill this one?" I said, "Praise be to God! Will boys be killed, for this is only a boy?" I went on arguing like that so that I kept all who came away from him until ʿUmar b. Saʿd arrived. He ordered, "No one should enter the tent of these women nor disturb this sick boy. Whoever has taken any of their belongings should return them." By God! No one returned anything. ʿAlī b. al-Ḥusayn said to me, "May you be a well-rewarded man, for by God, God kept evil away from me through your words."

People said to Sinān b. Anas, "You have killed Ḥusayn b. ʿAlī, the son of Fāṭimah, daughter of the Apostle of God. You have killed the greatest of the Arabs in nobility, who came to these people with the intention of taking them away from the despotism over them. So go to your leaders and ask them for your reward. If they give you their treasure houses for killing al-Ḥusayn, it would be little." Sinān went forward on his horse. He was a poet and there was an insanity (*lūthah*) in him. He went and stood at the entrance of ʿUmar b. Saʿd's tent and called out at the top of his voice:

[368]   Fill my saddlebag with silver and gold.
        I have killed the well-guarded king.
I have killed the man of noblest parents
        and when people trace descent his is the best.[527]

ʿUmar b. Saʿd declared, "I testify that you are mad. You could never be sane. Bring him in to me." When Sinān was brought in, ʿUmar struck him with a cane and said, "Madman, are you uttering these words? By God! If Ibn Ziyād heard you, he would have your head cut off."

ʿUmar b. Saʿd apprehended ʿUqbah b. Simʿān. He was the mawlā of al-Rabāb bt. Imruʾ al-Qays of Kalb, who was the mother of Sukaynah, daughter of al-Ḥusayn. He asked him who he was. He answered, "I am a slave who is possessed [by another]." So he let him go.

No one else among them escaped except for al-Muraqqaʿ b.

---

527. These verses came earlier. See p. 76, above.

Thumāmah al-Asadī.[528] He had been shooting arrows as he knelt on his knees and fought. A group of his own tribe had come to him and said, "You are guaranteed safe-conduct. Come out to us." He had gone out to them. When 'Umar b. Sa'd had gone with them to Ibn Ziyād and told him about al-Muraqqa', Ibn Ziyād sent him to al-Zārrah.

Then 'Umar b. Sa'd called out among his followers, "Who will volunteer [to go] to al-Ḥusayn and make his horse trample on al-Ḥusayn's body?" Ten volunteered. Among them was Isḥāq b. Ḥaywah al-Ḥaḍramī,[529] who was the one who stole al-Ḥusayn's shirt and later got leprosy, and Aḥbash b. Marthad b. 'Alqamah b. Salāmah al-Ḥaḍramī.[530] They trampled on the body of al-Ḥusayn with their horses until they had crushed his back and his chest. I learned that some time later an arrow from an unknown direction hit Aḥbash b. Marthad as he was standing in a battle. It split his heart, and he died.

Seventy-two men of the followers of al-Ḥusayn were killed. Some of the Banū Asad, who dwelt at al-Ghādiriyyah, buried al-Ḥusayn and his followers a day after they had been killed. Eighty-eight men of the followers of 'Umar b. Sa'd were killed apart from those who were wounded. 'Umar b. Sa'd prayed over them and buried them.

No sooner had al-Ḥusayn been killed than on the very same day his head was despatched with Khawalī b. Yazīd and Ḥumayd b. Muslim al-Azdī to 'Ubaydallāh to Ziyād. Khawalī traveled with the head. When he arrived at the palace, he found the door locked. He went to his own house and put the head under a washing tub in his house. He lived with two women, one from the Banū Asad tribe and the other from the Ḥaḍramīs. The latter was called al-Nawār bt. Mālik b. 'Aqrab.[531] That night was his night with the Ḥaḍramī woman.

According to Hishām b. Muḥammad al-Kalbī—his father (Muḥammad b. al-Sā'ib)—al-Nawār bt. Mālik: Khawalī came with the

[369]

---

528. Al-Muraqqa' b. Thumāmah al-Asadī was a supporter of al-Ḥusayn; he was not previously mentioned.

529. Isḥāq b. Ḥaywah al-Ḥaḍramī is not mentioned with regard to any other incident.

530. Aḥbash is not mentioned with regard to any other incident.

531. Al-Nawār is not mentioned with regard to any other incident.

head of al-Ḥusayn and put it under a washing tub in his house. He came into the room and went to bed. I asked him, "What is the news? What has happened to you?" He answered, "I have brought you the wealth of ages. There is the head of al-Ḥusayn with you in the house." I cried out, "Shame on you! People bring gold and silver, and you bring the head of the son of the Apostle of God. No, by God! You and I will never be together again in any room." I jumped from my bed and went out into the house. He called the Asadī woman and made her sleep with him. I sat on watch. By God! I began to see a light that spread like a pillar from the sky toward the washing tub and I saw white birds futtering round it. In the morning, Khawalī took the head to ʿUbaydallāh b. Ziyād.

ʿUmar b. Saʿd remained for the rest of that day and the next. Then he ordered Ḥumayd b. Bukayr al-Aḥmarī to announce the departure to al-Kūfah among the people. He took with him the daughters and sisters of al-Ḥusayn, the children who had been with him, and ʿAlī b. al-Ḥusayn, who was sick.

[370]   According to Abū Mikhnaf—Abū Zuhayr al-ʿAbsī—Qurrah b. Qays al-Tamīmī: I looked at those women. As they passed Ḥusayn and the members of his family and his sons, they shrieked and tore at their faces. I turned my horse toward them. I had never seen a sight of women more beautiful than the sight I saw of those women. By God! They were more beautiful than wild cows at Yabrīn. Among the things that I will never forget: I will never forget the words of Zaynab, the daughter of Fāṭimah, as she passed the prostrate body of her brother, al-Ḥusayn. She was saying, "O Muḥammad! O Muḥammad! May the angels of heaven bless you. Here is Ḥusayn in the open, stained with blood and with limbs torn off. O Muḥammad! Your daughters are prisoners, your progeny are killed, and the east wind blows dust over them." By God! She made every enemy and friend weep.

The heads of the rest were cut off and [these] seventy-two heads were sent with Shamir b. Dhī al-Jawshan, Qays b. al-Ashʿath, ʿAmr b. al-Ḥajjāj, and ʿAzrah b. Qays. They journeyed until they brought them to ʿUbaydallāh b. Ziyād.

According to Abū Mikhnaf—Sulaymān b. Abī Rāshid—Ḥumayd b. Muslim: ʿUmar b. Saʿd summoned me and sent me to his family to tell them the good news of his health, for God had given him victory. I journeyed until I came to his family. I informed them of his news. Then I went on to visit ʿUbaydallāh b. Ziyād. I found Ibn Ziyād holding an assembly for the people. I found that the delegation had already come to him. He had allowed them to enter and had given permission for the people to enter. So I went in with those who entered. There was the head of al-Ḥusayn placed in front of him. There he was, poking between its teeth with a cane. When Zayd b. Arqam saw that he continued to poke the head with his cane, he said, "Raise that cane from those teeth, for by God other than Whom there is no god, I have seen the lips of the Apostle of God kiss those lips." Then the old man began to weep. Ibn Ziyād said, "May God make your eyes weep, for, by God, if it were not for the fact that you are an old man, who has become silly and your mind has left you, I would cut off your head." Zayd b. Arqam stood up and left. When he had gone, I heard the people saying, "By God! Zayd b. Arqam said such words which, if Ibn Ziyād had heard, he would have killed him." I asked, "What did he say?" They replied, "As he passed us, he was saying: 'A slave has given power to a slave and he has made the people his inheritance. You, Arabs, are the slaves after today. You killed the son of Fāṭimah when Ibn Marjānah ordered you. He will kill the best among you and enslave the evil among you. You have accepted humiliation. Let destruction come to those who accept humiliation.'" [371]

When the head of Ḥusayn was brought in with his children, sisters, and womenfolk to ʿUbaydallāh b. Ziyād, Zaynab, daughter of Fāṭimah, had dressed in her dirtiest clothes, disguising herself with her maids surrounding her. She came in and sat down. Ibn Ziyād demanded, "Who is that woman who is sitting down?" She did not answer him. He repeated the question three times, but no one answered him. Then one of her maidservants said to him, "This is Zaynab, daughter of Fāṭimah." ʿUbaydallāh said to her, "Praise be to God, Who has disgraced you, killed you and revealed the false nature of your claims." Zaynab replied, "Praise be to God, Who has favored us with Muḥammad and has purified us completely from sin.[532] It is not as you say, for He only disgraces the great sinner and reveals the false nature of the profligate." He asked, "How do you consider God has treated your family?" She

---

532. A reference to Qurʾān, 33:33.

replied, "God decreed death for them, and they went forward to their resting places. God will gather you and us together. You will plead your excuses to Him and we will be your adversaries before Him." Ibn Ziyād became enraged and burnt with anger. ʿAmr b. Ḥurayth intervened, "May God make the governor prosperous, she is only a woman. Are women responsible for anything that they say? Do not hold her responsible for her words, or blame her for foolish talk." Ibn Ziyād said to her, "God has healed my soul from your tyrant and the rebellious, disobedient members of your family." Zaynab wept and then said: "By my life! You have killed the mature of my family; you have ruined my family; you have cut down my young branches; you have pulled out my root. If this satisfies you, then you have your fill."

ʿUbaydallāh declared, "By my life! This is real bravery. Your father was a brave poet." She answered, "What has a woman to do with bravery? Indeed, I have things to distract me from bravery, but what I say is just a spontaneous expression."

According to Abū Mikhnaf—al-Mujālid b. Saʿīd: When ʿUbaydallāh b. Ziyād noticed ʿAlī b. al-Ḥusayn, he said to one of the police, "See whether this one has attained the status of a man." After he had pulled his waistcloth from him, he said that he had. Ibn Ziyād ordered, "Take him away and cut his head off." ʿAlī said, "There is a kinship between you and these women. So send a man with them to look after them." Ibn Ziyād told him to go and sent him with them.

According to Abū Mikhnaf—Sulaymān b. Abī Rāshid—Ḥumayd b. Muslim: I was standing by Ibn Ziyād when ʿAlī b. al-Ḥusayn was presented to him. He asked him, "What is your name?" He replied, "I am ʿAlī b. al-Ḥusayn." Ibn Ziyād said, "Did not God kill ʿAlī b. al-Ḥusayn?" he was silent so Ibn Ziyād asked him, "What is wrong with you that you do not speak?" He answered, "I had a brother who was also called ʿAlī b. al-Ḥusayn, and the people killed him." Ibn Ziyād retorted, "God killed him." ʿAlī was silent. Ibn Ziyād demanded, "What is wrong with you that you do not speak?" He answered, " 'God receives the souls at the time of their death.'[533] 'It is not possible for a soul to die without

---

533. Qurʾān, 39:42 (43).

God's permission.' "[534] Ibn Ziyād shouted, "By God! You are one of them. See whether he has matured. By God! I think he is a man."

Murrī b. Muʿādh al-Aḥmarī[535] uncovered him and said, "Yes, he has matured." Ibn Ziyād ordered him to be killed. ʿAlī b. al-Ḥusayn asked him, "Who will you make responsible for these women?" Zaynab, his aunt, clung to him and pleaded, "O Ibn Ziyād haven't you had enough of us? Have you not sated yourself with our blood? Will you let any of us survive?" She embraced ʿAlī and continued, "I plead to you by God if you are a believer, that if you kill him, you kill me with him." ʿAlī b. al-Ḥusayn called to him, "Ibn Ziyād, if there is any kinship between you and the family of ʿAlī send a righteous man to accompany them in a proper Islamic way." Ibn Ziyād looked at Zaynab for a time and then he looked at the people and said, "How wonderful is kinship! By God! I think that she really wants me to kill her with him, if I kill him. Leave the boy. . . . Go with your women."

Ḥumayd b. Muslim reported: When ʿUbaydallāh had entered the palace, and the people had entered, the call—"the prayer is general"—was made and the people gathered in the great mosque. Ibn Ziyād ascended the pulpit. He said, "Praise be to God, Who has revealed the truth and the followers of truth. He has given victory to the Commander of the Faithful, Yazīd b. Muʿāwiyah, and his party. He has killed the liar who is the son of a liar, al-Ḥusayn b. ʿAlī, and his Shīʿah."

Ibn Ziyād had not finished his speech when up before him jumped ʿAbdallāh b. ʿAfīf al-Azdī al-Ghāmidī,[536] one of the Banū Wālibah. He had been one of the Shīʿah of ʿAlī, and his left eye had been lost in the Battle of the Camel alongside ʿAlī. At the Battle of Ṣiffīn, he had been struck on the head and had another blow on the eyebrow; as a result his other eye had been lost. He hardly ever left the great mosque, where he used to pray until night and then go. When he heard Ibn Ziyād's speech, he shouted, "Son of Marjānah, the ones who are liars and sons of liars are you

[374]

---

534. Qurʾān, 3:145 (139).

535. Murrī b. Muʿādh al-Aḥmarī is not mentioned with regard to any other incident.

536. Apart from the information given in the text, ʿAbdallāh b. ʿAfīf al-Azdī al-Ghāmidī is otherwise unknown.

and your father and the man who appointed you and his father. Ibn Marjānah, are you killing the sons of prophets and trying to speak the language of true men?" Ibn Ziyād ordered, "Get him for me." The soldiers jumped toward him and seized him but he gave the battle cry of al-Azd, "O Mabrūr" ("O blessed one"). ʿAbd al-Raḥmān b. Mikhnaf al-Azdī,[537] who was sitting there, declared, "You have brought trouble for others. You have destroyed yourself and you have destroyed your tribe." At that time there were seven hundred fighters of al-Azd present in al-Kūfah. Some of the young men of al-Azd moved quickly to ʿAbdallāh b. ʿAfīf and took him away. They brought him to his family. Then Ibn Ziyād sent to him some of those who would bring him back; they killed him. He had him crucified in the wasteland (al-sabakhah).[538]

According to Abū Mikhnaf: ʿUbaydallāh b. Ziyād had the head of al-Ḥusayn set up in al-Kūfah; he took it around al-Kūfah. Then he summoned Zaḥr b. Qays[539] and despatched him with the head of al-Ḥusayn and the heads of his followers to Yazīd b. Muʿāwiyah. With Zaḥr were Abū Burdah b. ʿAwf al-Azdī[540] and Ṭāriq b. Abī Ẓubyān al-Azdī.[541] They departed and took all the heads to Yazīd b. Muʿāwiyah in Syria.

According to Hishām (b. Muḥammad al-Kalbī)—ʿAbdallāh b. Yazīd b. Rawḥ b. Zinbāʿ al-Judhāmī[542]—his father[543]—al-Ghāz b. Rabīʿah al-Jurashī of Ḥimyar:[544]

---

537. ʿAbd al-Raḥmān b. Mikhnaf al-Azdī was a tribal leader of Azd and the great-uncle of Abū Mikhnaf; he died in 75 (695). See Sezgin, *Abū Miḥnaf*, 219.

538. Yāqūt records an area of salty marshy land called *al-sabakhah* in al-Baṣrah. See Yāqūt, *Muʿjam*, III, 30. There seems to have been an area called by the same name in al-Kūfah.

539. Zaḥr b. Qays was a Kūfan tribal leader; earlier he gave testimony against Ḥujr b. ʿAdī. Later he joined the supporters of Ibn al-Zubayr but then deserted them for ʿAbd al-Malik. See Ṭabarī, II, 134, 614, 804.

540. Abū Burdah b. ʿAwf al-Azdī is not mentioned with regard to any other incident.

541. Ṭāriq b. Abī Ẓubyān al-Azdī is not mentioned with regard to any other incident.

542. ʿAbdallāh b. Yazīd b. Rawḥ b. Zinbāʿ al-Judhāmī is only found here as an authority of Ibn al-Kalbī.

543. He is Yazīd b. Rawḥ. He is not mentioned with regard to any other incident but his grandfather was Rawḥ b. Zinbāʿ al-Judhāmī of Kalb, from Syria, who was appointed governor of Medina by Muslim b. ʿUqbah; he played a role in supporting Marwān for the caliphate. See p. 221, below; and Ṭabarī, II, 479.

544. Al-Ghāz b. Rabīʿah al-Jurashī is not mentioned with regard to any other incident.

By God! I was with Yazīd b. Muʿāwiyah in Damascus when
Zaḥr b. Qays came to see Yazīd b. Muʿāwiyah. Yazīd declared,
"Woe upon you! What [have you left] behind you? What have
you got?" He replied, "O Commander of the Faithful, I bring
good news of God's victory and support. Al-Ḥusayn b. ʿAlī came
against us with eighteen men of his House and sixty of his Shīʿah.
We went out to meet them and we asked them to surrender and   [375]
submit to the authority of the governor, ʿUbaydallāh b. Ziyād, or
to fight. They chose to fight rather than to surrender. We attacked
them as the sun rose and surrounded them on every side. Eventually our swords took their toll of the heads of the people; they
began to flee without having any refuge; they sought refuge from
us on the hills and in the hollows like the doves seek refuge from
a hawk. By God! Commander of the Faithful, it was only a time
for the slaughtering of animals, or for a man to take his siesta
before we had come upon the last of them. There were their
naked bodies, their bloodstained clothes, their faces thrown in
the dust. The sun burst down on them; the wind scattered [dust]
over them; their visitors in this deserted and desolate place were
eagles and vultures." Yazīd's eyes filled with tears, and he said, "I
would have been satisfied with your obedience without killing al-
Ḥusayn. May God curse Ibn Sumayyah. By God! If it had been I
who had accompanied him, I would have let him off. May God
have mercy on al-Ḥusayn." Yazīd gave the messenger nothing.

ʿUbaydallāh b. Ziyād ordered the women and children of al-
Ḥusayn to be made ready for traveling. He ordered ʿAlī b. al-
Ḥusayn to be chained with a chain around his neck. Then he
despatched them, to follow the heads, with Muḥaffiz b. Thaʿlabah
al-ʿĀʾidhī,[545] the clan of ʿĀʾidhah of Quraysh, and Shamir b. Dhī
al-Jawshan. They set out with them until they came to Yazīd.
ʿAlī b. al-Ḥusayn did not speak a word to either of them on that
journey until they arrived. When they reached the door of Yazīd,
Muḥaffiz b. Thaʿlabah raised his voice and shouted, "Here is   [376]
Muḥaffiz b. Thaʿlabah, who has brought the Commander of the
Faithful these vile profligates." Yazīd b. Muʿāwiyah answered

---

545. Muḥaffiz b. Thaʿlabah al-ʿĀʾidhī took part in the conquest of Persia; he
was one of those who gave testimony against Ḥujr b. ʿAdī. See Ṭabarī, I, 2460, and
II, 133.

him, "What the mother of Muḥaffiz gave birth to is more evil and grievous."

According to Abū Mikhnaf—Al-Saqʿab b. Zuhayr—al-Qāsim b. ʿAbd al-Raḥmān,[546] a mawlā of Yazīd b. Muʿāwiyah: When the heads were put in front of Yazīd—the head of al-Ḥusayn and those of his family and his followers—Yazīd recited:

[Swords] split the skulls of men who are dear
   to us; but they were more disobedient and oppressive.[547]

[Then he added,] "Yet, by God, Ḥusayn, if I had been to fight you, I would not have killed you."

According to Abū Mikhnaf—Abū Jaʿfar al-ʿAbsī[548]—Abū ʿUmārah al-ʿAbsī:[549] Yaḥyā b. al-Ḥakam, the brother of Marwān b. al-Ḥakam, recited:

The heads on the plain (ṭaff) were closer in kinship
   than Ibn Ziyād, the slave with the false lineage.
The offspring of Umayyah have become as numerous as stones
   while the daughter of the Apostle of God has lost her
   offspring.[550]

Yazīd b. Muʿāwiyah struck his hand against the chest of Yaḥyā b. al-Ḥakam and shouted, "Be quiet!"

When Yazīd b. Muʿāwiyah held an assembly, he summoned the Syrian nobles and sat them around him. Then he summoned ʿAlī b. al-Ḥusayn and the children and womenfolk of al-Ḥusayn. They were brought in to him while the people looked on. Yazīd said to ʿAlī, "ʿAlī, your father cut the bond of kinship with me, showed ignorance of my rights, and tried to deprive me of my position of authority. God has treated him in the way you have seen." ʿAlī replied, "'No misfortune strikes the earth or your-selves unless it has been written in a book before We bring it into

[377]

---

546. Al-Qāsim b. ʿAbd al-Raḥmān also reported about the Battle of Ṣiffīn, giving reports about the Syrians. See Ṭabarī, I, 3248, 3406.

547. The verse has been quoted earlier. See p. 76, above.

548. Abū Jaʿfar al-ʿAbsī only reported this account to Abū Mikhnaf. See Sezgin, Abū Mikhnaf, 188.

549. The only report Abū ʿUmārah al-ʿAbsī has given. See Sezgin, Abū Mikhnaf, 188.

550. Quoted by Balādhurī. See Ansāb, II/2, 222.

existence.'"[551] Yazīd urged his son, Khālid,[552] to answer him. However, Khālid did not know what to say in reply. So Yazīd answered, "Say: 'Whatever misfortune has struck you is because of what your hands have earned, and he excuses much.'"[553] At this he was silent.

Yazīd summoned the women and the children and they were made to sit in front of him. He saw a dreadful sight. He said, "May God detest Ibn Marjānah. If there had been any kinship between him and you, he would not have done this to you; he would not have sent you thus."

According to Abū Mikhnaf—al-Ḥārith b. Kaʿb—Fāṭimah, daughter of ʿAlī:[554] When we were made to sit before Yazīd, he showed pity to us, ordered things for us and was kind to us. Then a Syrian with a red face stood up before Yazīd and said, "Commander of the Faithful, give me this one." He meant me. I was a pretty young girl. I shuddered and moved away, for I thought that that would be allowed them. I caught hold of the skirt of my sister Zaynab. My sister Zaynab was older and cleverer than I. She said that that would not happen. She said to the Syrian, "By God! You are a liar! By God! You are too lowly born! Such a thing is not for you, nor for him!" Yazīd cried out angrily, "By God! You are a liar! That is for me. If I wish to do it, I can do it." She retorted, "No, by God! God would only let you do that if you left our faith and professed belief in another religion." Yazīd screamed, distraught with anger, "Dare you face me in this way! It is your father who has left the religion, and your brother." Zaynab replied, "You, your father and your grandfather have been guided by the religion of God, the religion of my father, the religion of my brother and my grandfather." He shouted, "Enemy of God, you lie!" She answered, "You, a commander who has authority, are vilifying unjustly and oppress with your authority." By God! It was as if he were ashamed; he became silent. The Syrian repeated,

[378]

---

551. Qurʾān, 57:22.

552. Khālid later studied alchemy and astronomy; he also became governor of Ḥimṣ for a time. He died during the caliphate of ʿAbd al-Malik. See Balādhurī, *Ansāb*, IV/1, 359–68.

553. Qurʾān, 42:30 (29).

554. According to Mufīd, Fāṭimah should be al-Ḥusayn's daughter, not ʿAlī's. See Mufīd, *Irshād* (trans.), 231.

"Commander of the Faithful, give me that girl." Yazīd said to him, "Go away! May God strike you dead!"

Then Yazīd b. Muʿāwiyah said, "Al-Nuʿman b. Bashīr, equip them with what will be useful for them and send a good, faithful Syrian with them. Send horsemen and helpers with him and let him go to Medina with them." Next he ordered the women to be lodged in an isolated house. With them [he sent] what would be useful for them. Their brother, ʿAlī b. al-Ḥusayn, was with them in the house. They left and went to Yazīd's house. There was not one of the women of the family of Muʿāwiyah who did not meet them with tears and weeping for al-Ḥusayn. They continued the lamentation for him for three days.

Yazīd never ate lunch or dinner without inviting ʿAlī b. al-Ḥusayn to join him. One day he invited him and he invited ʿAmr b. al-Ḥasan b. ʿAlī, who was still a young boy.[555] He said to ʿAmr, "Will you fight this boy?" meaning his son, Khālid. ʿAmr replied, "No, but give me a knife and give him a knife; then I will fight him." Yazīd rose, caught hold of him and embraced him. Then he said, "That is behavior that I recognize from the father.[556] Does the snake bring forth anything but a snake?" When they were about to leave, he summoned ʿAlī b. al-Ḥusayn and said, "God curse Ibn Marjānah, if I had been with your father, he would never have asked a favor from me without my granting it to him; I would have protected him from death with all my power, even through the destruction of some of my own children. But God has decreed what you have seen. Write to me from Medina and report everything that you need." He presented clothes to them, and entrusted them to the messenger. The latter went with them. He traveled with them at night so that they were in front of him but not out of his sight. When they stopped, he would go aside from them. He and his colleagues would spread out around them like a

[379]

---

555. ʿAmr b. al-Ḥasan b. ʿAlī survived Karbalāʾ but Mufīd does not mention a son of al-Ḥasan as ʿAmr. See Mufīd, *Irshād* (trans.), 176. Perhaps it is ʿUmar; there is some confusion about this son of al-Ḥasan.

556. An Arabic proverb. Literally: "This is a piece of flesh which I recognize from Akhzam." "Akhzam" can mean a snake but it is also the name of a man. The story is that Akhzam struck his father but died before his father. Akhzam's son attacked the grandfather and he said the words that became proverbial. See Ibn Manẓūr, *Lisān*, and al-Bustānī, *Muḥīṭ*, s.v. *khzm*.

group of guards; he would stay in such a position so that when anyone wanted to wash or carry out a [natural] need, he would not be ashamed. He never stopped asking them what they needed; he treated them gently until they arrived at Medina.

According to al-Ḥārith b. Kaʿb—Fāṭimah, daughter of ʿAlī: I said to my sister, Zaynab, "Sister, this Syrian has treated us well! Do you think we should give him a present?" She replied, "By God! We do not have anything that we can give him except our jewelry." I said, "Let us give him our jewelry." So I took my bracelet and armband, and she took her bracelet and armband, and we offered those to him. We apologized to him and said, "This is your reward for the good way in which you have accompanied us." He said, "If what I have done was only for worldly wealth, there would be satisfaction and more in your ornaments. However, by God, I have only done this for God and for your relationship to the Apostle of God."

According to Hishām (b. Muḥammad al-Kalbī)—ʿAwānah b. al-Ḥakam al-Kalbī: When al-Ḥusayn had been killed, and they had brought the baggage and prisoners to al-Kūfah to ʿUbaydallāh, [he imprisoned them]. While the people were imprisoned, a stone was thrown into the prison with a letter tied to it. In the letter, it said: "On such-and-such a day the courier was sent to Yazīd b. Muʿāwiyah for his instructions with regard to you. He will take so many days to go, and he will return on such-and-such a day. If you hear the pronouncement 'God is greater,' they have determined to kill you. If you do not hear the pronouncement 'God is greater,' it means security for you, God willing." Two or three days before the arrival of the courier, another stone was thrown into the prison with a message tied to it and a blade. In the message it said, "Make your last testimonies and wills; the courier is expected on such and such a day." The courier came and the pronouncement "God is greater" was not heard, for a letter had come saying, "Send the prisoners to me."

ʿUbaydallāh b. Ziyād summoned Muḥaffiz b. Thaʿlabah and Shamir b. Dhī al-Jawshan and said, "Take the baggage and the head to the Commander of the Faithful, Yazīd b. Muʿāwiyah." They went until they came to Yazīd. Muḥaffiz b. Thaʿlabah stood [at the door] and called out at the top of his voice, "We have come with the head of the stupidest and lowliest of men." Yazīd de-

[380]

clared, "What the mother of Muḥaffiz gave birth to is stupider and lowlier, but he was a disloyal relative and a wrongdoer." When Yazīd looked at the head of al-Ḥusayn, he recited:

[Swords] split the skulls of men who are dear
    to us; but they were more disobedient and oppressive.[557]

Then he said, "Do you know in what way this man was mistaken? He used to say, 'My father ʿAlī is better than his father; my mother Fāṭimah is better than his mother; my grandfather the Apostle of God is better than his grandfather, and I am better than he and have more right for this affair than he has.' As for his statement that his father is better than my father, my father disputed with his father, and the people know which of them the judgment was in favor of. As for his statement that his mother is better than my mother, by my life, Fāṭimah, daughter of the Apostle of God, is better than my mother. As for his statement that his grandfather is better than my grandfather, by my life, no [381] one who believes in God and the Last Day would regard any one among us as an equal or a rival to the Apostle of God. However, he has been mistaken through his lack of understanding, for he did not read: 'Say: O God, Master of the kingdom, You give the kingdom to whomsoever You wish and You take away the kingdom from whomsoever you wish. You strengthen those whom You wish and You make lowly whomsoever You wish. In Your hand is the decision. Indeed, You have power over everything.'"[558] Then the womenfolk of al-Ḥusayn were brought in to Yazīd. The womenfolk of Yazīd's family, the daughters of Muʿāwiyah and his family, shrieked with grief and lamentation. Fāṭimah, daughter of al-Ḥusayn—she was older than Sukaynah—asked, "Are the daughters of the Apostle of God prisoners, Yazīd?" Yazīd replied, "Cousin, I was unwilling for this to happen." She said, "By God! Not even an earring has been left to us" He answered, "Cousin, what will be given to you will be greater than what has been taken from you." Then they were taken out and taken to the house of Yazīd b. Muʿāwiyah. There was not a woman of Yazīd's family who did not begin to lament and grieve. Yazīd sent to each

---

557. A verse already cited. See pp. 76, 170, above.
558. Qurʾān, 3:26 (25).

of the women, "What has been taken from you?" No woman claimed anything, however expensive, without his giving double its value. Sukaynah used to say, "I never saw a man who did not believe in God who was better than Yazīd b. Muʿāwiyah."

The prisoners were brought to Yazīd. Among them was ʿAlī b. al-Ḥusayn. Yazīd asked him, "What is this, ʿAlī?" ʿAlī replied, "No misfortune strikes the earth or yourselves unless it has been written in a book before We bring it into existence; that is easy for God, so that you may not grieve for what He has caused to miss you or be proud at what He has given you. God does not love any arrogant boaster."[559] Yazīd replied, "Whatever misfortune has struck you is because of what your hands have earned and He forgives much."[560] Then he equipped him, gave him money and sent him to Medina. [382]

According to Hishām (b. Muḥammad al-Kalbī)—Abū Mikhnaf—Abū Ḥamzah al-Thumālī[561]—ʿAbdallāh al-Thumālī[562]—al-Qāsim b. Bukhayt:[563] When the delegation from al-Kūfah brought the head of al-Ḥusayn, they went into the mosque at Damascus. Marwān b. al-Ḥakam asked them, "How did you do it?" They told him, "Eighty men of them came against us. By God! We wiped them out to the very last of them. There are the heads and the women prisoners." Marwān jumped up and left. His brother Yaḥyā b. al-Ḥakam came to them and said, "What have you done?" They repeated the words to him. He said, "A curtain has been drawn between you and Muḥammad on Doomsday. I will never agree with any action of yours." He arose and left. They went in to Yazīd, put the head before him and told him the story. Hind bt. ʿAbdallāh b. ʿĀmir b. Kurayz,[564] who was married to Yazīd b. Muʿāwiyah, heard the story circulating. She put on her cloak and went out. She said, "Commander of the Faithful, is that the head

---

559. Qurʾān, 57:22–23.
560. Qurʾān, 42:30 (29).
561. Abū Ḥamzah al-Thumālī was Thābit b. Abī Ṣafiyyah, a traditionist and Qurʾān commentator of Shīʿite leanings; he died in 150 (767). See Sezgin, *Abū Mikhnaf*, 222.
562. This is the only report from ʿAbdallāh al-Thumālī used by Abū Mikhnaf.
563. This is the only report from al-Qāsim b. Bukhayt.
564. Hind's father, ʿAbdallāh b. ʿĀmir b. Kurayz of ʿAbd Shams, had been governor of al-Baṣrah for ʿUthmān and had fought vigorously against ʿAlī when the latter became Caliph. See *EI²*, s.v. ʿAbdallāh b. ʿĀmir.

of al-Ḥusayn, son of Fāṭimah, daughter of the Apostle of God?" Yazīd replied, "Yes. Lament for him and put on mourning garments for the son of the daughter of the Apostle of God, the son of the pure woman of Quraysh. Ibn Ziyād hurried against him and killed him. May God kill him." Then the people were summoned and they came in. The head was in front of him. In Yazīd's hand there was a cane and he was poking it into al-Ḥusayn's mouth. He said, "This man and our family were like al-Ḥusayn b. al-Ḥumām al-Murrī. Then he said:

[Swords] split the skulls of men who are dear
     to us; but they were more disobedient and oppressive."[565]

[383]   One of the Companions of the Apostle of God called Abū Barzah al-Aslamī, cried out, "Are you poking the mouth of al-Ḥusayn with your cane? Take your cane away from his mouth. How often have I seen the Apostle of God kiss it! As for you, Yazīd, you will come forward on the Day of Resurrection, and Ibn Ziyād will be your advocate. But this man will come forward on the Day of Resurrection, and Muḥammad will be his advocate." Then he got up and turned away.

According to Hishām (b. Muḥammad al-Kalbī)—ʿAwānah b. al-Ḥakam: When ʿUbaydallāh b. Ziyād had al-Ḥusayn b. ʿAlī killed and his head was brought to him, he summoned ʿAbd al-Malik b. Abī al-Ḥārith al-Sulamī[566] and told him, "Go to Medina to ʿAmr b. Saʿīd b. al-ʿĀṣ and give him the good news of the killing of al-Ḥusayn." ʿAmr b. Saʿīd b. al-ʿĀṣ was the governor of Medina at that time.

ʿAbd al-Malik went to plead excuses but ʿUbaydallāh chided him. ʿUbaydallāh was a person whose fiery spirit was unapproachable. He told him, "Go to Medina and do not let the news get there before you." He gave him money and then added, "Do not make excuses. If your mount stops under you, buy another mount."

ʿAbd al-Malik reported: I went toward Medina. One of Quraysh met me. He asked, "What is the news?" I answered, "The news is at the governor's." He said, "'We belong to God and to Him we

---

565. Verse already cited. See pp. 76, 170, 174, above.
566. ʿAbd al-Malik b. Abī al-Ḥārith is not mentioned elsewhere.

will return."[567] Al-Ḥusayn b. ʿAlī has been killed." When I went to ʿAmr b. Saʿīd, he asked, "What do you convey?" I answered, "What will please the governor. Al-Ḥusayn b. ʿAlī has been killed." He told me to announce his death. I announced his death. By God! I have never heard such wailing as the wailing for al-Ḥusayn by the women of Banū Hāshim in their houses. ʿAmr b. Saʿīd said, as he laughed:

The women of Banū Ziyād raised a great lament   [384]
    like the lamentation of our women mourning after the battle
    of al-Arnab.

Al-Arnab was a battle in which the Banū Zubayd defeated the Banū Ziyād of the Banū al-Ḥārith b. Kaʿb of the group of ʿAbd al-Madān. This verse is by ʿAmr b. Maʿdīkarib.[568]

ʿAmr b. Saʿīd exclaimed, "This lamentation is in return for the lamentation for ʿUthmān b. ʿAffān." Then he ascended the pulpit and informed the people about his death.

According to Hishām (b. Muḥammad al-Kalbī)—Abū Mikhnaf—Sulaymān b. Abī Rāshid—ʿAbd al-Raḥmān b. ʿUbayd Abū Kanūd:[569] When ʿAbdallāh b. Jaʿfar b. Abī Ṭālib learned of the death of his two sons, one of his mawālī entered while the people were consoling him. I think that the mawlā was none other than Abū al-Lislās.[570] The latter said, "This is what we have met and what has come upon us through al-Ḥusayn." ʿAbdallāh b. Jaʿfar struck him with his sandal, saying, "Son of a stinking woman! Are you saying this of al-Ḥusayn? By God! If I had been present with him, I would have preferred not to leave him in order that I would be killed with him. By God! It makes my soul more generous with their two lives and makes their fate easier for me that they were struck down with my brother and cousin, consoling him and enduring with him." He went forward to those who were sitting with him and said, "Praise be to God, Who has made life

---

567. Qurʾān, 2:156 (151).
568. Quoted in Mufīd, *Irshād* (trans.), 232. The poet, ʿAmr b. Maʿdīkarib, is a famous heathen poet and warrior who became a Muslim. See *EI*[2], s.v. ʿAmr b. Maʿdīkarib.
569. ʿAbd al-Raḥmān b. ʿUbayd Abū Kanūd was a Kūfan traditionist, who lived during the first (seventh) century. See Sezgin, *Abū Miḥnaf*, 218.
570. Abū al-Lislās is not mentioned elsewhere.

hard for me through the death of al-Ḥusayn. Even though I did not console al-Ḥusayn with my own hands, my two sons consoled him."

When news of the death of al-Ḥusayn came to the people of Medina, the daughter of ʿAqīl b. Abī Ṭālib came out. With her were her womenfolk. She was sighing with grief and twisting her clothes, as she recited:

What would you say if the Prophet asked you:
  What have you, the last of the religious communities,
[385] Done with my offspring and my family after my departure?
  Among them are prisoners and among them are those who
  have been stained with blood.[571]

According to Hishām (b. Muḥammad al-Kalbī)—ʿAwānah b. al-Ḥakam: ʿUbaydallāh b. Ziyād said to ʿUmar b. Saʿd after he had killed al-Ḥusayn, "ʿUmar, where is the letter in which I wrote to you concerning killing al-Ḥusayn?" ʿUmar answered, "I have carried out your order, and the letter has been lost." Ibn Ziyād ordered, "Bring it." ʿUmar repeated, "It is lost." Ibn Ziyād demanded, "By God! Bring it." ʿUmar said, "By God! It has been left behind so that it may be read to the old women of Quraysh, as my excuse to them in Medina. By God! I gave you good advice concerning Ḥusayn, which if I had given to my father, Saʿd b. Abī Waqqāṣ, I would have done my duty to him." ʿUthmān b. Ziyād, the brother of ʿUbaydallāh said, "True. By God! I would prefer that every one of the sons of Ziyād had a nose ring until the Day of Resurrection and that Ḥusayn had not been killed." By God! ʿUbaydallāh did not disown him for that.

According to Hishām (b. Muḥammad al-Kalbī)—one of his colleagues—ʿAmr b. Abī al-Miqdām[572]—ʿAmr b. ʿIkrimah:[573] We spent the morning of the day on which Ḥusayn was killed in Medina. One of our mawālī told us, "Yesterday I heard a voice calling out:

O men who have rashly killed Ḥusayn,
  do expect torture and chastisement.

---

571. These verses were quoted earlier. See p. 77, above.
572. ʿAmr b. Abī al-Miqdām is a little-known traditionist.
573. ʿAmr b. ʿIkrimah is not mentioned elsewhere.

All the people of heaven,
    prophets, angels, and tribes prosecute you.
You have been cursed by the tongue of the son of David,
    and of Moses, and of the bringer of the Gospels."[574]

According to Hishām (b. Muḥammad al-Kalbī)—ʿUmar b.
Ḥayzūm al-Kalbī[575] said that his father had heard that voice.

The Names of the Banū Hāshim Killed with al-Ḥusayn and the Number of Those Killed from Every Tribe Which Fought against Him[576]

According to Hishām (b. Muḥammad al-Kalbī)—Abū Mikhnaf: [386]
When al-Ḥusayn b. ʿAlī was killed, the heads of the members of
his House and his Shīʿah and supporters, who were killed with
him, were taken to ʿUbaydallāh b. Ziyād. Kindah brought thirteen
heads, and their leader was Qays b. al-Ashʿath. Hawāzin brought
twenty heads, and their leader was Shamir b. Dhī al-Jawshan.
Tamīm brought seventeen heads. Banū Asad brought six heads.
Madhḥij brought seven heads. The rest of the army brought seven
heads. That amounted to seventy heads.[577]

Al-Ḥusayn was killed. His mother was Fāṭimah, daughter of
the Apostle of God. Sinān b. Anas al-Nakhaʿī al-Aṣbaḥī killed
him, and Khawalī b. Yazīd took his head.

Al-ʿAbbās b. ʿAlī b. Abī Ṭālib was killed. His mother was
Umm al-Banīn bt. Ḥizām b. Khālid b. Rabīʿah b. al-Waḥīd. Zayd
b. Ruqād al-Janbī and Ḥakīm b. al-Ṭufayl al-Sinbisī killed him.

Jaʿfar b. ʿAlī b. Abī Ṭālib was killed. His mother was also Umm
al-Banīn.

ʿAbdallāh b. ʿAlī b. Abī Ṭālib was killed. His mother was also
Umm al-Banīn.

ʿUthmān b. ʿAlī b. Abī Ṭālib was killed. His mother was also
Umm al-Banīn. Khawalī b. Yazīd shot him with an arrow and
killed him.

---

574. These verses are also quoted in Mufīd, *Irshād* (trans.), 233.

575. ʿUmar b. Ḥayzūm al-Kalbī is not mentioned elsewhere.

576. Despite the title, the section only deals with the members of Banū Hāshim
and their family servants.

577. For the implications of those tribes designated to carry the heads, see
W. M. Watt, "Shīʿism under the Umayyads."

Muḥammad b. ʿAlī b. Abī Ṭālib was killed. His mother was a slave wife. One of Banū Abān b. Dārim killed him.

Abū Bakr b. ʿAlī b. Abī Ṭālib was killed. His mother was Laylā bt. Masʿūd b. Khālid b. Mālik b. Ribʿī b. Sulmā b. Jandal b. Nahshal b. Dārim. There is doubt about his death.[578]

[387]   ʿAlī b. al-Ḥusayn b. ʿAlī was killed. His mother was Laylā bt. Abī Murrah b. ʿUrwah b. Masʿūd b. Muʿattib al-Thaqafī, and her mother was Maymūnah bt. Abī Sufyān b. Ḥarb. Murrah b. Munqidh b. al-Nuʿmān al-ʿAbdī killed him.

ʿAbdallāh b. al-Ḥusayn b. ʿAlī was killed. His mother was al-Rabāb bt. Imruʾ al-Qays b. ʿAdī b. Aws b. Jābir b. Kaʿb b. ʿUlaym of Kalb. Hāniʾ b. Thubayt al-Ḥaḍramī killed him.

ʿAlī b. al-Ḥusayn was regarded as too young; he was not killed.

Abū Bakr b. al-Ḥasan b. ʿAlī b. Abī Ṭālib was killed. His mother was a slave wife. ʿAbdallāh b. ʿUqbah al-Ghanawī killed him.

ʿAbdallāh b. al-Ḥasan b. ʿAlī b. Abī Ṭālib was killed. His mother was a slave wife. Ḥarmalah b. al-Kāhil[579] killed him by shooting him with an arrow.

Al-Qāsim b. al-Ḥasan b. ʿAlī was killed. His mother was a slave wife. Saʿd b. ʿAmr b. Nufayl al-Azdī killed him.

ʿAwn b. ʿAbdallāh b. Jaʿfar b. Abī Ṭālib was killed. His mother was Jumānah bt. al-Musayyib b. Najabah b. Rabīʿah b. Riyāḥ of the Banū Fazārah. ʿAbdallāh b. Quṭbah al-Ṭāʾī al-Nabhānī killed him.

Muḥammad b. ʿAbdallāh b. Jaʿfar b. Abī Ṭālib was killed. His mother was al-Khawṣāʾ bt. Khaṣafah b. Thaqīf b. Rabīʿah b. ʿĀʾidh b. al-Ḥārith b. Taym Allāh b. Thaʿlabah of Bakr b. Wāʾil. ʿĀmir b. Nahshal al-Taymī killed him.

Jaʿfar b. ʿAqīl b. Abī Ṭālib was killed. His mother was Umm al-Banīn bt. al-Shaqr b. al-Ḥidāb. Bishr b. Sawṭ al-Hamdānī[580] killed him.

---

578. There is some confusion about the name Abū Bakr and whether he was present at Karbalāʾ. According to Mufīd, Abū Bakr's actual name was Muḥammad, which may account for some of the confusion. See Mufīd, *Irshād* (trans.), 269.

579. Kāhin has been emended to Kāhil as written by Balādhurī and later by Ṭabarī, where Ḥarmalah b. Kāhil is reported as having killed a member of al-Ḥusayn's family. See *Ansāb*, II/2, 201; and Ṭabarī, II, 678.

580. Ḥawṭ has been emended to Sawṭ as written earlier by Ṭabarī. See p. 152, above.

'Abd al-Raḥmān b. 'Aqīl was killed. His mother was a slave wife. 'Uthmān b. Khālid b. Usayr al-Juhanī killed him.

'Abdallāh b. 'Aqīl b. Abī Ṭālib was killed. His mother was a slave wife. 'Amr b. Ṣubayḥ al-Ṣaddā'ī shot him with an arrow and killed him.   [388]

Muslim b. 'Aqīl b. Abī Ṭālib was killed in al-Kūfah. His mother was a slave wife.

'Abdallāh b. Muslim b. 'Aqīl b. Abī Ṭālib was killed. His mother was Ruqayyah bt. 'Alī b. Abī Ṭālib and her mother was a slave wife. 'Amr b. Ṣubayḥ al-Ṣaddā'ī killed him, but it was [also] said that Asīd b. Mālik al-Ḥaḍramī killed him.

Muḥammad b. Abī Sa'īd b. 'Aqīl was killed. His mother was a slave wife. Laqīṭ b. Yāsir al-Juhanī[581] killed him.

Al-Ḥasan b. al-Ḥasan b. 'Alī was considered to be too young. His mother was Khawlah bt. Manẓūr b. Zabbān b. Sayyār al-Fazārī.

'Amr b. al-Ḥasan was considered to be too young; he was left and he was not killed. His mother was a slave wife.

Of the mawālī who were killed was Sulaymān, the mawlā of al-Ḥusayn b. 'Alī. Sulaymān b. 'Awf al-Ḥaḍramī[582] killed him. Munjiḥ, the mawlā of al-Ḥusayn b. 'Alī, was killed. [So] was 'Abdallāh b. Yuqṭur, the brother-in-nurture of al-Ḥusayn b. 'Alī.

According to Abū Mikhnaf—'Abd al-Raḥmān b. Jundab al-Azdī: After the killing of al-Ḥusayn, 'Ubaydallāh b. Ziyād searched for the missing Kūfan nobles. He did not see 'Ubaydallāh b. al-Ḥurr. Some days later the latter came and visited him. He asked him, "Where were you, Ibn al-Ḥurr?" He answered, "I was sick." Ibn Ziyād remarked, "Sick in heart or sick in body?" He replied, "My heart was not sick, but as for my body God has granted me health." Ibn Ziyād declared, "You are lying. Rather you were with our enemy." Ibn al-Ḥurr said, "If I had been with your enemy, my position would have been seen, for such a position as mine would not have been hidden." Ibn Ziyād, then, did not notice him for some time. Ibn al-Ḥurr departed upon his horse. Ibn Ziyād asked where Ibn al-Ḥurr was, and was told that he had just left. He

---

581. Laqīṭ b. Yāsir al-Juhanī is not mentioned elsewhere.
582. Sulaymān b. 'Awf al-Ḥaḍramī is mentioned earlier, making critical remarks about the Kūfans during 'Alī's caliphate. See Ṭabarī, I, 3322.

ordered them to return Ibn al-Ḥurr to him, and the police caught up with him. They told him to answer the governor. Ibn al-Ḥurr

[389]   urged on his horse and said, "Tell him that, by God, I will never come willingly." He departed and came to the house of Aḥmar b. Ziyād al-Ṭāʾī.[583] His followers gathered with him at his house. He set off and came to Karbalāʾ. He looked at the places where people were slain and sought God's forgiveness for them. Then he went on until he stopped at al-Madāʾin.[584] About this, he recited:

A treacherous governor, the very reality of a treacherous man,
>   says:
>   Should you not have fought against the martyr son of
>   Fāṭimah?
O how much I regret that I did not help him!
>   Indeed, every soul that does not set upon the right course
>   regrets.
Indeed, because I was not among his defenders,
>   I have a grief that will never depart.
May God constantly water with rain the souls of those who girt
>   themselves to help him.
I stood at their graves and their field of death.
>   My heart almost burst, and my eyes shed tears.
By my life! They were active in battle,
>   quick to war, noble defenders.

[390]   They helped to support the son of the daughter of their Prophet,
>   like lions from a covert, with their swords.
If they were killed, then every pious soul
>   on the earth has become downcast in grief for that.
Never have men been seen nobler than they
>   in the face of death, bright-faced generous lords.
Do you kill them unjustly and hope for our affection?
>   Leave a course of action that is not suitable for us.
By my life! You have antagonized us by killing them.
>   How many men and women of us detest you!

---

583. Aḥmar b. Ziyād al-Ṭāʾī is not mentioned elsewhere.
584. Al-Madāʾin is the site of the ancient city of Ctesiphon. See *EI*², s.v. al-Madāʾin.

Many times I intended to go with many supporters
    against an oppressive group who had deviated from the truth.
Refrain; otherwise I will come against you with ranks
    that [will attack] you more fiercely than the armies of al-
    Daylam.

In this year (61/680–81) Abū Bilāl Mirdās b. ʿAmr b. Ḥudayr[585]
from Rabīʿah b. Ḥanzalah was killed.

The Death of Mirdās b. ʿAmr b. Ḥudayr

Abū Jaʿfar al-Ṭabarī reported: There has already been in this book
an account of Abū Bilāl's revolt, ʿUbaydallāh b. Ziyād's sending
Aslam b. Zurʿah al-Kilābī[586] against him with two thousand   [391]
men, their battle at Āsak[587] and the defeat of Aslam and his army
by Abū Bilāl and his followers.[588]

According to Hishām b. Muḥammad—Abū Mikhnaf—Abū
al-Mukhāriq al-Rāsibī:[589] When ʿUbaydallāh b. Ziyād learned of
Aslam b. Zurʿah's defeat, he sent three thousand men against Abū
Bilāl under the command of ʿAbbād b. al-Akhḍar al-Tamīmī.[590]
ʿAbbād went in pursuit of Abū Bilāl until he caught up with
him at Tawwaj[591] and drew up his ranks against him. Abū Bilāl
Mirdās and his followers attacked them and were resolute. Then
ʿAbbād's army surrounded them, for they wcrc only a small group.
Abū Bilāl had said to his followers, "Whoever of you has come out

---

585. Abū Bilāl Mirdās b. ʿAmr b. Ḥudayr is a Khārijite rebel. On his earlier
exploits, see Ṭabarī, II, 185–87, and Wellhausen, *Religio-Political*, 40–42. His
name is usually given as Mirdās b. Udayyah. Udayyah was his mother and ʿAmr
was his father. See Balādhurī, *Ansāb*, IV/1, 180.

586. Aslam b. Zurʿah al-Kilābī was a leading tribesman who supported Muʿāwiyah b. Abī Sufyān. According to Wahb b. Jarīr, the leader of this expedition had
been Ibn Ḥiṣn. See Ṭabarī, II, 187. However, Abū Mikhnaf's report is confirmed by
Dīnawarī, *Akhbār*, 279; and Balādhurī, *Ansāb*, IV/1, 182.

587. Āsak is a town in Ahwāz. See Yāqūt, *Muʿjam*, I, 61.

588. See Ṭabarī, II, 186–87.

589. Abū al-Mukhāriq al-Rāsibī is one of the authorities of Abū Mikhnaf; he
probably lived until the first half of the second (eighth) century. See Sezgin, *Abū
Miḥnaf*, 189.

590. ʿAbbād b. al-Akhḍar al-Tamīmī was a supporter of ʿUbaydallāh b. Ziyād;
his mother's name was al-Akhḍar and his father's name was ʿAlqamah. According
to Balādhurī, he had four thousand men with him. See *Ansāb*, IV/1, 183.

591. Tawwaj is a town in a valley near Shīrāz. See Yāqūt, *Muʿjam*, I, 890.

in revolt in pursuit of worldly things, let him go, but whoever of you only wants the Hereafter and to meet his Lord, that was decreed earlier for him." He recited, "To him who desires the tillage of the Hereafter, We will give increase in his tillage. To him who desires the tillage of this world, We will give something of it, but he has no share in the Hereafter."[592] He stayed, and his followers stayed with him. Not one of them left him, and they were killed to the last one of them. ʿAbbād b. al-Akhḍar and the army that was with him returned to al-Baṣrah.

ʿUbaydah b. Hilāl[593] went there. There was a group of three men with him, and he was the fourth. He lay in wait for ʿAbbād b. al-Akhḍar as the latter was approaching the palace of the governorship with his son, a young boy, mounted behind him. They said, "Servant of God, stop so that we may seek a legal decision from you." He stopped, and they said, "We are four brothers, and our brother has been killed. What do you think we should do?" He said, "Implore the governor to act." They answered, "We have implored him to act, but he has not answered us." He told them, "Kill the man then, may God destroy him." They attacked him announcing their battle cry. He pushed his son aside, and they killed him.

In this year (61/680–1) Yazīd b. Muʿāwiyah put Salm b. Ziyād[594] in charge of Sijistān and Khurāsān.

[392]

The Appointment of Salm b. Ziyād

According to ʿUmar (b. Shabbah)—ʿAlī b. Muḥammad al-Madāʾinī—Maslamah b. Muḥārib b. Salm b. Ziyād:[595] Salm b. Ziyād visited Yazīd b. Muʿāwiyah when he was a man of twenty-four years of age. Yazīd said to him, "Abū Ḥarb (i.e., Salm b. Ziyād), I will appoint you to the province of your two brothers,

---

592. Qurʾān, 42:20.

593. ʿUbaydah b. Hilāl was a prominent Khārijite who was eventually killed in 77 (696–97). See Ṭabarī, II, 1032.

594. Salm was a brother of ʿUbaydallāh b. Ziyād; he died later while governor of Khurāsān for ʿAbd al-Malik b. Marwān between 65 (685) and 86 (705). See Balādhurī, *Ansāb*, IV/1, 371–72.

595. Maslamah b. Muḥārib was a grandson of Salm; he was also an authority for historical reports.

'Abd al-Raḥmān[596] and 'Abbād."[597] Salm said, "Whatever pleases the Commander of the Faithful." So he put him in charge of Khurāsān and Sijistān. Salm despatched al-Ḥārith b. Mu'āwiyah al-Ḥārithī,[598] the grandfather of 'Īsā b. Shabīb,[599] from Syria to Khurāsān while he went to al-Baṣrah to make preparations. Then he set out for Khurāsān. Al-Ḥārith b. [Mu'āwiyah] seized[600] Qays b. al-Haytham al-Sulamī, imprisoned him, beat his son Shabīb and put him in fetters.[601] Salm sent his brother Yazīd b. Ziyād[602] to Sijistān. 'Ubaydallāh b. Ziyād wrote to his brother 'Abbād, with whom he was friendly, informing him of the appointment of Salm. 'Abbād divided up the contents of the treasury among his slaves, and there was still some left over. Therefore his herald proclaimed, "Those who want payment in advance should collect it." He paid in advance all those who came to him. 'Abbād, then, left Sijistān. When he was at Jīraft,[603] he learnt of the place where Salm was. Between them was a mountain, so he turned aside from it. On that night a thousand slaves of 'Abbād went away and the least that they had was ten thousand dirhams for 'Abbād. 'Abbād passed through Fārs[604] and then went to Yazīd. Yazīd asked him, "Where is the money?" He replied, "I was the com-

---

596. 'Abd al-Raḥmān was a brother of 'Ubaydallāh b. Ziyād, governor of Khurāsān for Mu'āwiyah b. Abī Sufyān, and he was reappointed by Yazīd. It was said that he lived for a hundred years and spent a thousand dirhams every day. He died in al-Baṣrah. See Balādhurī, *Ansāb*, IV/1, 371.

597. 'Abbād is a brother of 'Ubaydallāh b. Ziyād, governor of Sijistān for Mu'āwiyah b. Abī Sufyān, and he was reappointed by Yazīd; he died in 100 (718–19). See Balādhurī, *Ansāb*, IV/1, 372–73.

598. Al-Ḥārith b. Mu'āwiyah was a supporter of Salm b. Ziyād, who died in 64 (683–84). See Balādhurī, *Ansāb*, IV/1, 409–10.

599. 'Īsā b. Shabīb was one of the leaders who brought about the succession of Yazīd III in 126/744. See Ṭabarī, II, 1792.

600. The Arabic text has been emended. It was *fa-akhadha al-Ḥārith b. Qays b. al-Haytham*. This would have to mean Salm seized an unknown al-Ḥārith b. Qays b. al-Haytham when he had not yet reached Khurāsān. However, it is reported that, after the death of al-Ḥusayn, 'Abd al-Raḥmān b. Ziyād had visited Yazīd and had left Qays b. al-Haytham as his deputy. See Ṭabarī, II, 189. Clearly it is al-Ḥārith b. Mu'āwiyah who seized Qays b. al-Haytham. Qays' son Shabīb is not mentioned elsewhere.

601. The Arabic is *aqāmahu fī sarāwīl*.

602. Yazīd b. Ziyād was killed in Sijistān in 64 (683–84). See Ṭabarī, II, 488.

603. Jīraft is a large town in Kirmān. See Yāqūt, *Mu'jam*, II, 174.

604. Fārs is a region to the southwest of Iran. See *EI²*, s.v. Fārs.

mander of a frontier post so that I divided whatever I came upon among the people."

Salm set out for Khurāsān. With him went ʿImrān b. al-Faḍīl al-Burjumī,[605] ʿAbdallāh b. Khāzim al-Sulamī,[606] Ṭalḥah b. ʿAbdallāh b. Khalaf al-Khuzāʿī,[607] al-Muhallab b. Abī Ṣufrah,[608] Ḥanẓalah b. ʿArādah,[609] Abū Ḥuzzābah al-Walīd b. Nahīk,[610] who was one of the tribe of Rabīʿah b. Ḥanẓalah, Yaḥyā b. Yaʿmar al-ʿAdwānī,[611] who was an ally of the tribe of Hudhayl, and a large group of the horsemen and nobles of al-Baṣrah. Salm b. Ziyād had brought a letter from Yazīd b. Muʿāwiyah to ʿUbaydallāh b. Ziyād for him to select a group of two thousand men. Others have reported that the group was six thousand. Salm chose the notables and the horsemen. Some people wanted to take part in the warfare (jihād) and asked him to take them. The first whom Salm wanted to take was Ḥanẓalah b. ʿArādah. ʿUbaydallāh asked him to leave him. Salm suggested, "Let him choose between you and me. If he chooses you, he is yours. If he chooses me, he is mine." He chose Salm.

The people spoke to Salm; they asked him to conscript them. Ṣilah b. Ashyam al-ʿAdawī[612] went to the office of conscription. The clerk would say, "Abū al-Ṣahbāʾ (i.e., Ṣilah b. Ashyam), shall I put your name down, for it is a mission in which there will be warfare and merit?" He would reply, "I will seek the decision of God and wait." When the arrangement for the enlistment of the people had been completed, he was still holding back. His wife

---

605. ʿImrān b. al-Faḍīl al-Burjumī was from al-Baṣrah; he had been in charge of Sijistān and Kirmān during the reign of ʿUthmān. See Ṭabarī, I, 2840–41.

606. ʿAbdallāh b. Khāzim al-Sulamī was a tribal leader in Khurāsān. See Shaban, *The ʿAbbāsid Revolution*, 39.

607. Ṭalḥah was also called Ṭalhat al-Ṭalaḥāt (the Ṭalḥah of the Ṭalḥahs). See Wellhausen, *Arab Kingdom*, 416.

608. Al-Muhallab b. Abī Ṣufrah was a great Arab general who transferred his allegiance to Ibn al-Zubayr, but later returned to the Umayyads. See Shaban, *Islamic History*, I, 98.

609. Ḥanẓalah b. ʿArādah was a tribal leader in al-Baṣrah; he is not mentioned elsewhere.

610. Abū Ḥuzzābah al-Walīd b. Nahīk was a tribal leader in Khurāsān; he is not mentioned elsewhere.

611. Yaḥyā b. Yaʿmar al-ʿAdwānī was a writer of eloquent Arabic, who became qāḍī in Khurāsān. See Ṭabarī, II, 1131.

612. Ṣilah b. Ashyam al-ʿAdawī is not mentioned elsewhere.

Mu'ādhah bt. 'Abdallāh al-'Adawiyyah[613] asked him, "Are you going to enlist yourself?" He answered, "I will wait." Then he prayed and sought the decision from God. He saw in his sleep a man approaching who came and said to him, "Go out, for you will gain profit, prosper, and be successful." He went to the clerk and said, "Put my name down." The clerk replied, "We have finished, but I will not leave you out," and he put his and his son's names down. Salm sent him with Yazīd b. Ziyād; he went to Sijistān.

Salm set out; he took with him Umm Muḥammad bt. 'Abdallāh b. 'Uthmān b. Abī al-'Āṣ al-Thaqafī.[614] She was the first Arab woman to be taken across the river.[615]

[394]

According to Maslamah b. Muḥārib and Abū Ḥafṣ al-Azdī[616]— 'Uthmān b. Ḥafṣ al-Kirmānī:[617] When the governors of Khurāsān went on campaigns and winter came, they would return from their campaigns to Marw al-Shāhijān.[618] When the Muslims withdrew, the kings of Khurāsān met in one of the towns of Khurāsān near Khwārazm[619] to make agreements with each other; they would not attack each other; no one would provoke anyone else; and they would consult with each other about their affairs. The Muslims would ask their leaders to raid that town, but they would refuse. When Salm came to Khurāsān, he set out on a campaign and wintered in the place where he had been conducting the campaign.

Al-Muhallab b. Abī Ṣufrah urged and requested Salm to send him to that town. He despatched him with six thousand men. It is also reported that it was with four thousand men. He besieged the people in the town; he demanded that they obediently submit to him. They asked him to make peace with them, for, if he did so, they would give a ransom for their lives. He agreed to that; they made peace with him on the payment of some twenty million dirhams. Among the terms of the peace agreement was that he

---

613. Mu'ādhah bt. 'Abdallāh is not mentioned elsewhere.
614. Umm Muḥammad is only mentioned on this campaign.
615. This is a reference to the river Oxus.
616. Abū Ḥafṣ Al-Azdī was a narrator of historical reports, who was alive in 137 (754–55), for he reported events of that date. See Ṭabarī, III, 117.
617. 'Uthmān b. Ḥafṣ al-Kirmānī is not mentioned elsewhere.
618. Marw al-Shāhijān is the full name of Marw, one of the four great cities of Khurāsān, situated near the Murghāb river. See Yāqūt, Mu'jam, IV, 507.
619. Khwārazm is to the east of the Oxus river.

should receive merchandise from them. He would take a head of cattle for half its price, a riding animal for half its price, and untanned leather for half its price. The value of what he took from them reached fifty million dirhams. As a result of this, al-Muhallab came to enjoy the favor of Salm. Salm chose from these the things that pleased him and sent them to Yazīd with the Persian governor (*marzubān*) of Marw[620] and he sent a delegation for that purpose.

According to Maslamah and Ishāq b. Ayyūb:[621] Salm campaigned against Samarqand[622] with his wife, Umm Muhammad bt. ʿAbdallāh; she bore him a son. He named him Sughdī.

According to ʿAlī b. Muhammad (al-Madāʾinī)—Al-Hasan b. Rashīd al-Jūzajānī[623]—a shaykh of the tribe of Khuzāʿah—his father—his grandfather: I took part in the campaign in Khwārazm with Salm b. Ziyād. They made peace with him on the payment of much wealth. Then he crossed into Samarqand, and its inhabitants made peace with him. His wife, Umm Muhammad, was with him and she bore him a son on that campaign. She sent to the wife of the leader of al-Sughd[624] to borrow some ornaments. The latter sent her her crown. Then they withdrew, and she took the crown.

In this year, Yazīd dismissed ʿAmr b. Saʿīd from his position as governor of Medina and appointed al-Walīd b. ʿUtbah.

According to Ahmad b. Thābit—those who transmitted to him —Ishāq b. ʿĪsā—Abū Maʿshar: Yazīd b. Muʿāwiyah dismissed ʿAmr b. Saʿīd on 1 Dhū al-Hijjah (August 21) and appointed al-Walīd b. ʿUtbah as governor of Medina. The latter led the pilgrimages of the year 61/681 and the year 62/682. Yazīd b. Muʿāwiyah's governor of al-Basrah and al-Kūfah in this year was ʿUbaydallāh b. Ziyād. His governor of Medina at the end of the year was al-Walīd b. ʿUtbah, and Salm b. Ziyād was in authority

[395]

---

620. Marw refers to Marw al-Shāhijān. See note 618, above.

621. Ishāq b. Ayyūb was a regular authority of the historian al-Madāʾinī, who was alive after 125 (743); he reported events of that date. See Tabarī, II, 1741.

622. Beyond the Oxus river, the capital of Sughd; see *EI*[1], s.v. Samarkand.

623. Al-Hasan b. Rashīd al-Jūzajānī was a regular authority of the historian, al-Madīʾinī, who was alive after 132 (749–50); he reported events of that date. See Tabarī, III, 38.

624. Al-Sughd was east of the Oxus river on its lower course. See *EI*[2], s.v. Khwārazm.

over Khurāsān and Sijistān. Hishām b. Hubayrah was qāḍī of al-
Baṣrah and Shurayḥ was qāḍī of al-Kūfah.

During this year, Ibn al-Zubayr made public his opposition to
and repudiation of Yazīd; the oath of allegiance was given to him.

Yazīd's Dismissal of ʿAmr b. Saʿīd as Governor of Medina and His Appointment of al-Walīd b. ʿUtbah

The reason for Yazīd's dismissal of ʿAmr and his appointment of
al-Walīd and the reason for Ibn Zubayr's making public the call to
himself are reported according to what Hishām (b. Muḥammad
al-Kalbī) has mentioned—Abū Mikhnaf—ʿAbd al-Malik b.
Nawfal[625]—his father:[626] When al-Ḥusayn was killed,[627] Ibn al-
Zubayr arose among the people of Mecca and declared his horror
at Ḥusayn's killing. He stigmatized the people of al-Kūfah in
particular and blamed the people of Iraq generally. After praising   [396]
and glorifying God and calling for blessings to be with Muḥammad, he said, "The people of Iraq have been treacherous and liars
except for a few. The people of al-Kūfah are the worst of the
people of Iraq. They summoned al-Ḥusayn so that they might
support him and put him in authority over them. When he came
to them, they rose up against him and told him that either he
should put his hand in theirs so that they could go with him to
Ibn Ziyād b. Sumayyah peacefully in order that that man could
carry out his judgment on Ḥusayn, or he should fight. By God! He
saw that he and his followers were few among many. Even though
God, the Mighty and Sublime, has not informed anyone of the
future, it was clear that he would be killed. However, he chose a
noble death rather than an ignoble life. May God have mercy
on Ḥusayn and punish the killers of Ḥusayn. By my life! In their
opposition and disobedience to him, there was a warning and

---

625. ʿAbd al-Malik b. Nawfal was an authority of Abū Mikhnaf, who probably
lived until the first half of the second (eighth) century. See Sezgin, *Abū Miḥnaf*,
193–94.
626. He was Nawfal b. Musāḥiq. He was said to have been in charge of Muslim
b. ʿUqbah's police at the Battle of al-Ḥarrah. See Ibn Ḥajar, *Tahdhīb*, X, 392–93.
627. The following report up until Marwān's verse is given in almost the exact
same words by Balādhurī. See *Ansāb*, IV/1, 304–5.

prohibition against them for men like him. However, what was decreed took place. If God wants something, He will never be thwarted. Now, after al-Ḥusayn, should we rely on these people? Should we believe their words? Should we accept their covenants? No! We do not regard them as worthy of that. Indeed, by God, they killed a man who stood in prayer at night for long hours, who fasted frequently during the day, who had more right to govern than they did, and one who was more entitled to it in terms of religion and outstanding merit. Indeed, by God, he would never exchange the Qurʾān for singing, nor would he exchange weeping out of fear of God for such [chanting], nor would he exchange fasting for drinking forbidden drinks, nor would he exchange gathering in religious groups to remember God for rushing off in pursuit of game." He was alluding to Yazīd. "They will meet destruction."[628]

Ibn al-Zubayr's companions rose to him and declared, "Man, make public your acceptance of the oath of allegiance to you, for no one remains now that Ḥusayn is dead who can dispute this affair with you." The people had been giving the oath of allegiance to him secretly,[629] while he was saying publicly that he was seeking refuge at the Sacred Mosque. He told them not to be too hasty.

[397] At that time ʿAmr b. Saʿīd b. al-ʿĀṣ was governor of Mecca and he was very hostile toward Ḥusayn and his followers. Despite his hostility toward them, he treated them gently and kindly. When it was confirmed to Yazīd that there were groups that Ibn al-Zubayr had gathered together in Mecca, he made a vow to God that he would have him bound in a chain; he sent a chain of silver. The messenger passed by with it to Marwān b. al-Ḥakam in Medina.[630] He gave him news of what he had brought for Ibn al-Zubayr and of the chain that was with him. Marwān recited:

---

628. Qurʾān, 19:59.

629. Balādhurī, *Ansāb*, IV/1, 304, says that Ibn al-Zubayr had been receiving the oath of allegiance on the basis of a *shūrā*, the consultative committee set up by ʿUmar b. al-Khaṭṭāb in order to choose the Caliph. This is a rather surprising difference between the two versions.

630. Balādhurī says that the messenger visited both Marwān b. al-Ḥakam and al-Walīd b. ʿUtbah. See *Ansāb*, IV/1, 304.

Take it. True It is not a course of action for a strong man.
Even a humiliated man would hesitate to accept it.[631]

The messenger left him to go on to Ibn al-Zubayr. He came to Ibn
al-Zubayr and told him of his passing by Marwān and of Marwān's
recitation of that verse. Ibn al-Zubayr declared, "No, by God! I
shall not be that man who is humiliated." He politely sent the
messenger back.

Ibn al-Zubayr became more powerful in Mecca and the people
of Medina wrote to him. The people said that since al-Ḥusayn had
been destroyed, there was no one who could dispute with Ibn al-
Zubayr.

According to Nūḥ b. Ḥabīb al-Qūmisī[632]—Hishām b.
Yūsuf[633]—ʿUbaydallāh b. ʿAbd al-Karīm[634]—ʿAbdallāh b. Jaʿfar
al-Madīnī:[635]

Hishām b. Yūsuf also transmitted to us the same words as in
the account of ʿUbaydallāh according to ʿAbdallāh b. Muṣʿab[636]—
Mūsā b. ʿUqbah[637]—Ibn Shihāb[638]—ʿAbd al-ʿAzīz b. Marwān:[639]
Yazīd b. Muʿāwiyah sent Ibn ʿIḍāḥ al-Ashʿarī[640] and [ʿAbdallāh

---

631. The verse was quoted on p. 15, above, and is repeated in a fuller version
with minor variations on p. 195, below.

632. Nūḥ b. Ḥabīb al-Qūmisī was a well-known traditionist, who died in 242
(856–57). See Ibn Ḥajar, *Tahdhīb*, X, 481–82.

633. Hishām b. Yūsuf was a traditionist and qāḍī of Ṣanʿā' who died in 197
(812–13). See Ibn Ḥajar, *Tahdhīb*, XI, 57–58.

634. ʿUbaydallāh b. ʿAbd al-Karīm was a traditionist but there are very few
reports from him; he cannot be identified.

635. ʿAbdallāh b. Jaʿfar al-Madīnī was a traditionist, who lived in al-Baṣrah and
died in 178 (794–95). See Ibn Ḥajar, *Tahdhīb*, V, 174–76.

636. ʿAbdallāh b. Muṣʿab was a descendant of Ibn al-Zubayr; he also was a poet
and reporter of historical traditions, who was executed in 187 (803). See Masʿūdī,
Murūj, VI, 296–99.

637. Mūsā b. ʿUqbah was a mawlā of the wife of Ibn al-Zubayr, and an expert
on the campaigns of the Prophet; he died between 141 (758) and 145 (762–63). See
Ibn Ḥajar, *Tahdhīb*, X, 360–62.

638. Ibn Shihāb was the famous scholar Muḥammad b. Muslim b. Shihāb al-
Zuhrī, who lived from 51 (671) to 124 (742). See *EI*[1], s.v. al-Zuhrī.

639. ʿAbd al-ʿAzīz b. Marwān was the father of the Caliph ʿUmar b. ʿAbd al-
ʿAzīz, who became governor of Egypt in 65 (685) and died in 84 (703). See Ṭabarī, II,
1171.

640. Ibn ʿIḍāḥ al-Ashʿarī was a supporter of the Umayyads. See Dīnawarī,
Akhbār, 273.

[398]   b.] Masʿadah[641] and their followers to ʿAbdallāh b. al-Zubayr in Mecca to bring him a chain so that the oath of Yazīd needed to be fulfilled. He sent with them a chain of silver and a cloak of silk and woolen material. My father sent me and my brother with them. He said, "When the messengers of Yazīd convey the message, stand before him and let one of you recite:

Take it. True it is not a course of action for a strong man.
    Even a humiliated man would hesitate to accept it.
O ʿĀmir, the people have offered you a course of action.
    It is a web spun on the spindle amid neighbors.
I see that, when you were the people's water carrier,
    to you it was said, 'Bring the bucket and take it away.' "[642]

When the messengers had delivered the message to Ibn al-Zubayr, we both stood before him and my brother said to me, "Do it for me." Ibn al-Zubayr listened to me and said, "Sons of Marwān, I have listened to what you have said and I know what you are saying. So tell your father:

I am of an origin (nabʿ, tree) that is hard to break.
    [It proves its firmness] when the [frail] reeds and the [hollow]
    ʿushar are easily bent [by the slightest breeze].[643]
I will not be tender toward anything except the right that I am
    demanding
    until the stone is tender to the tooth of one who chews."

[ʿAbd al-ʿAzīz] commented: I do not know which of the two of them was more surprised.

ʿUbaydallāh (b. ʿAbd al-Karīm) added in his account on the authority of Abū ʿAlī (i.e., ʿAbdallāh b. Musʿab) that he reminded Musʿab b. ʿAbdallāh b. Musʿab b. Thābit b. ʿAbdallāh b. al-Zubayr[644] of this account. He said that he had heard the same

---

641. The text has been emended to read ʿAbdallāh b. Masʿadah, who was a prominent supporter of the Umayyads. See Ṭabarī, II, 703.
642. The first verse was quoted on pp. 15, 191, above.
643. The verse means that he is firm in his purpose.
644. Musʿab was a son of ʿAbdallāh b. Musʿab, an accomplished scholar, who lived in the first half of the third (ninth) century. See Ibn Khallikān, *Wafayāt*, trans. McGuckin de Slane, I, 186.

report on the authority of Abū ʿAlī, but he did not remember its chain of authorities (*isnād*).

According to Hishām (b. Yūsuf)—Khālid b. Saʿīd[645]—his father, Saʿīd b. ʿAmr b. Saʿīd:[646] When ʿAmr b. Saʿīd saw that the people looked up to Ibn al-Zubayr and were anxious to support him, he thought that these matters would end in his favor. He sent to ʿAbdallāh b. ʿAmr b. al-ʿĀṣ, who was a companion of his; he had been with his father in Egypt. There he had read the books of Daniel.[647] At that time, Quraysh regarded him as a scholar. ʿAmr b. Saʿīd asked him, "Tell me about this man. Do you see his ambitions being successful for him? Tell me about my leader (i.e., Yazīd). How do you see that his situation will work out for him?" He answered, "I can only see that your leader is one of those kings whose affairs are successful for them until they die while they are still kings." From that time ʿAmr b. Saʿīd increased in vehemence against Ibn al-Zubayr and his followers despite the appearance of kindness and friendliness toward them.

Al-Walīd b. ʿUtbah[648] and other members of the Banū Umayyah with him told Yazīd b. Muʿāwiyah that, if ʿAmr b. Saʿīd wanted to, he could apprehend Ibn al-Zubayr and send him to Yazīd.

In this year, I mean 61/680−1, Yazīd dismissed ʿAmr [b. Saʿīd] from the Ḥijāz and appointed al-Walīd b. ʿUtbah as governor of that place.

Abū Jaʿfar (al-Ṭabarī) reported according to Muḥammad b. ʿUmar (al-Wāqidī): Yazīd dismissed ʿAmr b. Saʿīd b. al-ʿĀṣ at the beginning of Dhū al-Ḥijjah in 61 (August 21, 681). He appointed al-Walīd b. ʿUtbah who led the people on the pilgrimage in 61/681 and restored Ibn Rabīʿah al-ʿĀmirī[649] as his qāḍī.

According to Aḥmad b. Thābit—Isḥāq b. ʿĪsā—Abū Maʿshar: In the year 61/681, al-Walīd b. ʿUtbah led the people on the pilgrimage. This is one of the things about which there is no dis-

[399]

---

645. Khālid b. Saʿīd only seems to have been mentioned here as a reporter of a family story about his grandfather, ʿAmr b. Saʿīd.

646. Saʿīd b. ʿAmr b. Saʿīd went to live in al-Kūfah; he was reported to have been the most learned of Quraysh. See Sezgin, *Abū Miḥnaf*, 194.

647. This is probably a reference to the Old Testament.

648. The text says al-Walīd b. ʿUqbah but this seems to be a mistake.

649. Apart from his appointment as qāḍī, nothing more is known of Ibn Rabīʿah al-ʿĀmirī.

pute among the historians (*ahl al-siyar*). In this year (61/680–1), ʿUbaydallāh b. Ziyād was governor of both al-Kūfah and al-Baṣrah. Shurayḥ was qāḍī of al-Kūfah and Hishām b. Hubayrah was qāḍī of al-Baṣrah. Salm b. Ziyād had authority over Khurāsān.

The
Events of the Year

62

(September 20, 681–September 9, 682)

The Arrival of a Delegation of the People of Medina to Yazīd b. Muʿāwiyah

The reason for that was according to Lūṭ b. Yaḥyā (Abū Mikhnaf)—ʿAbd al-Malik b. Nawfal b. Musāḥiq—ʿAbdallāh b. ʿUrwah (b. al-Zubayr):[650] When Yazīd b. Muʿāwiyah sent al-Walīd b. ʿUtbah to the Ḥijāz as governor and dismissed ʿAmr b. Saʿīd, al-Walīd came to Medina and seized and imprisoned many servants and mawālī of ʿAmr. ʿAmr spoke to him about them, but he refused to free them saying, "Don't worry, ʿAmr." His brother Abān b. Saʿīd b. al-ʿĀṣ[651] said to him, "Can ʿAmr worry? If you caught hold of a burning coal, and he also caught hold of it, he would not let it go until you let it go." ʿAmr went away traveling until he stopped two nights' journey away from Medina. He wrote to his servants and mawālī—there were about three hundred of them: "I am sending a camel, a provision bag and equipment for each

---

650. ʿAbdallāh b. ʿUrwah was a traditionist and nephew of Ibn al-Zubayr.
651. Abān was a brother of ʿAmr, who was born in al-Kūfah. See Balādhurī, *Ansāb*, IV/1, 453–54.

man among you. The camels will be tethered in the market. When my messenger comes to you, break down the door of the prison. Then let every man among you get and mount his camel. Then come in my direction until you reach me." His messenger went and bought the camels. He made them ready with what was suitable for them and tethered them in the market. He went to the men in prison and informed them of ʿAmr's directions. They broke down the door of the prison, went to the camels, mounted them and set off in the direction of ʿAmr b. Saʿīd until they found him.

[401] When ʿAmr b. Saʿīd went to Yazīd and entered into his presence, Yazīd welcomed him and made him sit close. Then he reproved ʿAmr b. Saʿīd for his inadequacy, for he had not done the things that Yazīd had ordered him to do concerning Ibn al-Zubayr. ʿAmr had only carried out what he had wanted to. He replied, "Commander of the Faithful, one who was present would have seen what one who was absent could not have seen. The majority of the people of Mecca and Medina were inclined toward Ibn al-Zubayr; they favored him and gave their consent to him. They summoned each other both in secret and publicly. If I had struggled against him, I would not have had an army strong enough against him with these people. While he was being cautious toward me and on his guard against me, I was showing apparent kindness and friendliness so that I might deceive him in order to attack. However, I did restrict him and prevent him from many things which, if I had left them for him, would only have been of assistance to him. I positioned men in the roads and alleys of Mecca. My men did not let anyone enter Mecca until they had written down for me his name, the name of his father, from which part of God's land he came, what he brought, and what he wanted. If he was one of Ibn al-Zubayr's followers and one of those who I thought was coming to him, I would send him back ignominiously. If he was one of those whom I did not suspect, I would let him go. Now you have sent al-Walīd. Perhaps, as a result of his work and his effect, you will realize the merit of my efforts in your affair and, God willing, my sincere advice to you. May God act on your behalf and humble your enemy, Commander of the Faithful." Yazīd said, "You are truer than those who raised these matters about you and incited me against you. You are one of those whom

I trust, and whose help I hope for and whom I shall keep in order
to repair damage, to undertake an important task, and to uncover
the implications of great matters." 'Amr replied, "Commander of
the Faithful, no one is more fitting to strengthen your authority,
weaken your enemy, and do violence against those who oppose
you than I am."

Al-Walīd embarked on seeking for Ibn al-Zubayr but he found
that he was cautious and inaccessible.

Najdah b. 'Āmir al-Ḥanafī[652] came out in revolt in al-Yamāmah[653] after al-Ḥusayn had been killed. Ibn al-Zubayr also came   [402]
in revolt.

At the pilgrimage, al-Walīd led the procession (ifāḍah) from
'Arafah, and the general body of the people marched in the procession with him. Ibn Zubayr made the wuqūf[654] with his followers, and Najdah made the wuqūf with his followers. Then Ibn
Zubayr led the procession with his followers, and Najdah led the
procession with his followers. None of the three groups went in
the procession of the others. Najdah met Ibn al-Zubayr so frequently that the people thought that he would give the oath of
allegiance to him.

Then Ibn al-Zubayr worked a trick against the authority of al-
Walīd b. 'Utbah. He wrote to Yazīd b. Mu'āwiyah: "You have
sent us a stupid man who does not direct us to a straightforward
situation and will not listen to the advice of the wise. If you sent
us a man with an easy disposition and a gentle attitude, I would
hope that affairs that have seemed difficult would become easy
and what was at variance would become united. Consider that,
for there is benefit in it for our leaders (khawāṣṣ) and our ordinary
people ('awāmm), God willing. Peace be with you."

Yazīd b. Mu'āwiyah sent to al-Walīd, dismissed him and sent
'Uthmān b. Muḥammad b. Abī Sufyān[655] [in his place].

---

652. Najdah b. 'Āmir al-Ḥanafī was a leading Khārijite, who at one time came
to control nearly the whole of Arabia. He was killed after an internal dispute in 72
(691). See Wellhausen, *Religio-Political*, 47–50.

653. Al-Yamāmah was an area in central eastern Arabia. See *EI*[1], s.v. al-Yamāma.

654. The *wuqūf* is the ritual that involves gathering at 'Arafah in preparation
for the procession (*ifāḍah*) into the sanctuary of Mecca during the night of the
pilgrimage. See *EI*[2], s.v. Ḥadjdj.

655. 'Uthmān b. Muḥammad b. Abī Sufyān was a member of the Umayyad
family, and cousin of Yazīd. Apart from this incident, he was reported to have

According to Abū Mikhnaf—ʿAbd al-Malik b. Nawfal b. Musāḥiq—Ḥumayd b. Ḥamzah,[656] a mawlā of the Banū Umayyah: An inexperienced young man came, who had no knowledge of affairs, who had not learnt the lessons of age, and who had not been trained by experience; he could hardly understand anything about his authority and his task. He sent a delegation from the people of Medina to Yazīd. Among them were ʿAbdallāh b. Ḥanẓalah al-Ghasīl al-Anṣārī,[657] ʿAbdallāh b. Abī ʿAmr b. Ḥafṣ b. al-Mughīrah al-Makhzūmī,[658] al-Mundhir b. al-Zubayr and many of the nobles of the people of Medina. They came to Yazīd b. Muʿāwiyah, and he treated them generously and well. He gave them gifts, and then they left him. They all came back to Medina except for al-Mundhir b. al-Zubayr. He went to ʿUbaydallāh b. Ziyād at al-Baṣrah. Yazīd had made a gift of a hundred thousand dirhams to him. When those members of the delegation returned to Medina, they stood among the people and publicly cursed and vilified Yazīd. They said, "We have come from a man who has no religion, who drinks wine, who plays lutes, who passes his time with songstresses, who plays with dogs and spends his evenings talking to robbers and young men. We ask you to bear witness that we repudiate him." The people followed them.

[403]

According to Lūṭ b. Yaḥyā (Abū Mikhnaf)—ʿAbd al-Malik b. Nawfal b. Musāḥiq: The people went to ʿAbdallāh b. Ḥanẓalah al-Ghasīl and gave their oath of allegiance to him; they gave him authority over them.

According to Lūṭ (b. Yaḥyā Abū Mikhnaf)—Muḥammad b. ʿAbd al-ʿAzīz b. ʿUmar b. ʿAbd al-Raḥmān b. ʿAwf:[659] Al-Mundhir came back from Yazīd b. Muʿāwiyah and went to ʿUbaydallāh b.

---

had a daughter who married the Caliph al-Walīd b. Yazīd b. ʿAbd al-Malik. See Balādhurī, *Ansāb*, IV/1, 6.

656. A mawlā of the Banū Umayyah; Ḥumayd b. Ḥamzah is not mentioned except for this report.

657. ʿAbdallāh b. Ḥanẓalah al-Ghasīl al-Anṣārī was a leading man in Medina. His father had been killed at Uḥud and the Prophet said that he had seen angels washing his body. Hence *al-ghasīl*, the washed. See *EI*[2], s.v. ʿAbdallāh b. Ḥanẓala.

658. ʿAbdallāh b. Abī ʿAmr b. Ḥafṣ was a member of Quraysh who settled in Medina.

659. Muḥammad b. ʿAbd al-ʿAzīz was a descendant of the well-known Companion of the Prophet, ʿAbd al-Raḥmān b. ʿAwf. This is the only time he occurs as an authority of Abū Mikhnaf. See Sezgin, *Abū Miḥnaf*, 211.

Ziyād at al-Baṣrah. He was generous and hospitable to al-Mundhir, for he had been a friend of Ziyād. Then a letter came to ʿUbaydallāh from Yazīd b. Muʿāwiyah. In this letter, Yazīd told ʿUbaydallāh of the situation concerning his followers in Medina; he ordered ʿUbaydallāh to bind and imprison al-Mundhir until Yazīd's order about him came. ʿUbaydallāh b. Ziyād was reluctant to comply with his instructions because al-Mundhir was his guest. He summoned him and told him about the letter, which he read to him. He said, "You were friendly to Ziyād and you have become my guest. I am doing you a favor, for I want to act well in the whole matter. When the people gather with me, arise and say, 'Permit me to depart to my land.' When I say, 'No, rather stay with me, for you will have generous, munificent, and praiseworthy treatment,' say, 'I have an estate and work so that I must leave; permit me to go.' At that I will permit you to go. Then join your family." When the people gathered with ʿUbaydallāh, al-Mundhir arose and asked permission [to go]. He replied, "No, rather stay with me, for I will treat you nobly, generously, and praiseworthily." Al-Mundhir said, "I have an estate and work so that I must leave. So permit me to go." ʿUbaydallāh gave him permission. He set out until he reached the Ḥijāz. There he joined the people of Medina; he became one of those who urged the people against Yazīd. At that time among the things he used to say was, "By God! Yazīd made a gift of a hundred thousand dirhams to me but what he did to me does not prevent me from telling you about him; I will speak truthfully about him. By God! He drinks wine and gets so drunk that he misses the prayer." Al-Mundhir vilified him with not only similar vilifications but also harsher ones than the ones made by his companions.

[404]

Saʿīd b. ʿAmr was saying in al-Kūfah that Yazīd b. Muʿāwiyah had been informed of what al-Mundhir had said and he had declared, "O God! I treated him praiseworthily and generously. Then he did what You have seen. Remember him for lying and disruption of relations."

According to Abū Mikhnaf—Saʿīd b. Zayd Abū Muthallim:[660] Yazīd b. Muʿāwiyah sent for al-Nuʿmān b. Bashīr al-Anṣārī and

---

660. Saʿīd b. Zayd Abū Muthallim was an otherwise unknown authority of Abū Mikhnaf. See Sezgin, *Abū Miḥnaf*, 217.

said to him, "Go to the people of Medina and your own people; soothe them away from what they are intending to do. If they do not rise up in this matter, the people will not dare to oppose me. There are those of my clan who would not want to rise up in this discord (*fitnah*), for they fear destruction." Al-Nuʿmān b. Bashīr departed and went to his people. He summoned the people generally to him. He ordered them to obey and to adhere to unity and he warned them against discord. He told them, "You have no power against the Syrians." ʿAbdallāh b. Muṭīʿ said, "Al-Nuʿmān, what is making you split our unity and corrupt our affairs that God has set right?" Al-Nuʿmān answered, "By God! It is as if I can see that which you are calling for (i.e., civil war) taking place, with men mounting their horses and striking blows against the heads of the other party and their faces. The mill of death revolves between the two parties. It is as if I can see you flying on your mule and setting your face in the direction of Mecca, leaving these wretched people—meaning the Anṣār—behind to be killed in their alleys, in the mosques, and at the doors of their houses." The people struck out at him and he left. By God! It happened just as he said it would.

[405]

Al-Walīd b. ʿUtbah led the people on the pilgrimage in this year (62/682). The governors in Iraq and Khurāsān were the same in this year (62/681–2) as the governors that I mentioned in the year 61/680–1.

In this year (62/681–82) Muḥammad b. ʿAbdallāh b. al-ʿAbbās[661] was born according to what has been mentioned.

---

661. It was through Muḥammad b. ʿAbdallāh b. al-ʿAbbas's line that the ʿAbbāsid caliphs were descended. See *EI*², s.v. ʿAbbāsids.

The
Events of the Year

63

(SEPTEMBER 10, 682–AUGUST 29, 683)

Among the events that took place in the year of 63 was the expulsion by the people at Medina of Yazīd b. Muʿāwiyah's governor, ʿUthmān b. Muḥammad b. Abī Sufyān, from Medina, their public repudiation of Yazīd b. Muʿāwiyah, and their siege of those of the Banū Umayyah who were in Medina.

According to Hishām b. Muḥammad (al-Kalbī)—Abū Mikhnaf—ʿAbd al-Malik b. Nawfal b. Musāḥiq—Ḥabīb b. Kurrah:[662] When the people of Medina gave the oath of allegiance to ʿAbdallāh b. Ḥanẓalah al-Ghasīl to depose Yazīd b. Muʿāwiyah, they attacked ʿUthmān b. Muḥammad b. Abī Sufyān and the Banū Umayyah, their mawālī and those from Quraysh who held their views, who were in Medina. There were about one thousand of them. They left in a group and stopped at Marwān b. al-Ḥakam's house. There the people put them under a token siege. The Banū Umayyah

---

662. Ḥabīb b. Kurrah was a mawlā of the Umayyads, who was alleged to have led the party in pursuit of Ibn al-Zubayr when the latter had fled from Medina to Mecca in order to avoid giving the oath of allegiance to Yazīd. See note 25, above. From his account of his mission, he was obviously trusted by the Umayyads in Medina.

summoned Ḥabīb b. Kurrah. Those of them who sent for him were Marwān b. al-Ḥakam and ʿAmr b. ʿUthmān b. ʿAffān.[663] Marwān was the one who was organizing their affairs. As for ʿUthmān b. Muḥammad b. Abī Sufyān, he was only a young lad without any judgment.

[406]

According to ʿAbd al-Malik b. Nawfal—Ḥabīb b. Kurrah: I was with Marwān, and he and a group of the Banū Umayyah wrote a letter for me to take to Yazīd b. Muʿāwiyah. ʿAbd al-Malik b. Marwān[664] took the letter until he had come with me to Thaniyyat al-Wadāʿ.[665] He handed me the letter and said, "I will give you twelve days to go and twelve days[666] to return. Come to me in twenty-four days at this place. God willing, you will find me sitting and waiting for you at this time." The letter said: "In the name of God, the Merciful, the Compassionate.... We have been besieged in the house of Marwān b. al-Ḥakam. Good water has been stopped from getting to us, and we are having berries thrown at us. Help! Help!"

[Ḥabīb b. Kurrah] continued: I took the letter and went with it until I reached Yazīd. He was sitting on a chair with his feet in a brass basin filled with water; he was experiencing pain in them. It is said that he had gout. He read it and then, as we have been informed, he recited:

They have changed the clemency that was part of my nature.
    Therefore, I have substituted harshness toward my people
    for gentleness.[667]

Then he asked, "Are not Banū Umayyah and their mawālī in Medina a thousand men?" I said, "Yes, by God, and more." He

---

663. ʿAmr b. ʿUthmān b. ʿAffān was the eldest son of Caliph ʿUthmān. He does not seem to have been particularly pro-Umayyad, perhaps because he felt he had a better claim to the caliphate; he refused to give the oath of allegiance to Marwān b. al-Ḥakam when he became Caliph. He died in Minā. See Balādhurī, *Ansāb*, IV/1, 602.

664. ʿAbd al-Malik b. Marwān became Caliph after his father; he ruled the Islamic Empire from 65 (685) to 86 (705). See *EI*[2], s.v. ʿAbd al-Malik b. Marwān.

665. Thaniyyat al-Wadāʿ was a pass (*thaniyyah*) overlooking Medina on the road to Mecca. It was given this name in pre-Islamic times because it was the place where people said goodbye to travelers. See Yāqūt, *Muʿjam*, I, 937.

666. The Arabic is "nights" not "days."

667. The verse is not identified.

demanded, "Were they not able to fight for an hour in one day?"
I answered, "Commander of the Faithful, all the people united
against them, and they had no power against such a gathering of [407]
the people."

He sent for ʿAmr b. Saʿīd and made him read the letter and
gave him the news. He told him to go to them with the people.
ʿAmr answered, "I had kept a firm grip on that town for you, and
I had controlled its affairs on your behalf. Now, when it has come
to the blood of Quraysh being shed on the ground, I do not want
to be responsible for that. Let someone who is less closely associated with them than I am be responsible for that."

[Ḥabīb b. Kurrah] continued: He sent me with that letter to
Muslim b. ʿUqbah al-Murrī,[668] who was then a weak sick old
man. I handed him the letter and he read it. He asked me the
news, and I told it to him. Then he asked the same question as
Yazīd, "Aren't the Banū Umayyah and their mawālī and supporters in Medina a thousand men?" I replied, "Yes, they are." He
said, "Were they not able to fight for an hour in one day? These
are not worthy to be helped until they strive for themselves to
fight against their enemy and to strengthen their authority."
Then he went and visited Yazīd. He said to him, "Commander of
the Faithful, do not help these men, for they are contemptible.
Were they not able to fight for one day, or half a day, or even an
hour in a day? Leave them, Commander of the Faithful, until they
strive for themselves to fight their enemy and to strengthen their
authority. Then it will be clear to you which of them will fight
and endure in obedience to you or which will give in." Yazīd
exclaimed, "Shame on you! There would be no good in life without them. Depart! Keep me informed of what you do. Gather the
people and march with them."

His herald went out and proclaimed: "Set out for the Ḥijāz with
the condition of receiving your stipends in full and a grant of
a hundred dīnārs that will be put in the hand of each man immediately." Because of that, twelve thousand men volunteered.

---

668. Muslim b. ʿUqbah al-Murrī was one of the leaders of the Syrian Arabs,
who had served Muʿāwiyah at Ṣiffīn; he was a loyal supporter of Yazīd. See *EI*[1],
s.v. Muslim b. ʿUqba.

[408]   According to Ibn Ḥumayd[669]—Jarīr[670]—al-Mughīrah:[671] Yazīd wrote to Ibn Marjānah, "Attack Ibn al-Zubayr." He replied, "No, I will never bring two such actions together for that sinner as killing the son of the Apostle of God and attacking the House [of God]."

Marjānah was a truthful woman and after ʿUbaydallāh had killed al-Ḥusayn, she used to say to him, "Woe upon you! What have you done! What a crime you have committed!"

The account returns to that of Ḥabīb b. Kurrah, who reported: I came back to meet ʿAbd al-Malik b. Marwān at the place at that time or a little after it. I found him sitting under a tree with a cloak wrapped around him. I told him what had happened, and he was pleased with the news. We left and went into Marwān's house to the group of the Banū Umayyah. I told them the news that I had brought; they praised God, the Mighty and High.

ʿAbd al-Malik b. Nawfal informed us that Ḥabīb had come back in ten days. Ḥabīb recounted: I did not leave until I saw Yazīd b. Muʿāwiyah go out to inspect and look at the cavalry. He was wearing a sword and leaning on an Arab bow, and I heard him reciting:

Tell Abū Bakr:[672] When the nights have gone by
    and the people have descended on Wādī Qurā,[673]
If you see twenty thousand of the people, both mature and young,
    do you think that they have been gathered by a drunkard?
Or were they gathered by a wakeful man who has driven away
    sleep from himself?

---

669. Ibn Ḥumayd's full name was Abū ʿAbdallāh Muḥammad b. Ḥumayd al-Rāzī. He was a prolific traditionist and one of the authorities whose transmission of the *Sīrah* of Ibn Isḥāq Ṭabarī used. He died in 248 (862–63). See Ibn Ḥajar, *Tahdhīb*, IX, 127–31.

670. Jarīr's full name was Jarīr b. ʿAbd al-Ḥamīd al-Rāzī. He was a traditionist, who moved from al-Kūfah to al-Rayy and became a qāḍī. He died in 188 (804). See Ibn Ḥajar, *Tahdhīb*, II, 75–77.

671. Al-Mughīrah's full name was Abū Hāshim al-Mughīrah b. Miqsam. He was a traditionist from al-Kūfah, who died in 130 (747–48). See Ibn Saʿd, *Ṭabaqāt*, VI, 235.

672. Abū Bakr is a reference to Ibn al-Zubayr.

673. Wādī Qurā was a valley between Medina and Syria with many villages in it. See Yāqūt, *Muʿjam*, IV, 878.

I wonder about a man who strays from the truth (*mulḥid*)! I really wonder.
A man of deceit in religion, who slanders noble people.[674]

'Abd al-Malik b. Nawfal reported that that army had departed [409] from Yazīd with Muslim b. 'Uqbah in command. Yazīd had told him, "If anything happens to you, appoint Ḥuṣayn b. Numayr al-Sakūnī[675] as your deputy." He also instructed him, "Leave the people for three days. If they agree to your demands, so be it. Otherwise fight them and when you overcome them, give license to pillage the city for three days. Whatever property, silver coins, weapons, and food are found belong to the army. When the three days have passed, withdraw from the people. Look for 'Alī b. al-Ḥusayn, keep them away from him, give him kind treatment and make him stay close to you. He has not become involved in any of the things in which they have become involved. His letter has come to me." 'Alī did not know anything about what Yazīd b. Mu'āwiyah had instructed Muslim b. 'Uqbah to do with regard to him. In fact when the Banū Umayyah left for Syria, Marwān's goods and wife, 'Ā'ishah bt. 'Uthmān b. 'Affān[676]—she was the mother of Abān b. Marwān—were entrusted to 'Alī b. al-Ḥusayn.

According to Muḥammad b. Sa'd—Muḥammad b. 'Umar (al-Wāqidī): When the people of Medina expelled 'Uthmān b. Muḥammad from Medina, Marwān b. al-Ḥakam asked Ibn 'Umar if he would hide his family with him. Ibn 'Umar refused to do that. Marwān spoke to 'Alī b. al-Ḥusayn. He said, "Abū al-Ḥasan (i.e., 'Alī b. al-Ḥusayn), I have kinship with you. Let my women be with your women." 'Alī b. al-Ḥusayn agreed to do that. Marwān sent his women to 'Alī b. al-Ḥusayn, and the latter left with his own women and with Marwān's women until he

---

674. Mas'ūdī quotes part of these verses. See *Murūj*, V, 161. Balādhurī gives more verses. See *Ansāb*, IV/1, 323.

675. Ḥuṣayn b. Numayr al-Sakūnī was a leading supporter of the Umayyads but after Yazīd's death he was tempted to transfer his allegiance to Ibn al-Zubayr. However, he remained loyal to the Umayyads and was killed at the Battle of Khāzir fighting against Ibn al-Ashtar in 67 (686). See Crone, *Slaves*, 97, and *EI²*, s.v. Ḥuṣayn Numayr.

676. 'Ā'ishah is not mentioned in any other respect than being a daughter of 'Uthmān b. 'Affān, the third Caliph and also being the wife of Marwān. She bore Marwān several children. Her son Abān became governor of Palestine for his brother the Caliph 'Abd al-Malik. See Balādhurī, *Ansāb*, V, 164, 166.

settled them at Yanbuʿ.[677] Marwān was grateful to ʿAlī b. al-Ḥusayn in addition to the old friendship that had been between them.

[410]   The account returns to that according to Abū Mikhnaf—ʿAbd al-Malik b. Nawful: Muslim b. ʿUqbah advanced with the army. When the people of Medina heard of his coming, they attacked those of the Banū Umayyah who were with them and besieged them in the house of Marwān. They declared, "By God! We will not leave you alone until we overcome you and cut off your heads, or you give us a covenant and testimonies before God that you will not harm us. Also that you will not reveal the gaps in our positions and that you will not assist an enemy against us. In this respect, we will desist from doing any harm to you and will let you go out from our city." They gave them such a covenant and testimonies before God. They drove out the Banū Umayyah, who left Medina with their baggage until they met Muslim b. ʿUqbah at Wādī al-Qurā.

ʿĀʾishah bt. ʿUthmān b. ʿAffān left for al-Ṭāʾif and she passed by ʿAlī b. al-Ḥusayn. The latter was staying at a property of his outside Medina. He had withdrawn from it, as he was unwilling to have any association with their policy (amr). He asked her to take his son ʿAbdallāh with her to al-Ṭāʾif. She took him to al-Ṭāʾif until the affairs of the people of Medina were brought to an end.

When the Banū Umayyah reached Muslim b. ʿUqbah at Wādī al-Qurā, he summoned ʿAmr b. ʿUthmān b. ʿAffān, first of all, and demanded, "Give me information about the situation that you left behind; advise me." He answered, "I cannot give you any information, for covenants and sworn testimonies were made by us that we would not reveal gaps in their positions or help an enemy." Muslim b. ʿUqbah upbraided him and asserted, "By God! If it was not for the fact that you are the son of ʿUthmān, I would cut your head off. By God! I will never pardon a Qurashī for it after you!" ʿAmr b. ʿUthmān went out to his companions with the news of what treatment he had received from him. Marwān b.

---

677. Yanbuʿ was an estate near an oasis; it was located a day's journey from Mount Raḍwā and seven stages away from Medina. It was given to ʿAlī b. Abī Ṭālib and became the property of his descendants. See Yāqūt, Muʿjam, IV, 1039.

al-Ḥakam said to his son ʿAbd al-Malik, "Go in before me. Perhaps he will be satisfied with you instead of me." ʿAbd al-Malik went in. Muslim b. ʿUqbah demanded, "Come, what information do you have? Give me information about the people and how you see the situation." ʿAbd al-Malik said, "Yes, I think that you should go with those who are with you and avoid this road to Medina. [411] When you come to the palms lower down, stop there. Your army will be shaded by their shade, and they can eat from the palm dates. When night comes, appoint successive guards from the people in the camp for the whole night. In the morning, perform the morning prayer. Then go forward with them. Leave Medina to your left and go round it until you come toward them through al-Ḥarrah[678] coming from the east. Then you will be facing the people. When they face you, the east will be in front of them. When the sun shines, it will shine over the shoulder of your followers; it will not harm them but it will fall on the faces of the people of Medina; its heat will harm them and the harm from it will affect them. As long as you are coming from the east, they will see the dazzling brightness of your helmets, javelins, spears, swords, breastplates, and armlets. However, as long as they are coming from the west, you will not see any brillance from their weapons. Then fight them and ask for God's help against them. Indeed, God will be your helper, for they have opposed the imām and left the unity of the community (jamāʿah)." Muslim exclaimed, "God bless your father! What a man was born to him! When you were born to him, he saw a successor in you." Then Marwān entered. Muslim b. ʿUqbah asked him, "What is it?" Marwān said, "Hasn't ʿAbd al-Malik come to you?" Muslim replied, "What a man ʿAbd al-Malik is! Seldom have I spoken to a man from Quraysh like him." Marwān said, "When you met [412] ʿAbd al-Malik, you met me." He answered, "Indeed."

Muslim b. ʿUqbah departed from that place and the people departed with him until he stopped at the place that ʿAbd al-Malik had told him. There he did what ʿAbd al-Malik had told him to do. Then he went on into al-Ḥarrah until he stopped there.

---

678. Al-Ḥarrah is where the battle took place. It is a name meaning parched dry ground with black stones as if they had been burnt by fire. See Yāqūt, Muʿjam, II, 247.

He had come toward them from the east. Muslim b. ʿUqbah summoned the people of Medina and announced, "People of Medina, the Commander of the Faithful, Yazīd b. Muʿāwiyah, claims that you are the origin of Islam. I am reluctant to shed your blood. I will give you three days' respite. Whoever reverts from error and returns to the truth, we will accept that from him. I will leave you and go against this man who deviates from the truth (*mulḥid*), who is in Mecca. If you refuse, we will be excused for our treatment toward you."

That was in Dhū al-Ḥijjah, 64 (July 20–August 17, 684). Thus did I find it in my text (*kitāb*). It is a mistake because Yazīd died in the month of Rabīʿ al-Awwal 64 (November, 683). The Battle of al-Ḥarrah was on Wednesday, 28 Dhū al-Ḥijjah 63 (August 27, 683).[679]

When the three days had passed, he said, "What are you going to do? Are you going to make peace or are you going to fight?" They answered, "No, we will fight." He pleaded with them, "Don't do this. Rather enter into obedience, and we will use our vehemence and our weapons against this man who deviates from the truth, to whom heretics and libertines have gathered from every side." They shouted at them, "Enemies of God, by God, if you want to pass across to them, we will not leave you until we fight you. We will not let you go to the Sacred House of God to terrorize its inhabitants, to act impiously there, and to violate its sanctity. No, by God! We will not allow this."

The people of Medina had made use of a ditch at the flank of Medina. A great group of them stationed themselves there. In command of them was ʿAbd al-Raḥmān b. Azhar b. ʿAwf b. ʿAbd [413] ʿAwf,[680] who was the nephew of ʿAbd al-Raḥmān b. ʿAwf al-Zuhrī.[681] ʿAbdallāh b. Muṭīʿ was in charge of another quarter on

---

679. This correction seems to have been written by Ṭabarī.

680. The name given by Ṭabarī, ʿAbd al-Raḥmān b. Zuhayr b. ʿAbd ʿAwf, is clearly defective and Balādhurī, *Ansāb*, IV/1, 324, has the correct name that is used here. This man took part in the campaign to Ḥunayn; see Ṭabarī, III, 2380.

681. ʿAbd al-Raḥmān b. ʿAwf al-Zuhrī was a famous Companion of the Prophet, who became very rich; he was the man who appointed ʿUthmān in the consultative council (*shūrā*) for the appointment of the third Caliph. See *EI²*, s.v. ʿAbd al-Raḥmān b. ʿAwf.

the flank of Medina and Maʿqil b. Sinān al-Ashjaʿī[682] was in command of another quarter on the flank of Medina. The commander of their whole army (jamāʿah) was ʿAbdallāh b. Ḥanẓalah al-Ghasīl al-Anṣārī with the largest and most numerous of the quarters.

According to Hishām (b. Muḥammad al-Kalbī)—ʿAwānah b. al-Ḥakam al-Kalbī mentioned that ʿAbdallāh b. Muṭīʿ was in command of Quraysh among the people of Medina. ʿAbdallāh b. Ḥanẓalah al-Ghasīl was in command of the Anṣār and Maʿqil b. Sinān was in command of the emigrants.

According to Hishām (b. Muḥammad al-Kalbī)—Abū Mikhnaf—ʿAbd al-Malik b. Nawfal: Muslim b. ʿUqbah set forth with all of those with him. He advanced from the direction of al-Ḥarrah until he set up his tent on the road to al-Kūfah. Then he sent the cavalry against Ibn Ghasīl. Ibn Ghasīl attacked the cavalry with the foot soldiers who were with him until the cavalry was defeated. They went back to Muslim. The latter, with the foot soldiers, stood in their way and shouted at them. They went back and fought fiercely. Al-Faḍl b. al-ʿAbbās b. Rabīʿah b. al-Ḥārith b. ʿAbd al-Muṭṭalib[683] came to ʿAbdallāh b. Ḥanẓalah al-Ghasīl and fought well and fiercely alongside him with about twenty horsemen. He told ʿAbdallāh, "Order those horsemen with you to come to me and position themselves with me. When I attack, let them attack. By God! I will not stop until I reach Muslim; either I will kill him or I will be killed." ʿAbdallāh b. Ḥanẓalah ordered ʿAbdallāh b. al-Ḍaḥḥāk[684] of the Banū al-Ashhal of the Anṣār to proclaim to the cavalry that they should position themselves with al-Faḍl b. al-ʿAbbās. [ʿAbdallāh b.] al-Ḍaḥḥāk[685] proclaimed this among them and he joined them to al-Faḍl. When the cavalry   [414] gathered around him, he attacked the Syrians; they were put to flight. He cried to his companions, "Don't you see them miserably retreating? Attack again, may I be a sacrifice for you! By God! If I

---

682. Maʿqil b. Sinān al-Ashjaʿī was a Companion of the Prophet from the tribe of Ashjaʿ; as such, he was an emigrant from outside Quraysh. See Wāqidī, *Maghāzī*, II, 799, 820, 897.

683. Al-Faḍl b. al-ʿAbbās was a member of the Banū Hāshim; little is heard of him apart from this incident.

684. ʿAbdallāh b. al-Ḍaḥḥāk is not mentioned elsewhere.

685. ʿAbdallāh b. has clearly been omitted from the Arabic text.

see their leader, I will kill him or I will be killed. Perseverance for a time is followed by joy. Victory only comes after perseverance." Then he attacked and his companions attacked with him. The Syrian cavalry was separated from Muslim b. ʿUqbah, who was with about five hundred foot soldiers who were kneeling pointing their spears toward the people. Al-Faḍl b. al-ʿAbbās went as he was toward Muslim's standard so that he might strike the head of the standard bearer. The man was wearing a helmet but al-Faḍl cut through the helmet and split his skull. He fell dead. Al-Faḍl shouted, "I am the son of ʿAbd al-Muṭṭalib." He thought that he had killed Muslim and declared, "By the Lord of the Kaʿbah! I have killed the tyrant of the people." Muslim taunted him, "Your bottom missed the ditch,"[686] for that standard bearer was a brave servant of his called Rūmī. Muslim took his standard and called out, "People of Syria, is this the fighting of people who want to defend their religion and who want to strengthen the victory of their imām? May God abominate your fighting from today! How painful it is to my heart! How distressing it is to my soul! By God! Your reward for it will be nothing, for you will be deprived of your stipends and you will be posted to the most distant frontier posts. Attack with this standard. May God make your faces full of grief if you do not tuck up your trousers."[687] He went forward with the standard, and those foot soldiers attacked in front of the standard. Al-Faḍl b. ʿAbbās was brought down and killed. There were only about ten yards between him and the tent ropes of Muslim b. ʿUqbah. Zayd b. ʿAbd al-Raḥmān b. ʿAwf[688] and Ibrāhīm b. Nuʿaym al-ʿAdawī[689] were killed with him together with many foot soldiers from the people of Medina.

[415]   According to Hishām (b. Muḥammad al-Kalbī)—another account from ʿAwānah: Muslim b. ʿUqbah was sick on the day of the battle. He ordered a litter and a chair to be put between the two ranks. Then he said, "People of Syria, fight for your commander or leave." They advanced toward them. They did not set

---

686. Arabic proverb that is roughly equivalent to: "Look before you leap." See Bustānī, *Muḥīṭ*, s.v. ʿst.

687. An idiom roughly equivalent to: "Pull up your socks."

688. Zayd b. ʿAbd al-Raḥmān b. ʿAwf is only mentioned in connection with his death.

689. Ibrāhīm b. Nuʿaym al-ʿAdawī is not mentioned elsewhere.

themselves against one of those quarters without defeating it. They did not fight for long until their opponents had turned and fled. Then he came toward ʿAbdallāh b. Ḥanẓalah and fought the fiercest of battles against him. Those of the quarters who still wanted to fight gathered around ʿAbdallāh b. Ḥanẓalah. They fought a fierce battle. Al-Faḍl b. al-ʿAbbās b. Rabīʿah with a group of the nobles and horsemen of the people attacked, heading toward Muslim b. ʿUqbah while Muslim was sick on his litter. He called out, "Carry me and put me in the ranks." After they had carried him, they put him in front of his tent in the ranks. Al-Faḍl b. ʿAbbās and those companions of his attacked until he reached the litter. Al-Faḍl was fair-skinned. When he raised his sword to strike him, Muslim shouted to his followers, "The fair-skinned slave will be my killer. Where are you, sons of free women? Thrust your spears at him!" They attacked and stabbed him until he fell.

According to Hishām (b. Muḥammad al-Kalbī)—Abū Mikhnaf—ʿAbdallāh b. Munqidh:[690] The cavalry and foot soldiers advanced with their equipment toward ʿAbdallāh b. Ḥanẓalah al-Ghasīl and his foot soldiers until they were near him. Muslim b. ʿUqbah rode a horse of his; he went among the Syrians, urging them on and saying: "Syrians, you are not the best of the Arabs in lineage and descent, nor the most numerous of them, nor the ones with the broadest lands. God has only singled you out, as He has, with victory over your enemies and a good position with your imāms [416] because of your obedience and your integrity. These people and Arabs like them have changed, and God has changed toward them. Therefore, give the best obedience that you have, and God will give you the best victory and success that He can give you." He went back to his previous position and ordered the cavalry to advance against Ibn al-Ghasīl and his followers. When the cavalry began to advance against the foot soldiers, the latter raised their spears and swords in their faces. The cavalry were scared away, frightened off; they drew back in fear. Muslim b. ʿUqbah called out among them, "Syrians, God has not made anyone more entitled to the land than you. Ḥusayn b. Numayr, attack with your

---

690. ʿAbdallāh b. Munqidh was an otherwise unknown authority of Abū Mikhnaf. See Sezgin, *Abū Miḥnaf*, 107.

troops." He attacked with the people from Ḥimṣ.[691] He went toward them. When Ibn al-Ghasīl saw them approaching, marching under their standards toward him, he stood up among his followers and said, "Men, your enemy has achieved an attitude in the battle that it would have been more appropriate for you to have had to fight against them. I had thought that you would only have waited a short time before God made the decision between you and them, either for you or against you. Are you not people of clear sight, people from the place of emigration? By God! I do not think that your Lord has either become more pleased with the inhabitants of any Muslim land than He is with you, or more angry with the inhabitants of any Arab land than He is with these people who are fighting against you. Every man among you has only one death that he can die. By God! There is no better death than the death of

[417]   martyrdom. God has brought it to you. Seize it! By God! Not everything you want, you find!" Then he went forward a little way with his standard and stood there. Ibn Numayr came with his standard until he was close to it. Muslim b. ʿUqbah ordered ʿAbdallāh b. ʿIḍāh al-Ashʿarī to advance with a hundred archers until they were near Ibn al-Ghasīl and his followers. They began to shoot arrows at them. Ibn al-Ghasīl said, "Why are you being targets for them? Whoever wants to hurry to heaven, let him stay close to this standard." All of those who were prepared to face death came to him, and he said, "Accept the promise to your Lord. By God! I hope that soon you will be joyful." The people attacked one another, and for an hour of the day they fought the fiercest battle seen at that time. Ibn Ghasīl sent his sons forward in front of him, one by one, until they were killed in front of him while he was striking with his sword and reciting:

Destruction to those who want corruption and tyranny,
    who avoid the truth and the signs of guidance.
God will only destroy those who are disobedient.

He was killed and his brother on his mother's side, Muḥammad b.

---

691. Ḥimṣ is a town in Syria located in a rich agricultural plain on the eastern bank of the Orontes; it is bounded in the east by the desert and in the west by mountains. See *EI*[2], s.v. Ḥimṣ.

Thābit b. Qays b. Shammās,[692] was killed with him. He had gone forward and fought until he was killed. He declared, "I would not wish that the people of al-Daylam killed me instead of these people." Then he fought until he was killed. Muḥammad b. ʿAmr b. Ḥazm al-Anṣārī[693] was killed with him. Marwān b. al-Ḥakam passed by him. He was like an oblong stone of silver. Marwān said, "May God have mercy on you. How many pillars in the mosque have seen you standing long in prayer beside them!"

According to Hishām (b. Muḥammad al-Kalbī)—ʿAwānah: Muslim b. ʿUqbah was sitting on a chair; men were carrying him while he was fighting against Ibn al-Ghasīl at the Battle of al-Ḥarrah. He was reciting:

Hāshim b. Ḥarmalah revived his father   [418]
    at the Battle of al-Habātayn and the Battle of al-Yaʿmulah.
Through him all the kings were scattered dead,
    and his spear deprived many mothers of their sons.
The man [destined to killing] does not wait long until he knocks
    him down.
He kills those who have guilt and those who have no guilt.

According to Hishām (b. Muḥammad al-Kalbī)—Abū Mikhnaf: Muḥammad b. Saʿd b. Abī Waqqāṣ[694] came out to fight on that day. When the Syrians fled, he went after them striking at them until the defeat overcame him. Then he went away with the others who went away. Muslim gave up Medina to pillage for three days; they killed the people and seized goods. That frightened the Companions of the Prophet who were there. Abū Saʿīd al-Khudrī left and went to a cave in the mountain. One of the Syrians spotted him and came into the cave against him.

---

692. Muḥammad b. Thābit b. Qays b. Shammās's father had been a Companion of the Prophet from Medina; he reported traditions from his father and ʿUmar. See Wāqidī, *Maghāzī*, I, 273; and Ṭabarī, I, 1757, III, 2403.

693. Muḥammad b. ʿAmr b. Ḥazm al-Anṣārī's father had been a Companion of the Prophet from Medina; he had been sent as his representative to Yemen just before the Prophet's death. See Ṭabarī, I, 1727–29.

694. Muḥammad b. Saʿd b. Abī Waqqāṣ was a son of the famous Companion of the Prophet, who later took part in Ibn al-Ashʿath's revolution. He was captured and executed by al-Ḥajjāj b. Yūsuf in 83 (702). See Ṭabarī, II, 1120.

According to Abū Mikhnaf—al-Ḥasan b. ʿAṭiyyah al-ʿAwfī[695]—Abū Saʿīd al-Khudrī: The Syrian came in after me; he was walking with his sword. I drew my sword and walked toward him to frighten him so that perhaps he would leave me. However, he would do nothing but advance against me. I sheathed my sword and said, "If you stretch out your hand toward me to kill me, it is not for me to stretch out my hand toward you to kill you, for I fear God, the Lord of the universe."[696] He said, "Who are you, may your father be blessed?" I answered, "I am Abū Saʿīd al-Khudrī." He said, "The Companion of the Prophet?" I said, "Yes." Then he went away from me.

According to Hishām (b. Muḥammad al-Kalbī)—ʿAwānah: Muslim b. ʿUqbah summoned the people to give the oath of allegiance at Qubā.[697] Safe-conduct was sought for two men from Quraysh, Yazīd b. ʿAbdallāh b. Zamʿah b. al-Aswad b. al-Muṭṭalib b. Asad b. ʿAbd al-ʿUzzā[698] and Muḥammad b. Abī al-Jahm b. Ḥudhayfah al-ʿAdawī,[699] and also for Maʿqil b. Sinān al-Ashjaʿī. They were brought a day after the battle. Muslim demanded, "Give the oath of allegiance." The two Qurashīs declared, "We give the oath of allegiance to you on the basis of the Book of God and the Sunnah of His Prophet." Muslim asserted, "No, by God! I will never release you with that." He had them brought forward and their heads cut off. Marwān exclaimed, "Glory be to God! Are you killing two men of Quraysh who came to you to seek safe-conduct, and yet you cut their heads off?" Muslim pricked him in his hip with a cane and said, "And you too. If you say what they said, you will only see the sky for the time of a flash of lightning."

According to Hishām (b. Muḥammad al-Kalbī)—Abū Mikhnaf: Maʿqil b. Sinān came and sat with the people and he asked for a

[419]

---

695. Al-Ḥasan b. ʿAṭiyyah al-ʿAwfī was a traditionist, who was said to have died in 181 (797), but this would make him unusually old as an authority for Abū Mikhnaf. See Ibn Ḥajar, *Tahdhīb*, II, 294; and Sezgin, *Abū Miḥnaf*, 207.

696. Qurʾān, 5:31.

697. There is dispute about whether Qubā is the Prophet's mosque in Medina or a small village two miles south of Medina where an early mosque was built. Yāqūt, *Muʿjam*, IV, 23–24.

698. Yazīd b. ʿAbdallāh b. Zamʿah b. al-Aswad was only mentioned in connection with this incident, but his grandmother was Umm Salamah, wife of the Prophet. See Balādhurī, *Ansāb*, IV/1, 328.

699. Muḥammad b. Abī al-Jahm is not mentioned elsewhere.

drink to quench his thirst. Muslim asked him, "Which drink do you most like?" He answered, "Honey." Muslim ordered, "Give him a drink." Ma'qil drank until he had quenched his thirst. Muslim asked him, "Have you quenched your thirst with your drink?" He replied, "Yes." Muslim declared, "No, by God! You will never drink another drink after that except the boiling water in the fire of hell. Do you remember what you said about the Commander of the Faithful, 'I journeyed to him for a month, I spent a month returning from him and I have come back empty-handed. O God! Bring a change!' You were meaning Yazīd." He had him brought forward and his head cut off.

According to Hishām (b. Muḥammad al-Kalbī)—'Awānah b. al-Ḥakam: Muslim b. 'Uqbah sent 'Amr b. Muḥriz al-Ashja'ī,[700] and he brought Ma'qil b. Sinān to him. Muslim said, "Welcome, Abū Muḥammad (i.e., Ma'qil), I see you are thirsty?" Ma'qil said, "Yes." Muslim ordered, "Mix him some honey with the ice that you brought with us." Previously Ma'qil had been a friend of Muslim's. They mixed some honey with the ice for him. When Ma'qil had drunk, he said, "May God quench your thirst with the drink of heaven." Muslim asserted, "By God! You will never drink another drink after that until you drink the boiling water of hell." Ma'qil begged him, "I implore you before God and kinship."[701] However, Muslim said to him, "You are the one who met me at Tiberias[702] on the night when you had left Yazīd. You said, 'We journeyed for a month and we came back from Yazīd empty-handed. We will go back to Medina and depose this sinner. We will give the oath of allegiance to one of the sons of the emigrants (Muhājirūn).' What have the tribes of Ghaṭafān and Ashja' to do with deposing and installing a caliph? I swore an oath that I would not meet you in a battle without cutting your head off." Then he ordered him to be killed.

[420]

According to Hishām (b. Muḥammad al-Kalbī)—'Awānah: Yazīd b. Wahb b. Zam'ah[703] was brought. Muslim demanded, "Give the oath of allegiance." He declared, "I give you the oath of

---

700. 'Amr b. Maḥriz al-Ashja'ī is not mentioned elsewhere, but belonged to the same tribe as Ma'qil b. Sinān, whom he was sent to fetch.

701. Both men came from different clans of the tribe Ghaṭafān.

702. Tiberias is on the southwest coast of the Sea of Galilee in Palestine.

703. Yazīd b. Wahb b. Zam'ah is not mentioned elsewhere.

allegiance on the basis of the Sunnah of ʿUmar."[704] Muslim ordered him to be killed. Yazīd b. Wahb protested, "But I am giving the oath of allegiance." Muslim said, "No, by God! I will not save you from your fall!" Marwān spoke to him about the relationship that existed between the two of them. Then he ordered Marwān to be struck [with the fist] in the neck.[705] After that he announced, "Give the oath of allegiance on the basis that you are the servants of Yazīd b. Muʿāwiyah." Then he ordered Yazīd b. Wahb to be killed.

According to Hishām (b. Muḥammad al-Kalbī)—ʿAwānah and Abū Mikhnaf[706]—ʿAbd al-Malik b. Nawfal b. Musāḥiq: Marwān brought ʿAlī b. al-Ḥusayn. When the Banū Umayyah had been expelled, ʿAlī b. al-Ḥusayn had protected Marwān's goods and wife; he had given her refuge. ʿAlī b. al-Ḥusayn approached; he walked between Marwān and ʿAbd al-Malik, seeking safe-conduct from Muslim. He came and sat down with Muslim between the two men. Marwān asked for a drink so that ʿAlī might gain protection from Muslim.[707] A drink was brought for him, and Marwān drank a little from it. Then he handed it to ʿAlī. When he put it to his mouth, Muslim ordered, "Don't drink our drink."

ʿAlī's hand shook; he did not feel safe for his life. He held the cup in his hand without drinking from it and without putting it down. Muslim said, "You only came between these two men to [421] seek safe-conduct from me. By God! If that matter were just going to be due to them, I would kill you. But the Commander of the Faithful has ordered me to treat you kindly. He told me that you had written to him. That is what brings you benefit from me. If you want, drink your drink that is in your hand. If you want, ask

---

704. In this context a particularly provocative remark because the Sunnah of ʿUmar must refer to the consultative council (shūrā), which ʿUmar introduced to appoint the next Caliph and which had been ignored by Yazīd.

705. This appears to be somewhat harsh treatment of an Umayyad as important as Marwān.

706. The text is *qāla ʿAwānah ʿan Abī Mikhnaf* ("Awānah reported on the authority of Abū Mikhnaf"). This is highly unlikely as it has not occurred in the accounts given so far. I have followed Sezgin and changed the *ʿan* to *wa*. See Sezgin, *Abū Miḥnaf*, 193n.

707. The Arab custom of not killing a man who has shared one's food and drink seems irrelevant after the earlier incidents connected with Muslim b. ʿAqīl, but the others had been fighting against Muslim.

us for another." 'Alī b. al-Ḥusayn said, "I want the one that is in my hand." He drank it. Muslim told him to come to him and he made him sit beside him.

According to Hishām (b. Muḥammad al-Kalbī—'Awānah b. al-Ḥakam: When 'Alī b. al-Ḥusayn was brought to Muslim, he asked who he was. When they told him that it was 'Alī b. al-Ḥusayn, he welcomed him and made him sit with him on the couch and the cushions. He said, "The Commander of the Faithful told me to be kind to you but he also said that these wicked men would keep me occupied from you; they would stop my generosity to you." Then he suggested to 'Alī, "Perhaps your family are frightened?" He answered, "Yes, by God!" Muslim ordered his mule to be saddled. Then he took him and sent him back to his family.

According to Hishām (b. Muḥammad al-Kalbī)—'Awānah: 'Amr b. 'Uthmān [b. 'Affān] had not been among those of the Banū Umayyah who had left. One day he was brought to Muslim b. 'Uqbah, who said, "Syrians, do you know this man?" They answered, "No." He told them, "He is the wicked man who is the son of a good man. This is 'Amr, son of 'Uthmān b. 'Affān, the Commander of the Faithful. Hey, 'Amr! When the people of Medina have the upper hand, you say, 'I am one of you.' When the Syrians have the upper hand, you say, 'I am the son of the Commander of the Faithful, 'Uthmān b. 'Affān.'" He ordered his beard to be plucked out. Then he said, "The mother of this man used to put black beetles in her mouth. Then she would say, 'Commander of the Faithful, I challenge you to guess what is in my mouth.' And in her mouth was what was bad for her and what was painful for her." Muslim let 'Amr go. 'Amr's mother was from the clan of Daws.[708]

Abū Ja'far al-Ṭabarī reported according to Aḥmad b. Thābit—those who transmitted to him—Isḥāq b. 'Īsā—Abū Ma'shar: [422]

According to al-Ḥārith—Ibn Sa'd—Muḥammad b. 'Umar (al-Wāqidī):

Both Abū Ma'shar and al-Wāqidī reported that the Battle of al-Ḥarrah was on 26 Dhū al-Ḥijjah, 63 (August 28, 684).

Some of them say that it was on 25 Dhū al-Ḥijjah (August 27).

---

708. Daws is a clan of the tribe of al-Azd. See Balādhurī, *Ansāb*, IV/1, 601.

In this year (63/684) ʿAbdallāh b. al-Zubayr led the people in the pilgrimage.

According to al-Ḥārith—Ibn Saʿd—Muḥammad b. ʿUmar (al-Wāqidī)—ʿAbdallāh b. Jaʿfar[709]—Ibn Abī ʿAwf:[710] Ibn al-Zubayr led the people in the pilgrimage in the year 63/684. At that time he was called "one who seeks refuge" [in the sanctuary of Mecca]. The people thought that a consultative council (shūrā) was the appropriate course of action (amr) to decide the Caliph.

On the night of the new moon of al-Muḥarram (August 29) we were in our house when Saʿīd,[711] the mawlā of al-Miswar b. Makhramah,[712] came to us and told us what Muslim had done to the people of Medina and what had been taken from them. A great catastrophe had come upon them. I saw the people draw their swords, become serious, make preparations, and realize that he was going to attack them.

A different account of the Battle of al-Ḥarrah and the killing of Ibn Ghasīl from the one that has been related on the authority of Abū Mikhnaf from those from whom he reported, has been mentioned. That is according to Aḥmad b. Zuhayr[713]—his father[714]—Wahb b. Jarīr[715]—Juwayriyyah b. Asmāʾ[716]—what he heard the scholars of Medina transmitting:[717] When Muʿāwiyah was close to death, he summoned Yazīd and said to him, "There may be

---

709. ʿAbdallāh b. Jaʿfar was a regular authority of al-Wāqidī; he must have lived in the middle of the second (eighth) century. See Ṭabarī, index; and Wāqidī, *Maghāzī*, index.

710. Ibn Abī ʿAwf is never mentioned again and is unidentifiable; the *isnād* could be defective and the reporter could be a son of ʿAbd al-Raḥmān b. ʿAwf.

711. Saʿīd is not mentioned in any other context.

712. Al-Miswar b. Makhramah was a younger Companion of the Prophet, who came to Medina when still a boy. He died defending Ibn al-Zubayr. See Ibn Ḥajar, *Tahdhīb*, X, 151.

713. Aḥmad b. Zuhayr was an important traditionist and Ṭabarī's authority for the Baṣran tradition; he died in 280 (893). See Petersen, *ʿAlī and Muʿāwiya*, 110.

714. He was Zuhayr b. Ḥarb, a traditionist, who died in 234 (848–49). See Ibn Ḥajar, *Tahdhīb*, III, 342–43.

715. Wahb b. Jarīr was an important narrator of historical tradition that is rarely used by Ṭabarī; he died in 206 (821–22). See Ibn Ḥajar, *Tahdhīb*, XI, 161.

716. Juwayriyyah b. Asmāʾ was an important narrator of historical tradition from a school of history little used by Ṭabarī; he died in 173 (789–90). See Ibn Ḥajar, *Tahdhīb*, II, 124–25.

717. This report combines two separate reports given by Khalīfah b. Khayyāṭ. See *Taʾrīkh*, 237–38.

trouble for you one day from the people of Medina. If they do trouble you, then hurl Muslim b. ʿUqbah against them. He is a man whose sincere advice I have experienced."

When Muʿāwiyah died, a delegation of the people of Medina visited Yazīd. Among those who visited him was ʿAbdallāh b. Ḥanẓalah b. Abī ʿĀmir. He was a noble, an excellent man, a leader, and a man who worshiped God. With him were his eight sons. Yazīd gave him one hundred thousand dirhams. He also gave each one of his sons ten thousand dirhams, apart from the robes of honor and transport for them. When ʿAbdallāh b. Ḥanẓalah came back to Medina, he went to the people. They asked, "What was the situation back there?" He answered, "I have come to you from a man whom, if I only had these sons of mine, I would fight." They said, "We have been informed that he brought benefit to you, gave you gifts, and treated you generously." He replied, "He did that, but I only accepted that from him to make myself stronger through it." He incited the people, and they gave the oath of allegiance to him. Yazīd was informed of that and he sent Muslim b. ʿUqbah against them. The people of Medina sent men to every watering place between them and Syria; they poured a skin of tar into each one and spoiled it.[718] However, God sent down the rain on the Syrians, and they did not look for water to drink from a bucket [from the wells at the watering places] until they arrived at Medina. The people of Medina went out against them in many groups and in a manner the like of which has not been seen. When the Syrians saw them, they were terrified of them and were unwilling to fight them. Muslim was in severe pain. While the people were involved in fighting the Syrians, they heard the sounds of victorious cries of "God is greater" behind them in the hollow of Medina. The Banū Ḥārithah[719] had led the Syrians in against them while they were on the edge [of the trench]. The people were put to flight. More of the people at the trench were wounded than were killed. The Syrians entered Medina, and the people were defeated. ʿAbdallāh b. Ḥanẓalah was

[423]

---

718. ʿUwwira in the text has been emended to ʿawwarūhu following Khalīfah b. Khayyāṭ, Taʾrīkh, 238.

719. The Banū Ḥārithah are a subclan of the Aws in Medina; see Wāqidī, Maghāzī, I, 158.

leaning on one of his sons snoring in his sleep. His son woke him. When he opened his eyes, he saw what the people had done. He ordered his eldest son to go forward until he was killed. Muslim b. ʿUqbah entered Medina. He summoned the people to give the oath of allegiance on the basis that they were servants of Yazīd b. Muʿāwiyah, who would judge over their lives, their property, and their families as he wished.

The
Events of the Year
64
(AUGUST 30, 683–AUGUST 17, 684)

Abū Jaʿfar reported: Among those events was the advance of the
Syrians against Mecca to make war on ʿAbdallāh b. al-Zubayr and   [424]
those who held the same view as he in refusing to accept Yazīd
b. Muʿāwiyah. When Muslim b. ʿUqbah had finished fighting
the people of Medina and the three days of the plundering of their
property by his army, he set out with those of his army who were
with him in the direction of Mecca.

This is according to Hishām b. Muḥammad (al-Kalbī)—Abū
Mikhnaf—ʿAbd al-Malik b. Nawfal: Muslim set out with the
people toward Mecca with the intention of attacking Ibn al-
Zubayr. He appointed Rawḥ b. Zinbāʿ al-Judhāmī[720] as his deputy over Medina.

As for al-Wāqidī, he reported that Muslim appointed ʿAmr
b. Muḥriz as his deputy over Medina but he added that it was
reported that he appointed Rawḥ b. Zinbāʿ al-Judhāmī as his
deputy.

---

720. Rawḥ b. Zinbāʿ al-Judhāmī was a prominent supporter of the Umayyads,
particularly of ʿAbd al-Malik b. Marwān. See Ṭabarī, II, 1164–65.

The Death of Muslim b. ʿUqbah and the Bombardment and Burning of the Kaʿbah

The account returns to Abū Mikhnaf: When Muslim b. ʿUqbah reached al-Mushallal[721]—it was reported as Qafā al-Mushallal—death came upon him. That was toward the end of al-Muḥarram, 64 (toward the end of September, 683). He summoned al-Ḥusayn b. Numayr al-Sakūnī and said to him, "O son of a pack saddle of a donkey! If this matter were for me to decide, I would not have given you command over this army. However, the Commander of the Faithful has given you command after me, and the order of the Commander of the Faithful cannot be opposed. Take four pieces [of advice] from me: travel speedily; be quick in attack; keep the news unknown; and don't listen to a Qurashī." Then he died and was buried at Qafā al-Mushallal.

According to Hishām b. Muḥammad al-Kalbī—ʿAwānah: Muslim b. ʿUqbah set off aiming for Ibn al-Zubayr. When he reached the pass of Harshā,[722] death came upon him. He sent for the leaders of the troops and said, "The Commander of the Faithful has instructed me, if death were to come to me, to appoint Ḥusayn b. Numayr al-Sakūnī to take over command of you. By [425] God! If the decision were mine, I would not do so. However, I am unwilling to disobey the order of the Commander of the Faithful at the time of my death." Then he summoned Ḥusayn b. Numayr and said, "O son of a pack saddle of a donkey! Remember my advice to you: keep the news unknown; never listen to a Qurashī; don't hold the Syrians back from their enemy; only stay three days before you attack Ibn al-Zubayr, the sinful man." Then he said, "O God! After testifying that there is no god but God and that Muḥammad is His servant and Apostle, I have never done anything that I like better than my killing of the people of Medina or anything that I hope to be of such advantage to me in the Hereafter." He went on, "The Banū Murrah will have my estate at Ḥawrān[723] as a gift for them but whatever so-and-so keeps

---

721. Al-Mushallal is a mountain near Mecca. See Yāqūt, *Muʿjam*, IV, 542.

722. Harshā is a pass on the road to Mecca near al-Juḥfah; it is four stages away from Medina. See Yāqūt, *Muʿjam*, II, 19, and IV, 960.

723. Ḥawrān is a fertile district to the south of Damascus. See Yāqūt, *Muʿjam*, II, 358.

within her door belongs to her." He was referring to his slave wife. Then he died.

When he died, Ḥuṣayn b. Numayr departed with the people and advanced toward Ibn al-Zubayr and Mecca. The inhabitants of Mecca and the Ḥijāz had given the oath of allegiance to him.

According to Hishām—ʿAwānah: Before his will, Muslim said, "My son alleges that this slave wife has given me poison to drink. He is a liar. This disease attacks my family in our stomachs."

All the people of Medina came to him, that is, to Ibn al-Zubayr. Najdah b. ʿĀmir al-Ḥanafī came to him with people from the Khārijites to protect the Sacred House. Ibn al-Zubayr said to his brother al-Mundhir, "There is nobody to undertake this task and to drive off these people except you and me." His brother, al-Mundhir, was one of those who had been present at the Battle of al-Ḥarrah and had then joined him. Ibn al-Zubayr despatched his brother against them with the people. He fought against them fiercely for a time. Then one of the Syrians challenged al-Mundhir to single combat. The Syrian was on a mule of his, and al-Mundhir came out against him. Each of them struck the other a blow from which each fell dead. ʿAbdallāh b. al-Zubayr knelt down saying, "O Lord! Destroy it from its root and don't comfort it." He was praying against [the soul of] the one who had fought against his brother.

[426]

The Syrians made a dreadful onslaught against them, and Ibn al-Zubayr's followers were defeated. Ibn al-Zubayr's mule stumbled. He cried out, "How wretched!" He dismounted and shouted for his followers to come to him. Al-Miswar b. Makhramah b. Nawfal b. Uhayb b. ʿAbd Manāf b. Zuhrah and Muṣʿab b. ʿAbd al-Raḥmān b. ʿAwf came to him and fought alongside him until they were both killed. Ibn al-Zubayr remained steadfast against the Syrians fighting against them until night. Then they withdrew from him.

This was during the first siege. They stayed there fighting against him for the rest of al-Muḥarram and the whole of Ṣafar (from the end of September until October 28). On Saturday, 3 Rabīʿ al-Awwal, 64 (October 31, 683) they hurled [stones and wood] at the Sacred House with ballistae and they set it on fire. They began to recite:

A ballista with which we bombard the pillars of the mosque is
    like a raging stallion camel.[724]

According to Hishām (b. Muḥammad al-Kalbī)—Abū ʿAwānah:
ʿAmr b. Ḥawṭ al-Sadūsī began reciting:

How do you see the work of Umm Farwah
    as she takes them between al-Ṣafā and al-Marwah?[725]

He meant by "Umm Farwah" the ballista.

[427]   Al-Wāqidī reported that when Muslim b. ʿUqbah had been
buried at al-Mushallal on 21 al-Muḥarram (September 20), al-
Ḥusayn b. Numayr set out. He reached Mecca on 24 al-Muḥarram
(September 23). He besieged Ibn al-Zubayr for sixty days until
news of the death of Yazīd b. Muʿāwiyah reached him at the
beginning of Rabīʿ al-Ākhir (the end of November).
    In this year (64/683) the Kaʿbah was set on fire.

The Cause of the Burning of the Kaʿbah

Muḥammad b. ʿUmar (al-Wāqidī) reported that the Kaʿbah was
burned on Saturday, 3 Rabīʿ al-Awwal, 64 (October 31, 683),
twenty-nine days before news of the death of Yazīd b. Muʿāwiyah
came. The news arrived on Tuesday, 2 Rabīʿ al-Akhir (November
26).[726]
    According to Muḥammad b. ʿUmar (al-Wāqidī)—Riyāḥ b.
Muslim—his father: They were causing fires to be lit around the
Kaʿbah. There was a spark, which the wind blew; it set fire to the
veil of the Kaʿbah and burned the wood of the Sacred House on
Saturday, 3 Rabīʿ al-Awwal (October 31).
    According to Muḥammad b. ʿUmar al-Wāqidī—ʿAbdallāh b.

---

724. These verses are also quoted by Balādhurī from Abū Mikhnaf, who named
the poet as al-Zubayr b. Khuzaymah al-Khathʿamī from Palestine; he was said to
be also in charge of the bombardment. See *Ansāb*, IV/1, 339.
    725. This verse is also quoted by Balādhurī, who does not identify the poet. See
Ansāb, IV/1, 340.
    726. The Arabic is *hilāl*, literally "new moon," but this can also refer to the
first two days of the month. Clearly it is the second day here.

Zayd[727]—ʿUrwah b. Udhaynah:[728] I came to Mecca with my mother on the day the Kaʿbah was burned. The fire had reached it, and I saw that it was without its silk veil. I saw that the Yemeni corner of the Kaʿbah[729] was black and had been cracked in three places. I asked, "What has happened to the Kaʿbah?" They pointed to one of Ibn al-Zubayr's followers and said, "It has been burned because of this man. He put a firebrand on the tip of his spear; the wind made it fly off. It struck the veils of the Kaʿbah between the Yemeni corner and the Black Stone."

In that year (64/683) Yazīd b. Muʿāwiyah died. His death occurred in one of the villages of Ḥimṣ called Ḥuwwārīn in the land of Syria on 14 Rabīʿ al-Awwal, 64 (November 11, 683). He was thirty-eight years of age according to the report of some. [428]

According to ʿUmar b. Shabbah—Muḥammad b. Yaḥyā[730]—Hishām b. al-Walīd al-Makhzūmī: [Ibn Shihāb] al-Zuhrī wrote down the ages of the caliphs for his grandfather.[731] Among the things he wrote was: Yazīd b. Muʿāwiyah died when he was thirty-nine years of age.

His rule was for three years and six months according to the report of some. It is also reported that it was eight months.

According to Aḥmad b. Thābit—those who transmitted to him—Isḥāq b. ʿĪsā—Abū Maʿshar: Yazīd b. Muʿāwiyah died on Tuesday, 14 Rabīʿ al-Awwal (November 11).[732] His caliphate was for three years and eight months less three days. His son Muʿāwiyah b. Yazīd said the funeral prayer for him.

As for Hishām b. Muḥammad al-Kalbī, he reported a different version of the age of Yazīd from that of al-Zuhrī. What Hishām reported in the version that has been transmitted to us is: Abū

---

727. ʿAbdallāh b. Zayd is not mentioned by Ṭabarī elsewhere. However, it is possible that he is the traditionist ʿAbdallāh b. Zayd b. Aslam who died in 164 (780–81). See Ibn Ḥajar, *Tahdhīb*, V, 223–23.

728. ʿUrwah b. Udhaynah is not mentioned in any other context.

729. The Yemeni corner of the Kaʿbah is that corner facing Yemen. The Black Stone is in the corner to the right of it as one faces it. See *EI*[2], s.v. Kaʿba.

730. Muḥammad b. Yaḥyā was a well-known traditionist and a secretary. See Ibn Ḥajar, *Tahdhīb*, IX, 517–18.

731. There is some confusion as to whether this should be father or grandfather. In Ṭabarī, II, 199, Hishām b. al-Walīd reported that Ibn Shihāb answered questions about the ages of the caliphs for al-Walīd, which might mean Hishām's father.

732. Actually a Wednesday.

Khālid Yazīd b. Muʿāwiyah b. Abī Sufyān succeeded to the caliphate on 1 Rajab, 60 (April 8, 680), when he was thirty-two years and some months old. He ruled for two years and eight months and died on 14 Rabīʿ al-Awwal, 63 (November 21, 682), when he was thirty-five years of age. His mother was Maysūn bt. Baḥdal b. Unayf b. Waljah b. Qunāfah b. ʿAdī b. Zuhayr b. Ḥārithah al-Kalbī.

The Number of Yazīd b. Muʿāwiyah's Sons

Among Yazīd's sons were: Muʿāwiyah b. Yazīd b. Muʿāwiyah, whose *kunyah* was Abū Laylā.[733] Of him the poet says:

[429]   I see discord whose beginning has arrived.
       After Abū Laylā the kingdom will be for him who conquers.

Khālid b. Yazīd, whose *kunyah* was Abū Hāshim. It was reported that he acquired the skill of alchemy.[734]
Abū Sufyān.[735]
The mother of both of these was Umm Khālid[736] bt. Abī Hāshim b. ʿUtbah b. Rabīʿah b. ʿAbd Shams. Marwān married her after Yazīd. Of her the poet says:

Rejoice, O Umm Khālid;
       sometimes the results of one who strives are for one who
       sits.[737]

ʿAbdallāh b. Yazīd who was reported to be the finest archer of the Arabs at his time. His mother was Umm Kulthūm bt. ʿAbdallāh b. ʿĀmir. He was called al-Uswār.[738] Of him the poet says:

---

733. Muʿāwiyah b. Yazīd was ill when he succeeded his father; he survived only a few months before he died. See Balādhurī, *Ansāb*, IV/1, 356.

734. According to Balādhurī, Khālid b. Yazīd was also a poet and an astrologer; he is said to have remained silent when people with less knowledge spoke. He died during the caliphate of ʿAbd al-Malik, from 65 (685) to 86 (705). See *Ansāb*, IV/1, 359–64.

735. Abū Sufyān is not mentioned in any other context.

736. Umm Hāshim has been emended to Umm Khālid as in the poem below and in Balādhurī, *Ansāb*, IV/1, 365.

737. Similar verse quoted by Balādhurī. See *Ansāb*, IV/1, 290.

738. *Al-uswār* means "horseman" in Persian. He was in fact, a famous horseman. See Balādhurī, *Ansāb*, IV/1, 367.

The people claim that the best of all Quraysh
when they are mentioned is al-Uswār.

There were also 'Abdallāh al-Aṣghar,[739] 'Umar,[740] Abū Bakr,[741]
'Utbah,[742] Ḥarb,[743] 'Abd al-Raḥmān,[744] al-Rabī',[745] and Muḥammad.[746] Their mothers were various slave wives.

---

739. 'Abdallāh al-Aṣghar is not mentioned in any other context.

740. 'Umar was either struck by a thunderbolt or died of fright in a thunder-
storm. See Balādhurī, *Ansāb*, IV/1, 368.

741. Abū Bakr had a reputation for liking to eat food. See Balādhurī, *Ansāb*,
IV/1, 369.

742. The only report about 'Utbah is that he was said to have descendants in
Syria. See Balādhurī, *Ansāb*, IV/1, 370.

743. Ḥarb is not mentioned in any other context.

744. 'Abd al-Raḥmān had a reputation for piety and generosity. See Balādhurī,
Ansāb, IV/1, 368.

745. Al-Rabī' is not mentioned in any other context.

746. There are no further reports about Muḥammad other than that he had a
son called Muḥammad by a slave wife. See Balādhurī, *Ansāb*, IV/1, 370.

Bibliography of Cited Works

Ahlwardt, W. *The Divans of Six Ancient Arabic Poets*. London: Trubner & Co., 1870.

Ayoub, M. *Redemptive Suffering in Islam*. The Hague: Mouton, 1978.

al-Balādhurī, Aḥmad b. Yaḥyā. *Ansāb al-ashrāf*. Vol. II/1, edited by M. B. al-Maḥmūdī. Beirut: Muʿassasat al-ʿIlmī, 1974. Vol. II/2, edited by M. B. al-Maḥmūdī. Beirut: Dār al-Taʿaruf, 1977. Vol. IV/1, edited by I. ʿAbbās. Wiesbaden: al-Nasharāt al-Islāmiyyah, 1979. Vol. V, edited by S. D. F. Goitein. Jerusalem: Hebrew University Press, 1936.

al-Bustānī, Buṭrus. *Muḥīṭ al-muḥīṭ*. Beirut: Librairie du Liban, 1977.

Crone, P. *Slaves on Horses*. Cambridge: Cambridge University Press, 1980.

al-Dhahabī, Abū ʿAbdallāh Muḥammad. *Mīzān al-iʿtidāl*. 4 vols., edited by ʿA. M. al-Bajāwī. Cairo: Dār Iḥyāʾ al-Kutub al-ʿArabiyyah, 1964.

al-Dīnawarī, Abū Ḥanīfah Aḥmad b. Dāwūd. *Kitâb al-aḫbâr aṭ-ṭiwâl*. 2 vols., edited by V. Guirgass and I. Kratchkovsky. Leiden: Brill, 1888–1912.

Encyclopaedia of Islam. 1st edition (*EI*[1]). Leiden: Brill, 1913–38. 2nd edition (*EI*[2]). Leiden and London: Brill, 1960—.

Hinds, M. "Kûfan Political Alignments and Their Background in the Mid-Seventh Century A.D.," *International Journal of Middle East Studies*, 2, 1971: 346–67.

Hitti, P. *History of the Arabs*. London: Macmillan & Co., 1958.

Howard, I. K. A. "Accounts of the Martyrdom of al-Ḥusayn in Early Arabic Sources," *Papers from the Imam Ḥusayn Conference in London, July, 1984*. London, 1986.

————. "The Development of the *Adhān* and *Iqāma* of the Ṣalāt in Early Islam," *Journal of Semitic Studies*, 26, 1981: 219–28.

Ibn Aʿtham al-Kūfī, Abū Muḥammad Aḥmad. *Kitāb al-futūḥ*. 8 vols. Hyderabad: Dāʾirat al-Maʿārif al-ʿUthmāniyyah, 1968–75.

Ibn al-Athīr, ʿIzz al-Dīn Abū al-Ḥasan ʿAlī b. Muḥammad. *al-Kāmil fī al-taʾrīkh*. 13 vols. Beirut: Dār Ṣādir, 1385–87.

Ibn Ḥajar al-ʿAsqalānī, Aḥmad b. Nūr al-Din. *Tahdhīb al-tahdhīb*. Hyderabad: Dāʾirat al-Maʿārif al-Niẓāmiyyah, 1325–27.

Ibn Khallikān, Abū al-ʿAbbās Aḥmad b. Muḥammad al-Irbilī. *Wafayāt al-aʿyān wa-anbāʾ abnāʾ al-zamān*. 8 vols., edited by I. ʿAbbās. Beirut: Dār Ṣādir, 1968–72. Translated by Baron McGuckin de Slane under the title *Ibn Khallikan's Biographical Dictionary*. 4 vols. London: W. H. Allen, 1843–71.

Ibn Manẓūr, Jamāl al-Dīn Abū al-Faḍl Muḥammad b. Mukarram al-Anṣārī. *Lisān al-ʿArab*. 20 vols. Cairo: Būlāq, 1300–8.

Ibn al-Nadīm, Abū al-Faraj Muḥammad b. Isḥāq al-Warrāq. *Kitāb al-Fihrist*. Edited by G. Flügel. Leipzig: Vogel, 1871. Translated by B. Dodge under the title *The Fihrist of al-Nadīm*. 2 vols. New York: Columbia University Press, 1970.

Ibn Saʿd, Muḥammad. *Kitāb al-ṭabaqāt al-kabīr*. 9 vols., edited by E. Sachau *et al.* Leiden: Brill, 1905–40.

al-Iṣfahānī, Abū al-Faraj ʿAlī b. al-Ḥusayn. *Kitāb al-aghānī*. 20 vols. Cairo: Būlāq, 1285.

————. *Maqātil al-Ṭālibiyyīn*. Najaf: al-Maktabah al-Ḥaydariyyah, 1965.

Jafri, S. H. M. *The Origins and Early Development of Shīʿa Islam*. London: Longman & Librairie du Liban, 1979.

Khalīfah, Abū ʿAmr b. Khayyāṭ *Taʾrīkh*. Edited by A. Ḍiyāʾ al-ʿUmarī. Beirut: Muʾassat al-Risālah, 1977.

al-Khwārazmī, Akhṭab al-Muwaffaq. *Maqtal al-Ḥusayn*. 2 vols. Najaf: Muḥammad al-Samāwī, 1947.

al-Masʿūdī, Abū al-Ḥasan ʿAlī b. al-Ḥusayn. *Kitāb al-tanbīh wa-al-ishrāf*. Edited by M. J. de Goeje (Bibliotheca Geographorum Arabicorum VIII). Leiden: Brill, 1984. Translated by Baron Carra de Vaux under the title *Le livre de l'avertissement et de la revision*. Paris: Imprimerie Nationale, 1897.

————. *Murūj al-dhahab wa-maʿādin al-jawhar*. Edited and translated by C. Barbier de Meynard and Pavet de Courteille under the title *Les prairies d'or*. 9 vols. Paris: Imprimerie Nationale, 1861–1917.

al-Mufīd, Muḥammad b. Muḥammad b. al-Nuʿmān. *Kitāb al-irshād fī maʿrifat ḥujaj Allāh ʿala al-ʿibād*. Tehran: Dār al-Kutub al-Islāmiyyah, 1377/1957. Translated by I. K. A. Howard under the title *The Book of Guidance into the Lives of the Twelve Imams*. London:

Muhammadi Trust, 1981.

al-Najāshī, Abū al-ʿAbbās Aḥmad b. ʿAlī. *Kitāb al-rijāl*. Tehran: Nashr-e Kitāb, n.d.

Nicholson, R. A. *A Literary History of the Arabs*. Cambridge: Cambridge University Press, 1969.

Petersen, E. L. *ʿAlī and Muʿāwiyah in Early Arab Tradition*. Copenhagen: Scandinavian University Books, 1964.

Schacht, J. *The Origins of Muhammadan Jurisprudence*. Oxford: Clarendon Press, 1979.

Sezgin, U. *Abū Miḫnaf*. Leiden: Brill, 1971.

Shaban, M. A. *The ʿAbbāsid Revolution*. Cambridge: Cambridge University Press, 1970.

———. *Islamic History* I. A.D. 600–750. Cambridge: Cambridge University Press, 1971.

Shams al-Dīn, Shaykh Muḥammad Mahdī. *The Rising of al-Ḥusayn: Its Impact on the Consciousness of Muslim Society*. Translated by I. K. A. Howard. London: Muhammadi Trust, 1985.

al-Ṭabarī, Abū Jaʿfar Muḥammad b. Jarīr. *Taʾrīkh al-rusul wa-al-mulūk*. 16 vols., edited by M. J. de Goeje *et al*. Leiden: Brill, 1879–1901.

al-Ṭūsī, Muḥammad b. al-Ḥasan. *Fihrist kutub al-Shīʿa*. Edited by A. Sprenger *et al*. Calcutta: Asiatic Society of Bengal, 1853.

al-Wāqidī, Muḥammad b. ʿUmar. *Kitāb al-maghāzī*. 3 vols., edited by M. Jones. Oxford: Oxford University Press, 1966.

Watt, W. M. "Shīʿism under the Umayyads," *Journal of the Royal Asiatic Society*, 1960: 158–72.

Wellhausen, J. *The Arab Kingdom and Its Fall*. Translated by M. G. Weir. Calcutta: University of Calcutta, 1927.

———. *The Religio-Political Factions in Early Islam*. Translated by R. C. Ostle and S. M. Walzer. Amsterdam and Oxford: North Holland, 1975.

Wüstenfeld, H. F. *Der Tod des Ḥusein ben ʿAlī und die Rache. Ein historischer Roman aus dem Arabischen*. Abhandlungen der königlichen Gesellschaft der Wissenschaften zu Göttingen, 30, 1883.

al-Yaʿqūbī, Abū al-ʿAbbās Aḥmad b. Isḥāq. *Taʾrīkh*. 2 vols. Leiden: Brill, 1883.

Yāqūt, Abū ʿAbdallāh Yaʿqūb b. ʿAbdallāh al-Ḥamawī al-Rūmī. *Muʿjam al-buldān*. 6 vols., edited by F. Wüstenfeld. Leipzig: Brockhaus, 1866–70.

Index

The Arabic definite article *al-* and the abbreviations *b.* (*ibn*) and *bt.* (*bint*)
have been disregarded in the alphabetizing of entries.